Activities and Readings in Information Systems

Activities and Readings in Information Systems

Steven R. Gordon | *Babson College*
Judith R. Gordon | *Boston College*

THE DRYDEN PRESS
Harcourt Brace College Publishers

Fort Worth Philadelphia San Diego New York Orlando Austin San Antonio
Toronto Montreal London Sydney Tokyo

Activities Contents

ACTIVITY	**1**	Durley Hall Hotel A-4
ACTIVITY	**2**	The Mike O'Chip Maintenance Company A-8
ACTIVITY	**3**	Lewis Foods Fleet Management A-12
ACTIVITY	**4**	Connor Spring A-17
ACTIVITY	**5**	St. Thomas Psychiatric Hospital—A Strategic Planning Framework A-23
ACTIVITY	**6**	Three Minicases A-29
ACTIVITY	**7**	Lufkin-Conroe Telephone Exchange, Inc. A-32
ACTIVITY	**8**	The United States Postal Service A-35
ACTIVITY	**9**	Hisuesa (Hidroelectrica del Sur de Espana, S.A.) A-42
ACTIVITY	**10**	Bank Consolidates Data Processing Operations A-49
ACTIVITY	**11**	Airtour Vacaciones A-52
ACTIVITY	**12**	Shorko Films A-60
ACTIVITY	**13**	Benetton SpA A-72
ACTIVITY	**14**	Acme Engineering A-87
ACTIVITY	**15**	Norman Furniture Generation Ltd. A-95
ACTIVITY	**16**	Pinsos Galofré, S.A. A-103
ACTIVITY	**17**	Executive Information System Design for Frito Lay A-110
ACTIVITY	**18**	Implementing Business Process Reengineering: A Case Study A-115
ACTIVITY	**19**	Staying at the Top with Otis Elevator A-124
ACTIVITY	**20**	DMV A-143
ACTIVITY	**21**	A Case Study of Participative Systems Development A-147
ACTIVITY	**22**	It Won't Work in Kanji: The Case of Expert Systems Standardization at Global A-161
ACTIVITY	**23**	The Information Systems Infrastructure at AT&T A-170

Readings Contents

READING 1   "Hot New PC Services," by David Kirkpatrick   R-2

READING 2   "Mrs. Fields' Secret Ingredient," by Tom Richman   R-8

READING 3   "Prometheus Barely Unbound," by Tom Peters   R-15

READING 4   "Why Business Managers Are Empty-handed," by David Vaskevitch   R-29

READING 5   "Saving Time with New Technology," by Gene Bylinsky   R-34

READING 6   "In Search of the Perfect," by Steven Caniano   R-39

READING 7   "The Race to Rewire America," by Andrew Kupfer   R-48

READING 8   "A Multimedia Solution to Productivity Gridlock: A Re-Engineered Jewelry Appraisal System at Zale Corporaton," by Julie Newman and Kenneth A. Kozar   R-58

READING 9   "Will Toys "B" Great?" by Subrata N. Chakravarty   R-68

READING 10   "An Appraisal of Executive Management Information and Decision Systems," by Brian McNamara, George Danziger, and Edwin Barton   R-71

READING 11   "Networking with the Enemy," by Rochelle Garner   R-76

READING 12   "The End-user Developer: Friend or Foe?" by Jeff Papows and Joe King   R-80

READING 13   "No Set Rules for Systems Design," by Kathleen A. Gow   R-83

Activities

 **Durley Hall Hotel**

STEP 1: Read the Durley Hall Hotel case. (This activity is especially suited for use in conjunction with Chapter 2 of *Information Systems*.)

DURLEY HALL HOTEL

"Value for Money" is the motto of the Durley Hall Hotel. Originally, the hotel had 100 bedrooms—it now has 82 as the number of rooms with private facilities has been increased to 54 and the restaurant enlarged, which all helped to convince the AA and the RAC that the hotel deserved its recent three-star rating. The hotel is situated on the beautiful Westcliff of Bournemouth and is within easy walking distance of both the sea and the main shopping and entertainment area of the town. There is color TV, including a video receiver in each bedroom, a games room, and two bars and dancing featured in the Salisbury Bar every evening in the summer season (a different style of music each evening), and this coming winter will see off-season entertainment increased to include Thursday nights as well as the usual Friday and Saturday nights. There are "Mid-Week Bargain Breaks" and "Mini-Weekend Breaks" tariffs that put the accent on "Value for Money" during the winter, but conference business is taking on increasing importance during the off-season.

The hotel has two conference suites, the Canford Suite and the Forum Suite, both purpose-built and equipped with up-to-date audiovisual equipment. Both have two adjoining syndicate rooms. The Canford Suite has double doors so that large exhibits can be brought in for promotional events, air conditioning, recessed track lighting and plenty of power points. For training management courses, a capacity of 35 is appropriate, but 120 delegates can be accommodated theater-style and, as this suite has a portable dance floor, cocktail parties, dinner/dances, and discos can readily be held as well. The Forum Suite, which is situated in the Malborough Annex (adjacent to the main hotel), is very suitable for smaller, more intense meetings/courses, as it is set in quiet and peaceful surroundings overlooking the putting green and is completely self-contained.

Conference arrangements are made by the hotel, and it attracts a variety of clients—from carpet trade shows to training courses for major commercial and industrial organizations. "Getting the balance" right between individual guests and conference delegates is sometimes difficult, so bookings have to be carefully allocated. However, the main conference period is November to May, which does not conflict with the high-volume "holiday-maker" traffic prevalent in the summer season.

Increasingly, more municipal conferences are being held in Bournemouth during the summer months, and this type of delegate is seeking accommodation only in Bournemouth hotels. With training courses and "in-house" conferences, delegates require single occupancy of rooms, and all must have private facilities en suite. This is not always the case with municipal conference delegates as, in many cases, they are willing to share twin-bedded rooms. Within the last two years, quite a few larger Bournemouth hotels have tended toward the conference business—building conference suites and changing their facilities accordingly—but many more specialize in tourist business. There are also other specializations; for exam-

---

This case was made possible with the cooperation of the proprietor of the Durley Hall Hotel, Mr. M. J. Murray. It was prepared by Barbara Duchesne (B.A. Hons), Conference Officer of the Durley Hall Hotel as a basis for discussion and practical exercise rather than to demonstrate effective or ineffective handling of a particular situation.

Copyright © 1981 B. Duchesne.

ple, the Broughty Ferry Hotel in Boscombe caters exclusively to families with small children, and there are Orthodox Jewish hotels, Christian hotels, and indeed, "dry" hotels, that is, hotels that have no bar facilities whatsoever but rather encourage their clients to bring in their own drinks!

Although the conference facilities at the Durley Hall Hotel are not the largest in the area, they do rate among the very best in Bournemouth, especially in the "three-star" category, and the rates charged are extremely competitive. Generally speaking, the aim of the management team is for profitability rather than turnover and, apart from the revenue gained on its conference facilities, bars, restaurant, and accommodation, the hotel is constantly looking at ways to increase its sales while, at the same time, ensuring that it offers its clientele the best "value for money." At present, bar food has been introduced over the lunch-time period, which is proving extremely popular as the "traditional" lunch now seems to be fast losing its attraction except, of course, to conference delegates, where it is offered as part of the "all-inclusive" conference package. The new system seeks to attract nonresidents by providing a much needed facility—many of the smaller hotels on the Westcliff offer their guests dinner, room, and breakfast only. Similarly, traditional Sunday lunches are also on offer to residents and nonresidents alike at the Durely Hall Hotel with two choices of menu—regular and economy. In the winter months, candlelight dinner dances are held on Saturday nights, and the banqueting season brings into the hotel groups from local industry and commerce for annual celebrations such as office parties, dinner dances, and so on.

A four-night Christmas package is offered, which includes entertainment throughout for all tastes and age groups, and this has proved to be extremely popular, attracting regular guests year after year.

The hotel accommodation is sold in a variety of ways: from entries in the "Bournemouth Guide" produced by the Bournemouth Department of Tourism & Publicity, advertisements in the national press, mail shots, and so on, but much of it is now taken up by "repeat" business, that is, satisfied clients returning again to stay at the Durley Hall Hotel. Some accommodation is also sold via referrals from other hotels in the town full at the time, and vice versa. Of course, there is strong competition from other hotels, but it is of the friendliest kind and, as yet, there is little threat from the large "chains." Crest owns what used to be the Round House Hotel, Ladbroke has taken over the Savoy Hotel, and the De Vere group controls the five-star Royal Bath, the four-star Dormy Hotel, and others, but, generally, the buildings in Bournemouth that are available for purchase for hotel operation are too small to attract the interest of the major "chains." Similarly, planning applications for large purpose-built hotels seem unlikely to succeed, although this situation may change with the advent of the new municipal conference Center, which was under construction on the Westcliff and due for completion in 1984.

The Murray family, who own the Durley Hall Hotel, also own the Sun Court Hotel, a two-star family hotel also situated on the Westcliff and well known for its good food and friendly atmosphere. Mr. M. J. Murray operates from an office in the Durley Hall Hotel, whose Chief Executive is Mr. P. E. J. Williams. A new manager, Mr. S. J. Badger, has recently been appointed and is due to take up his duties shortly. Mrs. M. A. Murray works from the Sun Court, and the Murray's eldest son, Jon, is manager of the Sun Court Hotel.

Marketing is carried out on a "group" basis, and the two hotels are moving toward a "group" identity with the standardization within each hotel of literature/logos, and so on, used in brochures and correspondence and, to some extent, to staff uniforms, but styles do have to differ to reflect the unique image of each hotel. All the staff are aware of the role they play in the marketing of the hotel, and their interest in this respect is thoroughly encouraged by the management team. This generally results in a very high standard of customer service and promotion of the facilities while maintaining staff morale to equally enviable standards.

The Durley Hall Hotel was occupied by the Atomic Energy Commission as a training establishment for many years up to 1970. It was then taken over by the municipality to prevent its conversion into flats and leased to the Murray family in 1972. At the time it was in a fairly derelict condition and since then has needed a large injection of capital to bring it up to its present three-star standard. Capital expenditure is still necessary to constantly maintain and upgrade, where possible, both accommodation and facilities. Indeed, the hotel is presently involved in converting its small cocktail bar and "dry" lounge into a large but still intimate bar with a lounge that will also be licensed but that will still cater to the needs of clients who require soft drinks, coffee, and so on. Also, more and more, bathrooms en suite are being demanded by clients as expectations have been raised via foreign holidays and, of course, for business occupancy, they are essential. It has, therefore, become increasingly difficult to sell rooms without private facilities. Special offers attractively discount rooms without bath, but there is still a wish by the management to steadily increase the number of rooms with bath. Plans are now also being made to modernize the reception area and thereby use the space more efficiently while, at the same time, offering a better and faster service to customers. Tourism is a vital "sterling earner," and Mr. Murray feels that aid should be available, perhaps in the form of government grants or cheap loans, to improve Britain's accommodation stock. At the present time, however, assistance is only available for these types of projects in so-called "development" areas of the country.

As far as the home tourist market is concerned, the Bournemouth season, which used to stretch from Whitsuntide right through to the end of October, is now curtailed to the five or six weeks of the school summer holidays, and there is a strong attraction for tourists without families to go abroad on holiday. Therefore, the Durley Hall Hotel management team are constantly seeking conference business for a considerably longer period each year; but, in the main, the emphasis still lies on the winter months.

After a poor 1980–81 winter conference season, due to the cancellation at a very late stage of prebooked regular weekly training courses by a large motor company, October and November 1981 were looking extremely healthy as far as conference bookings were concerned, and the hotel was awaiting confirmation of further regular weekly training courses from two major British companies. Conference advertising expenditure, as such, was pared down to the bone during 1981 because of economic necessity, but regular attendance at the now biannual "Meet Bournemouth" exhibitions (arranged by the Bournemouth Department of Tourism & Publicity in conjunction with Bournemouth's "Conference" hoteliers and held usually in the major centers like London over a two-day period) helped to secure new business as well as cement existing client relationships, and the Durley Hall Hotel entered 1982 confident in the knowledge that it had both a firm and wide base on which to build further conference business.

General tourist advertising is done via the national press and various specialist publications such as "Let's Go," the "Michelin Guide," the "Bournemouth Guide," and "Bargain Breaks," the latter being published by the Bournemouth Department of Tourism & Publicity and specifically geared to the promotion of off-season business. Moreover, in 1981, in view of the particularly difficult situation in which hotels were finding themselves, the English Tourist Board sponsored part of the cost of specific advertisements carried in the national press to promote Bournemouth and her hotels. These advertisements were produced by the hoteliers and coordinated by the Bournemouth Department of Tourism & Publicity. Analysis of the bookings received carried out by the Durley Hall Hotel as a result of these advertisements showed them to have been most effective, and it is therefore their policy to continue to take part in all such future advertising. No advertising agency is employed by the hotel, but the services of a professional layout artist are called upon to advise on the more ambitious promotions and advertisements.

In addition to the information gleaned from the hotel register, client feedback is also obtained by means of questionnaires left in rooms for completion. These give a constant appraisal of the standards and service of the hotel along with information on the effectiveness of advertising by requesting the clients to say how this particular hotel came to their notice, why they made their booking, and so on. The questionnaires also form the basis of a "Mail Shot Club" by which clients are regularly mailed with details of special offers, new tariffs, and so on, and from this Mail Shot, it is encouraging to see that the hotel is attracting more and more "repeat" business. At the same time, it also helps in the judgment and assessment of how special offers do appeal to a mass clientele.

Plans to expand "in-house" sales, as mentioned above, are tempered by experience in that, in the past, guests have traditionally been alienated by the idea of a large number of separate charges. "Simplicity is the key," as Mr. Murray puts it—"the client generally wants a package tied up in a single charge and it is always our policy to give the client what he wants." Interestingly enough, however, a change in client thinking is becoming apparent in that full-board terms no longer seem to be the requisite of holiday visitors—dinner, bed, and breakfast or bed and breakfast terms are very popular so the hotel, as well as offering bar food at lunch-time, is now looking into ways of changing its traditional lunch service in the restaurant. Of course, capital investment is always worthwhile if it means a cut in labor requirements, but dramatic changes would not be acceptable to regular clients.

The management team of the Durley Hall Hotel feels that the hotel industry is undergoing a major change, a tendency toward "business" custom and away from traditional "holiday-maker" business, and this is duly reflected in their actions regarding tariff structuring and pricing, advertising, and so on, but certainly, caution still remains the byword. One must try to foresee changes and adjust to them accordingly, but sweeping changes cannot be made until the market research has been thoroughly carried out. Customer satisfaction has to go hand in hand with profitability.

STEP 2: Prepare the case for class discussion.

STEP 3: Answer each of the following questions, individually or in small groups, as directed by your instructor:

Diagnosis
1. What are the information needs of the Durley Hall Hotel management team?

Evaluation
2. What market research has the team already done?
3. What market information does the team still need?
4. What other information does the team need to adjust for anticipated changes?
5. What needs could computer systems meet?

STEP 4: In small groups, with the entire class, or in written form, share your answers to the questions above. Then answer the following questions:

1. What information needs exist in this situation?
2. What types of information management are required?
3. What aspect of these information management requirements might be computerized?
4. What issues would be associated with computerizing the systems? ●

The Mike O'Chip Maintenance Company

STEP 1: Read the Mike O'Chip Maintenance company case.* (This activity is especially suited for use in conjunction with Chapter 2 of *Information Systems*.)

Bits and Pieces is a retail supplier of microcomputer systems and associated products with four outlets, all situated in Sheffield area. They used to market the products of four manufacturers of international repute together with ancillary equipment and software products. Most of their buyers are local small businesses.

However, the business microcomputer market has become more sophisticated. Distributors of the market-leading products expect higher standards from authorized dealers, and will not supply nonauthorized dealers any longer. Authorized dealers are expected, among other things

to stock an extensive minimal product range;

offer consultancy;

offer a range of introductory and advanced training courses;

offer an implementation service;

offer hotline support.

Only dealer staff who have attended courses run by the distributor are allowed to operate these services.

Accordingly, B & P have taken the strategic decision to become an authorized dealer for one main hardware distributor only, and to discontinue the arrangements with the other three as the contracts expire.

Among the problems created by this major decision is the question of honoring maintenance contracts, especially to customers of the discontinued ranges.

At present, maintenance as a function is treated as a necessary after-sales service, administered by the sales department. Even without the impetus of the new policy, it was becoming clear that the existing arrangements have become too inflexible for the maturing market base. There is evidence that sales have been lost because of this.

Since their establishment seven years ago, B & P have offered all new customers the benefits of a hardware maintenance contract administered by B & P. For an annual outlay of 10 percent of the purchase price, paid in advance, all servicing and repair work is carried out promptly and subject to no additional charges. The customer brings the item to any of the outlets and collects it again on notification of completion of the job, usually within 48 hours. Each day items for attention are collected and taken to the repair center on site at one of the outlets, whose serviced products are delivered back to the appropriate outlet.

A small number of products are not subject to maintenance contract, for example, those where it is known that replacement parts are in irregular supply and the terms of the contract would be difficult to honor.

This case was compiled from generalized experience. It was prepared by the author specifically for class discussion on the "IT in Management" option of the University of Sheffield MBA.

Copyright © 1990 R. F. Morgan, University of Sheffield

*All names in this case study are fictitious. Any similarities with real names are purely coincidental.

Once a contract has been entered into, B & P are obliged to renew it on demand for three more years on the same terms. After this time, B & P reserve the right to cancel the whole contract or remove selected items from it following an inspection. In addition, or as an alternative, the annual charge may be increased, often by as much as 50 percent per annum.

Where new equipment is added to the system (such as extra storage or a printer), the customer is offered a separate maintenance contract on this equipment. This happens quite often. In effect, a separate contract is issued for each self-contained piece of computer hardware such as visual display screen (monitor), keyboard, system unit, and so on. In practice this is complicated by the fact that suppliers may integrate some separate components into a single cabinet (e.g., hard disk and system unit, keyboard and system unit).

During the past 12 months problems of increasing severity have afflicted the maintenance function. A significant number of customers are complaining of matters such as undue delays in repair work, damage to cabinets of goods undergoing maintenance, and being offered the wrong goods for collection.

On inspection, it is discovered that most of the delays are being caused by increased workload plus a scarcity of parts for the older products. It appears that long-standing maintenance contracts are being automatically renewed on existing terms without the stipulated conditional inspection because of poor communications between sales and the maintenance section. Again, there is a suspicion that repeat sales are being lost because of this.

B & P management believe that the long-term solution lies in setting up a separate maintenance function which is better organized to anticipate and serve the needs of the customer base. In the short term, however, they are more concerned with the plans to reorganize the business.

Matters are brought to a head when B & P's maintenance engineer, Mike O'Chip, announces his intention to quit and set up on his own. He is tired of suffering avoidable customer complaints, has recognized the long-term opportunities in computer maintenance, and wishes to start his own business.

B & P Management immediately enter into negotiations and do a deal with Mike which they hope will ensure a friendly parting and the creation of a new long-standing and mutually beneficial relationship.

The essence of the deal is as follows:

1. For an agreed nominal amount, B & P will transfer all of its maintenance contracts to a company set up by Mike and cease all maintenance work of its own.
2. Mike will honor all existing maintenance contracts although he may alter the terms of fresh ones. In addition, Mike will have the option of purchasing at cost price all maintenance spares and equipment he wants.
3. B & P will provide Mike with a list of all customers not presently covered by maintenance contracts.
4. In the future, B & P will attempt to sell maintenance contracts on behalf of Mike's company to all purchasers of new equipment. For each successful sale, B & P will take a once-only introduction fee of 20 percent of the value of the contract in its first year. B & P will also provide Mike with the names and addresses of other purchasers who do not take out maintenance contracts.

By means of this agreement, B & P seek to offload their maintenance problems permanently and present customers with a better service at a stroke.

For his part, Mike O'Chip is acquiring an ongoing business at minimal cost with development potential in a number of directions.

He has several ideas for improving customer service. He intends to innovate an on-site contract at once. Repairs and servicing will be carried out at the place of use of the computer. If a case proves too difficult, the offending part will be removed to his workshop and, whenever possible, a substitute part fitted to leave the customer with a working machine. There will be a premium charge for this service.

Mike believes that this change will also smooth his workload and enable him to run the business single-handedly for a year or so, with the aid of an efficient administration, his wife. Peaks can be coped with by evening and weekend work, or so he hopes.

Most of his other ideas will be shelved until he decides which way to develop the business.

For example, he would like to break away from the rigid charging structure. Given sufficiently detailed information he would like to offer a 'No-claims' bonus to customers as an incentive not to call him out for trivialities. Likewise he would like to offer preferential terms for customers owning products with a proven reliability record.

At the moment he sees 3 broad alternatives, but others may present themselves in time, and anyway nos. 2 & 3 are not mutually exclusive.

The alternatives he sees are as follows:

1. Expand passively—that is, employ staff in response to additional work generated by B & P.
2. Expand aggressively—that is, generate new business by such methods as advertising his improved services to current users without maintenance contracts or by attempting B & P-type deals with other computer system suppliers.
3. Expand selectively—offer a superservice (at super-charges) to the larger business machine sector operating Local Area Networks.

Mike made his original decision to start the business through "back-of-an-envelope" figuring and personal frustration. However, he resolves to base future development decisions on sound information about the industry and his own operations.

He believes there are 3 essential ingredients of a good internal information system.

1. Determination in advance of what information he will need.
2. Carefully designed records and an easy way to use the system to provide such information from these records.
3. A simple, effective system for updating the records.

B & P had never bothered much about maintenance records. Being sales oriented, each shop kept a file for each customer, and following a maintenance operation a note would be entered containing the date, the nature of the maintenance, labor time and total parts cost. Parts were ordered centrally by telephone from the original equipment suppliers, following a telephone call from Mike. Purchase orders seldom got recorded on paper.

No attempt had ever been made to reconcile the total cost of the maintenance function against income. The original policy had been to set the annual maintenance charges at the level which would ensure that income would comfortably cover the operational costs, and everyone assumed, probably correctly, that this was still the case. Maintenance had never been seen as a profit-generating function.

Because his overall aim is growth, Mike decides to be ready and computerize his information system from the start using a relational database package. Hardware will, of course, be no problem and there are sufficient software writers around who owe him favors to enable him to get a system off the ground in the three months he has before the new business commences. In the longer term, the customer records system should be integrated with the accountancy system (i.e., items such as cost of parts employed on a callout should be picked up directly from the inventory control system). However, to keep things manageable in the short term, some such items will be input from data transcribed onto the callout form from manual records. In other words, he sees the customer records system primarily as a sales aid and information system.

Information on which Mike based his decision to start the business:

Number of customers of B & P to date = 2,100

Number of maintenance contracts to be transferred to Mike O'Chip's company = 500

Average value of each complete business hardware system sold = £2,760

Estimated number of new customers next year = 1,000

Estimated proportion of customers taking out hardware maintenance contracts = 5%

Estimated number of callouts/customer/year = 2

Estimated number of callouts dealt with per day = 5

Estimated average cost of parts/callout = £80

STEP 2: Prepare the case for class discussion.

STEP 3: Answer each of the following questions, individually or in small groups, as directed by your instructor:

Diagnosis
1. What are Mike's information needs?
2. How, if at all, have they changed since his split with Bits and Pieces?

Evaluation
3. What were the deficiencies in Bits and Pieces's information systems regarding maintenance services?
4. How could Mike use a computer to help with information management?

STEP 4: In small groups, with the entire class, or in written form, share your answers to the questions above. Then answer the following questions:

1. What information needs exist in this situation?
2. What types of information management are required?
3. What computer systems could be introduced to help manage information?
4. What are likely to be the issues associated with computerizing the management of information? ●

Lewis Foods Fleet Management

STEP 1: Read the Lewis Foods Fleet Management case. (This activity is especially suited for use in conjunction with Chapter 3 of *Information Systems*.)

LEWIS FOODS FLEET MANAGEMENT

On June 1, Lee Foods, an Omaha-based distributor of cheese and other foodstuffs, acquired Wisconsin Food Distributors, a similar company also based in Omaha, Nebraska, to form Lewis Foods. Lee Foods distributed cheese and other foodstuffs to fast food restaurants, pizzerias and Mexican restaurants throughout the states west of the Mississippi River. Lee Foods owned a fleet of 160 tractors and 230 refrigerated trailers. Wisconsin Foods was a distributor of perishables to retail grocery stores in a nine-state area centered in Omaha. Wisconsin Food Distributors had 90 tractors and 160 refrigerated trailers. A total of 26.5 million miles was driven by the two fleets in 1988 and that figure is remaining constant this year. Management anticipated that a total of 31.5 million miles, an additional 5 million miles, will be driven next year to support new customers.

At Lee Foods, John Richards, the chief mechanic, had also been serving as the dispatcher/fleet supervisor for the past year. At Wisconsin Foods, Al Lopez was the chief dispatcher with responsibilities similar to John's. After talking to both Al and John, Harlan Highsmith, the President of Lewis Foods, had the uneasy feeling that in the excitement generated by the potential savings in overhead costs, the increased productivity and efficiency due to economies of scale, and the larger market area, upper management may have overlooked some major issues in the merger of the two fleets.

As a result, he created the position of fleet manager to oversee the entire fleet. John Richards was to be named chief mechanic for Lewis Foods, the newly formed company and Al Lopez was to take the position of chief dispatcher when the merger of the two fleets was completed. Harlan Highsmith knew whom he wanted as fleet manager. He contacted Bill Carnes and offered him the job. He voiced his uneasy feelings and emphasized that he wanted a smooth changeover.

On July 15th, Bill Carnes became the Fleet Manager for Lewis Foods, the newly formed company. His first concern was to merge the operation and management of the two groups of trucks into a single fleet rather than continue to operate two separate fleets. The warehouse division of the company had completed their plans and expected to close the Wisconsin Foods facility in about 90 days. At that time all route planning and dispatching of loads would be out of the main warehouse.

Bill began his job of integrating the two groups into a single unit by evaluating the past performance of the two fleets. The major expenditures in fleet operations are for fuel, engine maintenance and tires. The staff anticipated Bill's information needs and prepared a report on fuel economy, maintenance and tire life for the trucking industry as shown in Table I and a comparison of the two fleets as shown in Table II. This report failed to identify the strengths and weaknesses of the operations of the two fleets. Bill Carnes visited both terminals and obtained the following additional information.

At Lee Foods, John Richards, the chief mechanic, provided much of the information Bill wanted. The Lee fleet consists of tandem Kenworth and Peterbilt tractors. Eighty percent of

---

This case was written by Carl R. Ruthstrom, University of Houston–Downtown, David Cross, Robert Bosch Power Tool Corp., and Arthur Nelson, Lufkin Industries. Published with the permission of the North American Case Research Association.

Table I Operating Performance-Industry Averages

Fuel Economy	5.7 mpg
Engine Overhauls	Every 450,000 miles to 475,000 miles
Tire Life	Recapped at every 150,000 miles, replaced at 500,000 miles

Table II Lee/Wisconsin Performance Comparisons

	Lee Averages	Wisconsin Averages
Fuel Economy	5.0 mpg	5.8 mpg
Engine Overhauls	330,000 miles	450,000 miles
Tire Life	Recapped at every 100,000 miles, replaced at 345,000 miles	Recapped at every 150,000 miles, replaced at 500,00 miles

the tractors are powered by the Cummins 350 Big Cam III governed at 1800 RPM. The phrase "governed at 1800 RPM" means that a governor or speed control device is installed on the engine to limit the maximum engine speed to 1800 revolutions per minute. This extends the operating life of the engines. The other twenty percent of the fleet's engines are Caterpillar 3406Bs governed at 1600 RPM.

The Lee fleet uses eight Goodyear 167 radial tires, four on each of the two drive axles, and two Goodyear Unisteel IIs on the single steering axle of each tractor. The trailers have another eight tires, four on each of the two axles. Tires removed from the steering axles are recapped and used on trailers. At the third recap, drive axle tires are moved back to the trailers. Only recapped tires are used on the trailers.

Two years ago, Lee had improved the fuel economy to 5 miles per gallon (MPG) by using fuel saving devices such as Paccar's Varashield air deflectors, Rudkin Wiley cab extenders, Rockford viscous fans, and lower horsepower engines. "But, somehow we seem to have hit a plateau and cannot get above 5 MPG," said John Richards.

Driver comfort and safety have always been important considerations at Lee Foods as shown by the cabs with their deluxe carpeted interiors, AM/FM radio-tape players, air conditioning and seats with air-ride suspensions. The estimated cost of upgrading the interiors is $2000 per tractor. In addition, Lee has awarded drivers completing one million miles of safe driving with a $1000 bonus check. Every month, each driver attends a half-day driver safety and improvement class conducted by company instructors. As a result, Lee, with a turnover rate of three percent, has one of the lowest driver turnover rates in the trucking industry.

John Richards said, "There are not any labor problems at Lee. The only new drivers we have hired replaced those lost to retirement or physical disability."

At the Wisconsin Foods terminal, Al Lopez, the chief dispatcher, provided similar information. The Wisconsin fleet is entirely Kenworth tractors powered by the Cummins 350 Big Cam III engines governed at 1800 RPM. Fuel saving devices similar to those used by Lee are installed on all the tractors. Drivers are allowed to customize their tractors at their own expense resulting in interiors similar to the Lee tractors.

Two and one-half years ago, Wisconsin implemented a transportation improvement (TRIM) program. The program includes Stemco's on-board computer monitoring system (trip recorder) and Stemco's vehicle management system (VMS) software package. The recorders are installed in all Wisconsin's tractors. The hardware for this system averages $2200 per tractor. The memory cartridges are in the tractors when drivers are dispatched. At the end of a trip, the last thing a driver does is to remove the cartridge and turn it into dispatch. There he is given a blank cartridge, which he installs before leaving for the day. The driver enters his identification, the vehicle number and the route number at the start of each trip. In addition, he enters the number of gallons of fuel purchased for the trip. The computerized recorder stores times, engine RPM, speed in MPH, foot brake applications, and stops.

The data for each trip is downloaded from the memory cartridge to an IBM PC and subsequently stored on a floppy disc. The VMS program analyzes the data and prints out a Basic Trip Summary. Included in this summary are the statistics of various performance criteria management selected to evaluate driver performance, such as engine on time, idle time, road time, speed RPM, and fuel consumption plus a grade (from 0 to 100) of the driver's performance.

The drivers were introduced to the TRIM program in meetings of 10 to 15 drivers. In these meetings, the emphasis was on improving fleet performance by identifying the problem areas in each driver's performance. Initially, the computer trip summaries showed 50% to 60% of the drivers were speeding (running above 58 MPH).

Al Lopez said, "We knew that the greatest savings for large tractors can be achieved through improved gas mileage and reduced wear on the vehicle. Better efficiency in either area would make a very visible difference in costs. We started informally counseling the drivers with emphasis on driver awareness of economical driving habits. The non-threatening approach produced dramatic results in reducing our fleet costs. Our fuel economy rose rapidly to 5.8 MPG where it remains today. Tire wear and engine maintenance costs have declined noticeably."

The single most noteworthy incident occurred when one of the drivers blew a Cummins engine in Texas. Cummins claimed it was attributable to over-revving and speed. The driver brought the memory cartridge with him when he flew back to Omaha. The VMS program analyzed the data and showed no speeding or over-revving, saving the company a $17,000 engine repair bill.

"The most disappointing thing about the TRIM program is that we have never reached the anticipated 6-7 MPG that the Stemco salesmen assured us could be attained. In addition, we seem to be continually training new drivers on the system. Over 40% of our drivers have less than one year with the company," volunteered Al Lopez.

Further discussion with Al Lopez revealed that while 20 to 25% turnover of drivers was not unusual in the trucking industry, other underlying problems did exist. Both the chief dispatcher and the drivers feel that all the benefits of the computerized vehicle management system are reserved for the company.

The drivers are of the opinion that having "a cop" in the cab limits their potential earnings and does not allow the driver much freedom in terms of length of driving day, breaks, and sleeping time. Therefore, most of the turnover of drivers is generated by the lure of higher incomes and more individual freedom in other trucking companies.

Upon his return to his office, Bill Carnes decided to review that data in Tables I and II to compare the performance differences in fuel consumption, maintenance and tire wear. After reviewing the data in Table II, he decided to visit accounting and acquire cost data comparisons for the two fleets. Since the two fleets had continued operating separately, accounting had maintained separate books. The data Bill needed was readily available and Bill constructed Table III.

Before leaving, he questioned the accounting supervisor, Shirley Williams, about the differences in operating costs per mile between the two fleets. Shirley confirmed his finding that the Lee trucks were reporting higher fuel, tire and engine repair costs per truck than the Wisconsin fleet. Shirley Williams had begun investigating the differences in operating costs and found that both fleets were reporting approximately the same unit costs for fuel, tires,

Table III Lee/Wisconsin Cost Comparisons

	Lee Averages	Wisconsin Averages
Cost per mile		
Equipment	$0.82	$0.65
Drivers	$0.61	$0.58
Miles per year		
Per tractor	112,708	94,075
Per driver	77,420	73,127

Table IV Unit Costs

Item	Unit Price
Engine Overhauls	$7000 per engine
Diesel fuel	$1.15 per gallon
New tires	
Steering Axles	$175 per tire
Drive Axles	$195 per tire
Recapping	$65 per tire

and engine overhauls as listed in Table IV. Shirley also found that the company policies for both fleets included the replacement of 15 percent of the fleet with new tractor-trailer rigs each year.

At first she was puzzled by the difference in the drivers' cost per mile. "Both groups of drivers are paid union scale. I'll have to look into this for you," Shirley said. As Shirley reviewed the records used to calculate the drivers' cost per mile for the two fleets, the only differences she could find were the safe driving bonuses paid to Lee drivers and lower pay to Wisconsin drivers during their initial probationary period. Shirley did find that the total pay and benefits package was larger for the Lee drivers because of the greater number of miles driven annually.

As Bill Carnes walked back to his office, he remembered Al Lopez's final remark, "Over 40% of our drivers have less than one year with the company." He made a mental note to confirm this with Shirley Williams in the morning.

When Bill Carnes returned to his office at 4:00 p.m., his secretary handed him a message to call Harlan Highsmith, President of Lewis Foods, immediately. Bill was surprised when Harlan Highsmith answered the phone without the assistance of a secretary.

After preliminary salutations, Harlan Highsmith said, "Bill, you have been with the company long enough to evaluate our current fleet operations. I've scheduled you to present your plans for integrating the Lee and Wisconsin fleet operations into a single fleet for 3:00 p.m., tomorrow. Have a good evening."

Bill Carnes realized that his recommended program must address both fleet operating costs and employee relations. He realized that capital investments may be needed in both fleets to achieve improvements in these areas.

At 6:00 p.m., before leaving the office, he called both John Richards and Al Lopez at home. He explained why he was calling and solicited their help in preparing for the 3:00 p.m. meeting. Both men agreed to be in Bill Carnes' office at 9:00 a.m. the next morning to assist in developing the plans for integrating the two fleets.

At 9:00 a.m., the next morning John Richards and Al Lopez report to Bill Carnes' office. By this time, Bill Carnes has begun to feel the same uneasiness that Harlan Highsmith, the President, had expressed when he hired Bill.

Bill Carnes begins, "After tossing and turning all night, I finally got dressed and prepared this list of questions that need to be answered."

1. What problems do you anticipate from the employees related to the merging of the two fleets if we do not make any changes in the treatment of the two groups of drivers?
2. What issues do you anticipate will cause the most concern among the drivers and what approach should we use to integrate the two fleets without alienating drivers?
3. Some of the drivers already qualify for the safe driving bonus. Could we continue this and add a bonus of $.03 per mile for every mile driven under 58 MPH?
4. Since any changes or improvements will cost money, where will we get the money to implement our plans?
5. Assuming that we decide to upgrade the tractors, would your first action be to install the Stemco trip recorders in all the Lee tractors or upgrade the driver comfort items in the Wisconsin tractors? Why?

"I have been listening to all of the drivers' comments at Lee and can give you a long list of answers for those first two questions," exclaimed John Richards.

"I'll bet my list of gripes is longer," said Al Lopez.

"Great! John, if you and Al will work on the first two questions, I'll get to work on the last three. Remember that we need more than just a list of gripes. We need a plan detailing how we are going to integrate the two groups of drivers without creating more problems. Let's meet back here at 11:00 a.m. and see what progress we have made."

STEP 2: Prepare the case for class discussion.

STEP 3: Answer each of the following questions, individually or in small groups, as directed by your instructor.

Diagnosis
1. What management processes and roles does Bill perform?
2. What information does he need to manage the fleet merger?

Evaluation
3. What systems exist for collecting, analyzing, and reporting the information?
4. Are these systems computerized?
5. What problems exist in securing the necessary information?

STEP 4: In small groups, with the entire class, or in written form, share your answers to the questions above. Then answer the following questions:

1. What types of information do managers at Lewis Foods Fleet Management require?
2. What systems exist to supply this information?
3. How effective are these systems?
4. What changes should be made in the information systems? ●

Activity 4

Connor Spring

STEP 1: Read the Connor Spring case. (This activity is especially suited for use in conjunction with Chapter 4 of *Information Systems*.)

THE KNOWLEDGE FACTORY

By the mid-1980s Joe and Henry Sloss, the twin brothers who had built up the family business, were getting on in years and were thinking about retirement. Joe's son Bob, the only member of the next generation on the payroll, was ready to take over.

Ready. OK, that might be an understatement. More like chomping at the bit. Pounding at the door. Because Robert Sloss, then in his thirties, had discovered not just a job but a mission.

The company he was inheriting was a small metal-spring manufacturer, successful in its day but exactly the kind of old-line, low-tech business likely to be eaten alive by aggressive and innovative Far Eastern competitors. Young Bob—an alumnus of Stanford's summertime executive-education program and a fan of Tom Peters—set out to search for excellence right in his own backyard. American industry, he decided, could be revived, its loyal employees rewarded and reinspired. The Japanese and Taiwanese and Singaporeans could be repulsed. Spearheading the attack would be the Sloss family business, Connor Spring.

Once in charge, Sloss made all the right moves. He bought state-of-the-art machinery. He decentralized the company, ceding day-to-day authority to the managers of its four plants. He set up an employee stock ownership plan (ESOP) and instituted a quarterly cash bonus based on each plant's profits. He plunged into statistical process control and the other accoutrements of modern quality assurance. And he made sure—through stylish videos, glossy brochures, slick sales presentations—that customers heard about the all-new, world-class Connor.

The blitz almost worked. Connor's shipments rose from $12.4 million in 1985 to $16.4 million in 1989. The company landed new jobs from big customers such as Aerojet; it became a certified vendor to the likes of Hewlett-Packard and Xerox. Japanese transplants searching for U.S. suppliers began sniffing around Connor. Employees seemed more content and more committed. What else could Sloss want? Really, just one little thing. He would have been happier if the company were making decent money.

He knew that Connor's loses in 1989, the first year in at least two decades the company actually wound up in the red, could be chalked up to the closing of a plant in Phoenix and the transfer of many employees to Connor's Dallas facility. But he also knew the financial problems ran deep and that they weren't being solved by all his fancy footwork. The Dallas operation, established in 1984, hadn't yet seen a profitable year. The flagship plant in Los Angeles, Connor's biggest, was barely squeaking by. Only the little shops in Portland, Ore., and San Jose, Calif., were solidly in the black, and at best they pulled the company a few percentage points above break-even. Something had to be done.

It was then that Sloss, almost unwittingly, found himself presiding over a change that would leave Connor Spring looking remarkably different, not only from its most recent incarnation but from most other companies in the United States. The change didn't involve yet another hotshot management philosophy, only a new tool for making the company run bet-

---

Reprinted with permission, *Inc.* magazine, October 1991. Copyright 1991 by Goldhirsh Group, Inc. 38 Commercial Wharf, Boston, MA 02110. "The Knowledge Factory" John Case.

ter. Or so it seemed at the time: today, midway through the process, the tool seems to be transforming Connor's whole culture.

The tool—the driving force behind this ongoing metamorphosis—is information. Now, the astute use of information is one hot topic among management gurus these days. Gather more data about your customers! Communicate more with your employees! Analyze those critical financial indicators! Such injunctions never hurt. But they may not help much either, because they address maybe 10% of a business's information flow.

The other 90%, the part that never shows up in market-research studies or employee newsletters or monthly P&Ls, is the mundane, nuts-and-bolts information that permeates a company every minute of every day, determining how managers allocate resources and how employees spend their time. Why Customer X is complaining. Which jobs absolutely, positively have to be done by Friday. How much money we stand to make this month on the National Widgets account, why Bill in sales has been spending so much time in Chicago, what's causing the bottleneck in shipping. Small companies' chief executives typically know or learn the answers to those and a hundred similar questions: that's why they feel—and frequently are—indispensable to smooth operations and why they intuitively understand bigger-picture issues such as cost ratios or market trends. Most CEOs, however, never think about sharing what they know with any but a few top managers.

But ask yourself—suppose all employees in the company had easy access to everyday knowledge of this sort? And suppose they could not only receive but exchange information, adding what they know to the pool and thereby enabling everyone to work just a little more intelligently? As Harvard Business School professor Shoshana Zuboff argues in her book *In the Age of the Smart Machine,* modern computer and communications systems allow knowledge that once resided "in people's heads, in face-to-face conversations, in metal file drawers, and in widely dispersed pieces of paper" to be disseminated throughout an organization, moving upward and sideways as well as downward. People with access to all that information work differently—work smarter—because they suddenly know a whole lot more about what they and everyone else in the business are doing.

Bob Sloss hadn't read Zuboff. But he did want to boost his bottom line, and he figured Connor's information systems were a good place to start tightening things up.

Connor Formed Metal Products, as the company has recently been rechristened, is a jobshop manufacturer, making springs and other components to a customer's specifications. In some ways it's a prototypical business enterprise. Like a professional-services firm, it has hundreds of customers, each one with unique, complex, and usually urgent needs. Like a retailer, it has to manage a sizable and varied mix of products, and like a high-tech manufacturer, it has to guarantee near-flawless quality.

And like many, many small American companies, Connor was, less than two years ago, processing information much as information was processed in 1950. In the Los Angeles plant, engineers cranked out cost estimates by hand, penciling in figures for raw materials and machine speeds and labor hours, then erasing and starting over when the bottom line seemed too high or too low. Salespeople kept handwritten trip reports and copies of letters in cumbersome loose-leaf notebooks. In the office, clerical workers typed out highly detailed shop orders, 10 carbons deep, using Wite-Out on errors. Out in the shop, supervisors did their best to read specs off a finger-smudged copy of the order.

Even managers were often flying blind. Once a job was out the door, for example, no one could be sure whether it had been profitable. For a while, Connor kept labor-time records for each job by hand. But the data were never collated or analyzed, in part because their accuracy was suspect. Ironically, Sloss had spent nearly $300,000 on computers a few years earlier, installing several IBM System 36 minicomputers. But the big machines and their canned software proved too clumsy for daily plant-level chores such as estimating or job costing, and managers mostly ignored them.

By 1989 Sloss had begun thinking about using personal computers, which were getting more powerful by the day, and about custom software. His San Jose plant manager had already begun experimenting with PCs, albeit with packaged programs. And now here was this young man named Michael Quarrey looking for a job.

Quarrey had some unusual credentials. He had worked for the National Center for Employee Ownership and was an ESOP expert. He was also an experienced programmer and was just leaving a position with another job shop. After a moment's hesitation—"the idea of a little company like ours hiring a computer programmer was mind-boggling"—Sloss hired him and installed him in Los Angeles with instructions to develop an effective job-tracking and job-costing system. On Quarrey's recommendation he immediately began buying PCs and networking software.

Before long Quarrey was writing programs to computerize the L.A. operation's information flow. Before long, too, the two men realized they shared an agenda going well beyond computerization.

Ever since he took over, Sloss had been chipping away at Connor's old-fashioned, secretive style of management. Employees had become part owners of Connor through the ESOP, he argued; they should be treated like owners. So he explained the company's financial statistics to them, and he made a point of walking around the plant, answering questions. Now, he figured, the new computer system gave him a chance to disseminate day-to-day operating data, exactly what owners ought to see. Quarrey, similarly inclined toward employee involvement, designed his system to ensure broad access. He also designed a two-way flow of information: each electronic shop order would contain "notes" areas, so that engineering or quality control, for example, could enter comments about a particular job.

But it was Roy Gallucci, a blunt-spoken machinist in Connor's coiling department, who may have had the biggest impact on the new system.

"Gallucci stopped me one day in the shop," remembers Sloss, "and pretty soon we were talking in the plant manager's office behind closed doors." The machinist's message to the boss was simple. At least one computer should be out in the shop. Blue-collar employees should have the ability not only to enter comments about a job but to somehow force the office to pay attention. He didn't know exactly how it might work, but if the company was going to put in a whole new system, it had better do it right.

Bingo, thought Sloss: Gallucci was touching on a perennial complaint, namely, that the office never listened to the shop. Here was a chance to deal with it.

Quarrey agreed—not that he had much choice. "There was no discussion," he remembers. "Bob said, 'do it.'" By May of 1990 Quarrey had his unusual new system up and running.

Pull up to Connor's L.A. plant—it's actually in Monterey Park, on the outskirts of the city—and you won't be immediately impressed. It's housed in a standard-issue industrial building. Inventory spills out from the shipping door into the weed-rimmed, California-size parking lot. Inside, Connor looks like a company on a bare-bones budget. There's no receptionist: visitors are invited to use the phone in the lobby. The office staff—which, it turns out, handles customer service, invoicing, purchasing, bookkeeping, personnel, production scheduling, and all related paperwork—numbers exactly six.

But don't be misled by the seeming austerity: this is not a company done in by the recession. In the last two years the plant's head count has dropped (through attrition) by 15—yet its sales have *risen* 28%, to an annual level of $10 million. In 1990 Connor's L.A. division turned a 5% pretax profit. It's maintaining that pace this year, despite the downturn in the economy.

On the face of things, the difference between today's Connor and 1989's is purely technological. Customer-service reps now prepare shop orders on a quietly humming PC—no more carbons and Wite-Out. Engineers use an estimating program to calculate trial quotes in minutes, not hours.

But dig a little deeper—talk to people throughout the company about what's different now—and the magnitude of Connor's ongoing transformation becomes apparent. Plenty of companies computerize their information systems. Not many disseminate information to every nook and cranny of the organization—let alone share the power all that knowledge carries with it.

At Connor, that's pretty much what is happening.

Thanks to Roy Gallucci, for example, every employee has full and instant access to data about the jobs he or she is working on. Not just the customer's name and the specs, but a full history of the job to date, special notes or instructions from engineering or customer service, and management information once thought of as sensitive, such as the price and the margin. An employee who spots (or develops) a problem with a job can go to the computer and put a "shop hold" on it. Until the engineering department investigates—and makes a formal written disposition of the problem—the software won't allow Connor to take any new orders for the same part.

In one recent six-week period, Quarrey counted 117 holds emanating from machine operators and their supervisors. "This grinding can only be done by A-1 Surface Grinding," read one, adding the address, a contact name, and the price per part that the preferred outside vendor would charge. "OK, will change the master," responded engineering. "Change run speed from 850 pcs/hr to 700 pcs/hr," answered the not-totally-compliant engineer. Gallucci himself admits to using the feature regularly—for example, to propose sending a three-part order out for heat treating all together rather than one batch at a time. And Quarrey points out that similar holds can be put on a shop order by quality control, by engineering ("Don't allow this estimate to become an order until we have a clean blueprint"), or by customer service ("Don't ship without clearance from us").

A direct effect of sharing information and power is that problems get nipped in the bud and jobs that cause difficulties the first time around rarely cause the same difficulties the second time. Closing the loop, Quarrey calls it: the people who need feedback get feedback. That effect shows up most graphically in a number calculated monthly by Armando Lopez, Connor's head of quality control, and posted on the bulletin board outside the lunchroom. In 1989 Connor's "cost of discrepant material"—rejects, rework time, and so on—came to 4.28% of sales. A year later the figure was just over 1%; through May of this year it was .5%.

But the indirect effect of Connor's unusual system may be even more dramatic: just as Harvard's Zuboff might have predicted, it is altering the way the company operates. Information is now both widely available and easily accessible, so employees all over the organization have begun to ask questions and to learn more about matters affecting their own jobs. Then too, the company evidently welcomes initiative—so plenty of employees have begun to propose new ways of doing things. Consider four examples:

- Javier Castro, a setup man working the second shift, has begun making it a practice to consult the computer about upcoming jobs. Noticing that a part for Hughes Aircraft was being done in two steps, he checked the price, then calculated that he could do it more cheaply in one step on his computer-numerical-control machine. So he proposed the change to his supervisor, Ron Washburn. "Within three days I had the job, with no secondary operations," says Castro. "We saved probably 200 hours of secondary operations per order."
- Judy Quinn and Jan Morgan, who handle most of Connor's customer service, always knew they were spending a sizable chunk of their time handling change orders on jobs, but couldn't figure out where all those changes were coming from. Earlier this year they asked Quarrey if the new system would allow them to track the orders. It would. Pulling up the

reports, the two women found that roughly one out of every five change orders was internally generated—and that a significant fraction of those were caused by initial errors in entering an order. "So we developed a purchase-order checklist," says Quinn, "a list of items to be checked to make sure we didn't miss anything. That's cut down on the internal change orders significantly."

- Karla Penalba, in charge of purchasing, was hearing from top management that raw-material quality was key to Connor's manufacturing quality. Yet she realized she had no systematic information on individual vendors' performance in such areas as on-time delivery. So last February she and Quarrey set up a spreadsheet-based program to track every shipment; since then she has produced reports rating Connor's suppliers. Later this year new purchasing software will be integrated with the shop-order system, making it possible for anyone in the building to learn the status of raw-material deliveries.
- Jeff Applegate, an outside sales manager, asked for and got a laptop computer last January. Until then he had relied on phone calls and occasional handwritten reports to keep the shop up to date about his customers' needs; since then he has been generating a flood of neatly printed memos, which are circulated to the appropriate people and posted on the bulletin board. "The more information people get from me, the more they understand the customer's needs," says Applegate. "Pretty soon the toolmaker and the production foreman and engineering are anticipating, not just reacting." Later this year Applegate and Connor's other salespeople will get high-speed modems allowing them, too, to tie into the shop-order-system—and to check a job's progress or enter comments from remote sites.

Sloss and Quarrey themselves have plenty of ideas for the future. The "quality alert" notices issued for troublesome jobs by Lopez's quality-control department will soon pop up automatically on shop orders. Late deliveries will automatically be flagged for later analysis. Most ambitious, each step in every job will soon be coded, so the corporate office can then calculate and produce a P&L statement not only by plant but also by department. That information, too, will be shared. The rationale? "We're taking the knowledge necessary for business decision making and giving it to people in the shop," says Quarrey. "That has been the philosophical objective—to give people enough information to change their roles."

Introducing the new system in the Los Angeles plant cost close to $100,000 in computer hardware, plus maybe half of Quarrey's time over two years. Spreading the system to the other plants, a process that will be completed by the end of 1991, won't be so expensive, but some plants will have to buy PCs, and employees will have to learn the system. Connor's information mania is not coming cheap.

The payoff, however, is already plain, at least for the L.A. division. Late jobs have declined over the past two years, from 10% of backlog to less than 1%. Connor's scores in the annual quality ratings provided by many of its customers have climbed to near perfection. The company's service and quality record commands a premium in the marketplace. An Indiana customer hired Connor as the sole source for several items, even though Connor's price was considerably higher than the other bids. A Los Angeles County customer invented the acronym CDBWGDCS, for Cost of Doing Business with Goddamn Connor Spring. "That was my purchasing manager," chuckles Al Wentzell, materials manager for Anthony Industrial Products. "Every time I wondered why we were paying this much for a part, he'd put those letters on the board. But the quality and service they give us are phenomenal."

The information systems also reduce Connor's costs. In 1989, 14% of defective jobs had similar problems the second time around. By 1990 that figure was down to 4%. Credits issued to customers fell from almost 4% of sales, in 1989, to slightly over .5%, in 1990. The company's overall sales per employee have risen about 20% in the past two years.

There are other payoffs as well.

For the employees and managers of Connor, there's the knowledge that they own 42% of a company whose stock value rose 35% last year—and that increased earnings will be reflected in fat bonus checks. Arguably, it's that financial interest in the company that makes the information system work. There's a tangible reward for making the kind of improvements the new system encourages.

For Bob Sloss, the payoffs are both tangible and intangible. His family's 55% interest in Connor is worth as much as its 100% interest was worth when the ESOP was started, in 1985. His company is once again profitable and seems to be weathering the national recession well.

Maybe more important, he has the satisfaction of accomplishing at least part of that original mission to revive American industry. Spring making as a whole hasn't done too well in recent years. But Connor has taken on all comers and won its share of victories.

"We're competing with the best house in Japan, and the best in Germany, and the best in Korea," says Sloss. "And we're still in the game."

STEP 2: Prepare the case for class discussion.

STEP 3: Answer each of the following questions, individually or in small groups, as directed by your instructor:

Diagnosis
1. What business problems was Connor Spring experiencing?
2. What strategy did the top executives at Connor Spring develop?
3. How did they plan to secure a competitive advantage over other companies in the industry?
4. What information did the management and employees of Connor Spring require to obtain this advantage?

Evaluation
5. Did Connor Spring have any information systems for meeting these needs?
6. How effective were these systems?
7. What types of information systems did Connor Spring introduce?
8. How well did they provide the information the company required to compete effectively?

Implementation
9. What costs were incurred in implementing these information systems?

STEP 4: In small groups, with the entire class, or in written form, share your answers to the questions above. Then answer the following questions:

1. What information needs existed in this situation?
2. How would meeting these needs give the company a competitive advantage?
3. What computer systems were introduced to meet these needs?
4. What have been the costs and benefits of these systems? ●

St. Thomas Psychiatric Hospital—A Strategic Planning Framework

STEP 1: Read the St. Thomas Psychiatric Hospital case. (This activity is especially suited for use in conjunction with Chapter 4 of *Information Systems*.)

Chris Bailey, Coordinator of Planning and Management Services at the St. Thomas Psychiatric Hospital in St. Thomas, Ontario, met with Bob Cunningham, the hospital administrator, late July 1989. "You mentioned that we should get together to discuss my proposal for a hospital strategic planning process," she said. "What do you think of it so far?"

THE HOSPITAL

St. Thomas Psychiatric Hospital (STPH) was one of ten provincial psychiatric hospitals operated by the Ontario Ministry of Health, the government body responsible for overseeing personal, community, and institutional health care in Ontario. It was a 500-bed hospital with 2000 registered outpatients and 800 staff. Its mandate was to serve people aged 16 and over living in St. Thomas and five nearby southwestern Ontario counties. The psychiatric services offered to patients included assessment, diagnosis, treatment, rehabilitation, consultation, and education. STPH provided out-patient and crisis services, and acted as a resource for general hospitals in the counties served. Patient treatment at times involved individual, group, and family therapy, occupational therapy, physiotherapy, rehabilitation for community living, as well as vocational and recreational services.

STPH Computing Resources

The hospital had a Data General MV4000 minicomputer with five Megabytes main memory, and a 354 Megabyte disk drive. Installed on the Data General were ADT (admission, discharge, transfer), pharmacy, and business application software, and a query language, Forthwriter.

Several STPH departments had also installed PC-based information systems, as depicted in Exhibit 1. These systems utilized Epson Equity II+ personal computers and IBM-compatible software. Department heads and program directors used the PC-based information to supplement the data available from the minicomputer when analyzing departmental and program efficiency and effectiveness. This information was especially valuable to them at this time because of increasing government cost control requirements.

MOTIVATION FOR STRATEGIC PLANNING

In recent years, government cutbacks had resulted in annual hospital budget increases below the inflation rate. It had thus become important for hospitals to allocate scarce funds optimally, in a manner consistent with their overall objectives. Government hospitals, STPH included, were now placing greater emphasis on proactively managing the services provided. At STPH, Bob Cunningham had asked Chris Bailey a few weeks earlier to recommend a

---

This case was prepared by Yolande Chan, under the direction of Professor Sid L. Huff, as the basis for classroom discussion. Copyright 1989 the University of Western Ontario.

Exhibit 1 Organizational Overview—St. Thomas Psychiatric Hospital

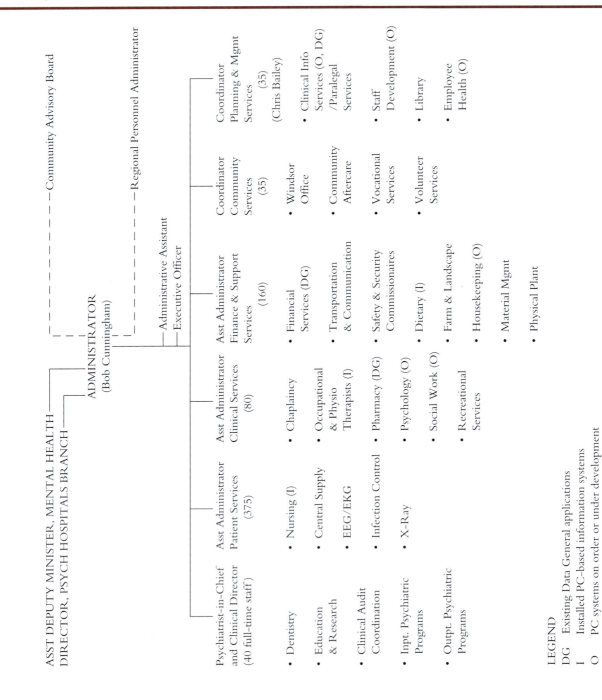

planning strategy that might serve as a basis for future hospital resource and program planning. A 32-year-old with an MBA from York University, she had been with the hospital for just over three years and was keen to make her contribution.

THE VISION FOR STRATEGIC PLANNING AT STPH

Chris envisioned that strategic planning at STPH would involve the formalized ongoing process of developing, evaluating, and implementing STPH goals, and guiding hospital decision-making processes. Information collected could be used to determine departmental and program strengths, weaknesses, and utilization. In this way, strategic planning could assist the hospital in optimizing its service levels.

Chris had recommended that a corporate database be created to support the STPH strategic planning effort. Her goal was to have enough departmental, program, and environmental information available so that management could track past, present, and expected required hospital services and performance. It would be necessary to quantify what the hospital was already doing, analyze departmental and program effectiveness, and identify possible cost savings through, for example, resource sharing.

Chris had recently recommended to Bob Cunningham the strategic planning framework depicted in Exhibit 2. She believed that strategic analysis should begin with an environmental assessment which could be used to refine the STPH mandate. Hospital operations could then be evaluated relative to the mandate in terms of effectiveness, efficiency, technological change and possible risk. The results of these ongoing evaluations could be used also to further refine the hospital mandate. The process would be iterative.

The *environmental assessment* that Chris was considering for STPH included monitoring:

1. Demographics, i.e. population trends and socio-economic statistics
2. Canadian and provincial disease incidence statistics
3. Designated service area psychiatric diagnosis statistics
4. STPH admission statistics
5. Socio-political conditions
6. Local hospital profile and image
7. Financial conditions including funding trends and forecasts
8. Competitive analysis including:
    - Substitute services and technologies provided by other facilities such as nursing homes and psychiatric wards of general hospitals
    - Suppliers of professional and technical resources, i.e. staff
    - Buyers of services, i.e. the agencies, facilities, and individuals who referred patients to STPH
    - Potential entrants and providers of similar services

This environmental analysis might highlight factors which could influence specific services or even the entire hospital.

Chris expected *STPH's mandate,* encompassing its stated mission, goals and objectives, to change over time to meet future requirements. The mandate could be formally stated and updated annually to reflect changes in:

1. Key problems faced by the hospital
2. A prediction of how these problems would change and what new challenges would be faced
3. A statement of the services to be provided and to whom
4. A description of the ongoing relationship the hospital had with the local community, other institutions, and agencies

Exhibit 2   A Proposed Framework for Strategic Planning at STPH

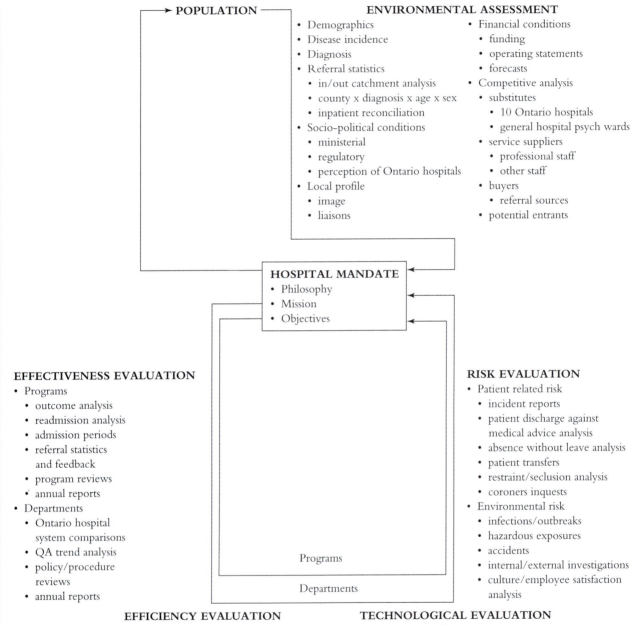

5. A description of the hospital's commitment to education and research
6. A description of the hospital's culture and a summary of its history

Chris felt sure that a *service effectiveness evaluation* would be key to any successful strategic planning effort. The important questions to be asked here included:

1. What is the business of this department or departmental program?
2. How effectively are these services being provided?
3. Are these services appropriate for the department or program?

Information on individuals, programs, and departments could be collected on a monthly basis and then spreadsheet and trend analyses carried out. On an annual basis, the following information also could be analyzed and reviewed:

1. Departmental quality assurance statistics
2. Comparisons with other departments in the Ontario hospital system
3. Feedback from patients who had used departmental services

Chris thought that *efficiency evaluation* might involve quantifying both departmental and program inputs and outputs. These inputs would include people (both direct and indirect staff involved in patient care), equipment, supplies, etc. Program outputs could be reflected in statistics on patient days, staff/patient ratios, and so on. Departments might also be asked to specify more detailed breakdowns of their services and to conduct more frequent operational reviews.

Technological evaluations could be carried out at the department or program level. It would be difficult to do technological planning centrally because of the large volume of information and the specific technical expertise required. Ongoing monitoring of the following could take place:

1. Changes in state-of-the-art techniques for patient care
2. Changing availability of equipment
3. Changes in drug usage

Risk evaluation would involve capturing information to assist with identifying and preventing action that might lead to patient, employee, or visitor injury, or damage to hospital property. Patient incident reports, disturbances, accidents, etc. could be monitored. Trend analyses also could be carried out.

The STPH strategic planning process would be followed by strategy implementation. This would involve determining specific action plans, resource allocation and budgetary processes, as well as monitoring newly acquired hospital resources.

THE ADMINISTRATOR'S RESPONSE

Chris Bailey had recommended a strategic planning process to be followed and the information to be gathered. It was now up to Bob Cunningham, the Administrator, to give Chris his feedback.

STEP 2: Prepare the case for class discussion.

STEP 3: Answer each of the following questions, individually or in small groups, as directed by your instructor:

Diagnosis
1. Why did the hospital engage in strategic planning?
2. What information did it require as part of its strategic planning effort?
3. How could the hospital secure a competitive advantage?
4. What information did the hospital need to obtain this advantage?

Evaluation

5. What information systems does the hospital have to meet these needs?

Design

6. What changes would help the hospital obtain the needed information more cost effectively?

Implementation

7. What costs might the hospital incur in implementing its strategic planning effort?

STEP 4: In small groups, with the entire class, or in written form, share your answers to the questions above. Then answer the following questions:

1. What information needs existed in this situation?
2. How would meeting these needs give the hospital a competitive advantage?
3. What computer systems exist to meet these needs?
4. Do the existing systems appear to be adequate? ●

Activity 6: Three Minicases

STEP 1: Read each of the minicases. (This activity is especially suited for use in conjunction with Chapter 5 of *Information Systems*.)

MINICASE 1: AN INTERORGANIZATIONAL SYSTEM

Certain lines of insurance such as personal property, health, and travel, involve large numbers of customers who each take out relatively small dollar amounts of coverage. Processing insurance claims requires a great deal of information, usually supplied in written form by the insured party, which is then manually entered into the company's database. Often information on a single claim comes from multiple sources as a car accident may involve claims for auto repair, hospitalization, and personal liability.

Filing claims is frequently complicated because many insurance accounts originate at independent insurance agents. Much of this information is transferred by public mail, which is slow and is becoming increasingly more expensive. Reducing the paperwork flow between the insurance company, its customers, and its independent agents is an important cost-cutting strategy for the insurance firm: it simplifies the reporting tasks for the independent agents and customers, and it provides the customer with a speedier claims settlement.

Because of these advantages, linking independent agents to the insurance company's information system support functions will induce independent insurance agents to favor that company when signing up new customers for insurance. This benefits the company because it obtains a strategic advantage over its competitors.

With this in mind the Finnish insurance firm SAMPO started a pilot project to link its mainframe-based information system with the PC-based information systems of car dealers and trucking firms. The car dealers provided insurance to new car buyers, and the trucking firms purchased insurance for their trucking fleets. The software required in these interorganizational information systems was designed by the insurance firm with the cooperation of, but at no cost to, the participating organizations.

This business operates in a highly competitive environment and its information system is considered to be essential to achieving its corporate totals. Management would be averse to buying off-the-shelf software if this software would negate the company's advantage over its competitors. Furthermore, the application requires the exchange of large quantities of data between the insurance company's information system and the information systems of its independent agents.

MINICASE 2: A SYSTEM FOR COMPUTER-ASSISTED DISPATCHING

A police car dispatching sequence typically begins with a call from a citizen for police assistance. The call is answered by a complaint evaluator who selects one of four courses of action:

1. no need exists for a police response (e.g., caller requests the local town hall's address);
2. no need exists for a police response, but a police report is required (e.g., caller reports his car stolen);

Minicase 1 is reprinted from Carl R. Ruthstrom and Charlene A. Dykman, *Information Systems for Managers; Casebook* (St. Paul: West, 1992). Minicase 2 is adapted from Marius A. Janson, University of Missouri, St. Louis, Evidence to support the continuing role of the information systems department in organizations, *Journal of Management Information Systems* (Fall 1989): 22–31. Minicase 3 is reprinted by permission of M. E. Sharpe, Inc., Armonk, NY 10504.

3. a police response and a police report are required (e.g., crime is in progress), and
4. a police response but no police report is required (e.g., police involvement is limited to directing traffic in an emergency situation).

Only in the last two situations is a police car required and the complaint evaluator places the request for assistance in a queue, where it awaits processing by the next available dispatcher.

Computer-assisted car dispatching (CAD) systems have been operating successfully for nearly 20 years. Thus, when the St. Louis Police Department required such a system, it was natural to look for standard off-the-shelf software that could operate on the department's mainframe. However, police departments differ in how they perform this day-to-day task. Additionally, police information systems, rather than being isolated entities, communicate and exchange data with regional and national information systems.

With these issues in mind, the department's database administrator, accompanied by several members of the police force, visited four cities with CAD systems similar in specifications to those needed in St. Louis. They selected a system in use in Kansas City because it used dispatching procedures in close agreement with those followed by St. Louis dispatching personnel. The only obstacles to implementing an exact duplicate of the Kansas City system in St. Louis were the dissimilar database systems of the two applications. The database administrator planned to bridge these differences by a partial rewrite of the software, which was not thought to affect the success of system implementation.

To ensure a smooth implementation, police personnel initially operated the modified system at approximately 20% of its intended capacity alongside the existing manual dispatching system. The entire cycle of dispatching a car requires information displayed on four different screens. In the modified system the dispatcher had to look at two screens at a time; thus, the completion of a dispatching task required alternating between screens. The time needed to alternate between screens was only a few seconds, but the St. Louis dispatchers considered this time to be much too long because it had the potential of placing police officers in undue jeopardy during crisis situations. Displaying all four screens simultaneously on one video display terminal, however, required significant changes in hardware and software.

MINICASE 3: AN INFORMATION SYSTEM FOR ENERGY CONSERVATION

Adequate information about energy consumption by end-use type is crucial in any effective energy conservation program. This case relates the failure of an energy information system installed to support the energy conservation effort for a midwestern state's publicly owned buildings. The energy agency purchased standard off-the-shelf software that had already been extensively used in other states to target buildings for energy consumption measures. The software was part of a system consisting of data collection, system operating manuals, and instruction manuals for staff members at individual buildings to help them complete the self-administered data collection forms. The agency collected data on approximately 300 variables for several thousand buildings and prepared reports indicating whether energy conservation measures were desirable. Subsequent analysis of these results by agency personnel revealed that the recommendations contained in the reports were erroneous and the system was abandoned.

This application seems a fitting candidate for commercial software because demand for similar information existed at other state energy agencies. Thus the availability of standard off-the-shelf software was likely, and no data exchange with other systems was required. Then what were the causes of its failure?

First, the energy agency was unaware that its objectives differed from those of the software house. The software house wanted a database for its own future use that contained as much information as possible on the energy consumption of publicly owned buildings. Thus, the amount of data collected was far in excess of what was needed for the energy agency's limited goal of targeting buildings for energy conservation measures. The data collection and data entry processes became unnecessarily complex and were sources of many data errors. The resulting poor quality data demonstrates that end-user computing without adequate attention to data integrity can place an organization at considerable risk.

Second, the software contained an engineering model for identifying buildings that consumed excessive amounts of energy compared to buildings with similar structural and operational characteristics. Because the model was incorrectly calibrated for climatic conditions and building characteristics unlike those found in the midwestern state, grossly inaccurate predictions resulted. The problems with the model and the data were uncovered after an indepth study that required expertise on energy conservation, information technology, and statistical techniques for improving data quality.

STEP 2: Prepare the cases for class discussion.

STEP 3: Answer each of the following questions for each minicase, individually or in small groups, as directed by your instructor:

Diagnosis
1. What are the information needs in this situation?

Evaluation
2. What type of software is currently used?
3. How well does it meet the information needs?

Design
4. What are the relative advantages and disadvantages of horizontal applications software, off-the-shelf software, customized software, and home-grown software in the situation?
5. What type of software should be used to meet the information needs in the situation?

Implementation
6. What issues exist in purchasing, installing, and using the new software?

STEP 4: In small groups, with the entire class, or in written form, share your answers to the questions above. Then answer the following questions:

1. What are the information needs in each situation?
2. What types of software best meet these needs?
3. What are the assets and liabilities of each type of horizontal and vertical applications software?
4. How can the required changes in software be implemented? ●

Lufkin-Conroe Telephone Exchange, Inc.

STEP 1: Read the Lufkin-Conroe Telephone Exchange, Inc. case. (This activity is especially suited for use in conjunction with Chapter 6 of *Information Systems*.)

LUFKIN-CONROE TELEPHONE EXCHANGE, INC.

The Lufkin-Conroe Telephone Exchange, Inc. (LCTX), incorporated in 1986, is an independent local telephone exchange operating as a privately held public utility with administrative and operating offices located in Lufkin, Texas. Customers are located in Lufkin and its surrounding areas, in Alto (30 miles away), and in Conroe (approximately 85 miles south of Lufkin). The company serves approximately 66,000 access lines and is located in the Houston Local Access Transport Area (LATA). The service area extends over 1400 square miles and includes a network of nearly 4,000 miles of telephone cable.

The company employs over 400 people with 28 working in the Information Systems Department. The department has 19 programmers, three operators, and six people in administration and technical support. The computers and Information Systems staff are located in Lufkin. The computers discussed in this paper are used for company operations and commercial business. These are not the computers used by LCTX to record telephone call data. The latter, Northern Telecom digital switches, are located separately from the application computers with the only communication being via magnetic tape.

LCTX provides operator services for the Lufkin area and Southwestern Bell provides operator services for the Conroe customers. Typical user applications include billing inquiries from customers who call LCTX with billing questions and the accounting department staff making inquiries regarding accounts payable issues. One of the major systems supported by the Information Systems Department is the Toll Processing System which records and processes the billable telephone traffic traveling throughout the Lufkin-Conroe Telephone Exchange network.

THE TOLL PROCESSING SYSTEM

The Toll Processing System processes records entering the system from three different points. The first is LCTX (Northern Telecom switches) recorded calls that are long distance, mobile traffic, or directory assistance calls. The second entry point is calls recorded outside of the LCTX service area yet billable by LCTX. Included are credit card, collect, and third-party billing calls. The third point of entry is conference calls originating in the Lufkin area. These are recorded manually and entered through a CRT. Also included here are Centralized Ticket Investigation (CTI) rebills following customer initiated inquiries regarding billing irregularities.

The information comes into this system in hexadecimal and is converted to character format. Calls not billed individually are separated out as are Access Usage Records. The latter are used to apportion out the monies to various companies whose facilities may have been used for the calls. The information goes through a rating process that involves a search of tables for the correct rate given the start time of the call, the call date, etc. Service charges

---

This case was written by Charlene A. Dykman and Carl R. Ruthstrom, University of Houston–Downtown, and Chris B. Copenhaver, Lufkin-Conroe Telephone Exchange, Inc. Reprinted with permission from C. R. Ruthstrom and C. A. Dykman, *Information Systems for Managers: A Casebook* (St. Paul, Minn.: West, 1992).

for activities such as operator assistance are added at that time. The system then goes through a settlement process using industry guidelines and the Access Usage Records to set the actual value of the money to be shared between the phone companies.

Following this processing, a sampling process is conducted resulting in 5% of LCTX's traffic being sent by tape to Southwestern Bell each week. This is then sent to AT&T where the information is used for trend analysis. A third process divides out LCTX, Southwestern Bell, and Contel traffic. LCTX records some of Contel's traffic in one area. A tape containing this information is sent to Southwestern Bell and Contel each week.

LCTX uses different billing cycles to spread out the printing and mailing work load. Customers' billing cycles are determined by the first three digits of the phone number. There are two cycles for the Conroe area and three for the Lufkin area. This printing and mailing process occupies one full-time person. It is easy to see the heavy processing requirements that result from the complexity of today's telecommunication networks.

THE TECHNOLOGY

LCTX processed all applications and development work on a single IBM System 38 until 1986. The Conroe and Alto areas were connected to the computer via modems and Lufkin was direct wired. Conroe users began to experience unacceptable response time as business grew dramatically during the 1980s. This was accompanied by growth in the size of the programming staff and the amount of development work being performed. A second System 38 was installed in October, 1986 and was dedicated to the Conroe users. Lufkin and Alto users, as well as the programming staff, used the larger of the two System 38s.

In July, 1988, IBM announced the introduction of the AS/400 line of computers. This line was to replace the System 38 in the IBM midrange family line and was to be much faster, more reliable, and have more memory than the System 38. The System 38 would no longer be manufactured by IBM and at some point in the future IBM would no longer offer service for the System 38. The 38 model would become what is known as "orphaned" and users would need to rely on private vendors for support and service.

IBM's long range plans for the AS/400 include increasing the potential of the computer over the next decade. This will be accomplished by new operating systems with minor changes to the hardware. When IBM announced the phase-out of the System 38, LCTX had to make several critical decisions about the future of the computer hardware they were using. LCTX was totally dependent on these computers and the enormous amounts of code, written in RPG3, which resides on these computers.

ALTERNATIVES

LCTX Information Systems personnel were now faced with alternatives to consider. What about making no changes? This would not require any capital investments or hardware or software changes. However, over time, support for the 38s would become a major issue and this prevented serious consideration of the "do nothing" alternative.

The second option was to purchase two AS/400 computers and configure them in the same manner as the 38s with a small one dedicated to Conroe users and a larger one for Lufkin and Alto users and developmental activities. This offered possibilities for one computer serving as a backup for the other, avoided problems with user competition for batch processing resources, assured good response time for Conroe users, gave flexibility to the operations staff for scheduling the nightly production jobs, and gave the programming staff easy access to test data on the same machine. This configuration had some disadvantages also. Production jobs requiring data from both machines meant operator intervention and tape handling. Program changes had to be installed on two machines and complex interfaces were needed for access to common applications that shared data because these applications resided on one machine. Redundant programs and data existed and this required more memory. With programmers doing testing on a production machine, there was always vulnerability to erroneous updates of production data.

The third alternative considered was to purchase two AS/400s and configure one as a developmental platform and the larger one to serve the entire user population. This would eliminate complex hardware interfaces, separate development work from the production data, reduce memory requirements caused by program and data redundancy, and eliminate the competition for resources between the users and the programming staff. There were disadvantages associated with this configuration also. Program testing now would require the importing of live data to the development machine. Nightly production scheduling would become much more difficult and the volume of production jobs on one machine would nearly double. Jobs that shared data could no longer be run at the same time. Response time for the users in Lufkin, who access the system through modems, might degrade during peak periods.

The manager of Information Systems at LCTX has to make a decision that will have a long-term impact on the department, the entire company, and its users. Neither of the viable alternatives is without risks. The manager contemplates the future, weighing the various advantages and disadvantages, and finally develops a proposal and recommendation for the acquisition and implementation of the AS/400 computers.

STEP 2: Prepare the case for class discussion.

STEP 3: Answer each of the following questions, individually or in small groups, as directed by your instructor.

Diagnosis
1. What information needs did the Toll Processing System meet?

Evaluation
2. How effective were the System 38 minicomputers in meeting the company's needs?
3. How well would they meet those needs in the future?
4. What limitations exist to the continued use of System 38 computers?

Design
5. What alternatives were available to the LCTX Information Systems Department in dealing with IBM's phase-out of the System 38 computers?
6. What are the advantages and disadvantages of each alternative?

Implementation
7. What issues should the LCTX Information Systems Department consider in choosing among the alternatives?

STEP 4: In small groups, with the entire class, or in written form, share your answers to the questions above. Then answer the following questions:

1. What information needs does the Toll Processing System meet?
2. How effectively do the System 38 computers meet these needs?
3. What options for replacing the System 38 computers exist?
4. What implementation issues must be considered in replacing this hardware?

The United States Postal Service

STEP 1: Read the United States Postal Service's Address Management System case. (This activity is especially suited for use in conjunction with Chapter 7 of *Information Systems*.)

Every day, Americans mail over ½ billion letters, parcels and magazines. Each piece of mail then begins a processing journey during which it is collected, postmarked, sorted and delivered to one of over 120 million final destinations throughout the country. Mail processing is a labor-intensive operation which is occurring around the clock in every town and city across the country.

Mail volume, which grew over 300 percent in the past two decades, exploded in the 1980s. In 1992, the United States Postal Service (USPS) processed over 170 billion pieces of mail. In contrast, twelve years earlier, 97 billion pieces of mail were processed. Although alternative forms of communication are rapidly becoming available, mail volume is projected to continue to grow into the foreseeable future. Along with this increasing demand for service, millions of business and residential addresses are created or changed every year.

Although this demand from today's rapidly changing environment suggests an ominous growth in personnel and infrastructure support, the unacceptable cost implications of such growth, which would ultimately be passed on to the public via price increases, necessitates a dynamic approach to mail processing. Postal managers realized the strategic importance of automating mail sortation processes and, thus, initiated an aggressive automation plan which seeks to continuously maximize emerging information technology. As part of this plan, the USPS undertook a major corporate effort to design, develop, and implement an information system with a consistent and current address database. This paper discusses the innovative information system developed to meet this challenge—the Address Management System (AMS). AMS is the official record of all addresses in the U.S. and its territories; its database contains the critical information resource of the U.S. Postal Service.

BACKGROUND

The initial implementation of the Address Management System (AMS) involved consolidating three independently-supported, concurrent address files into a single database. Prior to consolidation, these three distinct files—the Five Digit ZIP Code file, the Carrier Route Information System file, and the ZIP+4 file—reported common information inconsistently (such as duplicate address data) and required users to update each file using independent system methods. Since a more accurate and centralized address management system was needed, a network-based software database management system was proposed to create an on-line, real-time data entry and query system.

The AMS project team faced an array of start-up challenges. The size and functional requirements of the new database pushed the limits of what was technically achievable at the time AMS was conceptualized. There were no similar-sized existing models on which the proposed system could be based. Numerous physical design options were possible. Technical expertise in a new system development technology did not exist and needed to be developed. A national structure of over 300 AMS support personnel had to be positioned, trained, and equipped to handle address information and maintenance functions. A compressed development and implementation schedule, which was dictated by business needs, generated skepticism from peers and experts outside the organization.

Extracted from Joseph M. Feliu and Harry Aldstadt, The address management system: Improving customer information flow, *Journal of End User Computing* (Winter 1994): 26–32.

THE FUNCTION OF AMS

The true power of AMS lies in its role as the source database for all address information products necessary for the essential business processes involved in moving America's mail. AMS' primary function is maintaining, extracting, and distributing the data used by 1) all automated mail sorting machines, 2) other internal systems, and 3) mailing customers via products needed to create 'automation ready' mail (Figure 1). AMS is critical to effectively managing the USPS' huge capital investment in automation technology and to realizing the intended benefits.

A new generation of highly sophisticated automated mail processing equipment sorts mail using information extracted from the AMS database. This equipment constitutes the backbone of the Postal Service's automation strategy. It scans the address on a mail piece, matches it against the AMS directory, and then sprays a bar code representing that address on the envelope. In a manner similar to the way price scanners are used in supermarkets, the mail can then be sorted by bar code at a rate of nine letters per second into the exact sequence that letter carriers walk their routes. The efficiency of the automated equipment is dependent on the accuracy of address data which AMS provides. Automation reduces the volume of mail that must be sorted by manual or mechanized processes and provides greater accuracy of delivery.

AMS also provides data for other internal systems such as the Computerized Delivery Sequence File, the Computerized Mail Forwarding System, and ZIP+4 Encoding Services. These subsidiary systems all utilize the AMS database for accurate address information. By directly supporting these systems, AMS further unifies and advances the automation of mail processing and delivery functions. Additionally, significant cost savings are realized. For example, the National Change of Address and the Address Change Service systems realize a savings of $9,000,000 a week by utilizing AMS data.

Business mailers, mailing houses, list management firms and service bureaus depend on AMS products to maintain and improve the accuracy of their address records, to target specific customer areas, and to qualify for presort discounts. USPS customers use AMS products in conjunction with commercially available ZIP+4 conversion and bar coding software to increase the quality and efficiency of their internal business mailing operations and to realize immediate cost savings. Customers using 4-digit add-on codes or a unique Five-Digit ZIP Code, can direct mail to specific departments within their company. Payments and time sensitive replies can be separated from other correspondence as incoming mail is sorted. When AMS products are used by businesses to prepare their mailings, the Postal Service is then able to process their mail faster and with greater accuracy.

AMS products are available on paper, microfiche, magnetic tape, cartridge, and CD-ROM. The Postal Service also provides monthly and quarterly address subscription services to over 8,600 mailers. These products currently generate more than $1.3 million in annual revenue for the USPS. The demand for them has increased every year since these services began.

The following high-level AMS process flow chart illustrates the flow of data through the primary address information functions (Figure 2).

CONTINUAL SYSTEMS DEVELOPMENT

Currently, the on-line AMS database contains 28 million address block records representing areas serviced by over 40,000 Postal Service facilities. Weekly directory updates ensure the most current information is available. Direct file maintenance is performed on-line by 200 postal facilities where analysts report new building and housing starts, demolitions, letter carrier route changes and other delivery information. AMS provides consistent up-to-date data and, on a daily basis, averages 500 users who generate over 500,000 transactions.

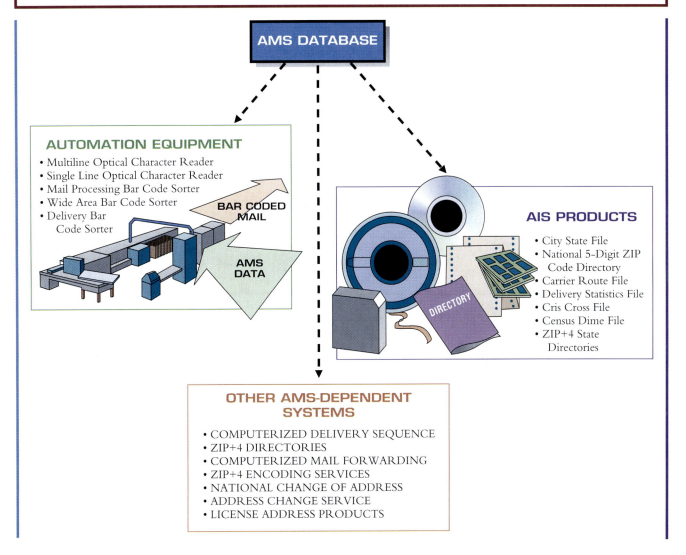

FIGURE 1 Address Management System-Primary Address Data Source

The Address Management System is continuously evolving as both technology and business needs change. By late 1993, AMS will be expanded from 28 million address block records to 125 million delivery point addresses. The 242 billion character database will soon have the capacity to store over 150 million records. These enhancements will further support sorting mail in letter carrier walk sequence and will consolidate additional existing address information support systems. A client/server-based front-end system for AMS is also under development. This system promises revolutionary change in internal business practices because it allows distribution of the centralized data store to local processing and distribution sites.

Employing emerging technologies as they become available has further enhanced AMS applicability. For example, the increased availability of CD-ROMs provides the USPS with an additional medium on which to provide the entire ZIP+4 database to AMS products

FIGURE 2 Address Management System–Process Flow

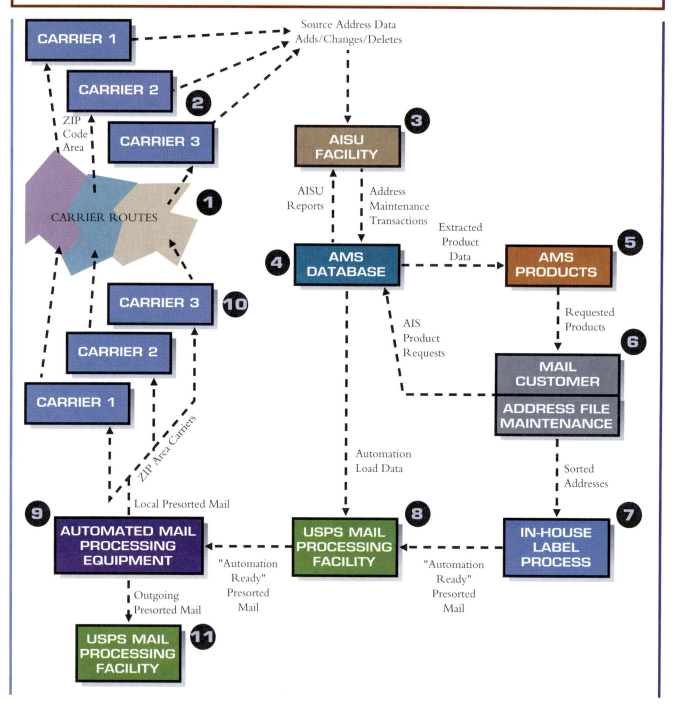

FIGURE 2 Continued

Address Management System Process Flow

Flow #
1. **ZIP Code Area**
   - Basic defined delivery area
   - Served by multiple letter carriers having route identifiers
   - Can contain other "unique" ZIP codes for businesses, hospitals, government buildings, etc.
   - Defined to AMS database via data elements
   - 43,274 ZIP codes in database
2. **Carrier Routes**
   - Streets and delivery points within ZIP code area assigned to a single carrier
   - Initial source of address change data via letter carrier
   - 501,046 carrier routes in database
3. **Address Information Support Unit**
   - Update AMS database using on-line terminals from address change information received from carriers
   - 167 screens provide required database update capability
   - Receive updated listings/reports for updated ZIP codes
   - 200 facilities serve all USPS delivery areas
4. **AMS Database**
   - Hierarchical database containing USPS organizational address and product fulfillment/customer data
   - 45 million records - 106 billion characters
   - 200 data elements define AMS data
   - Update, extract, report, audit, and fulfillment processes via 850 programs/utilities that comprise the Address Management System
5. **Address Management System Products**
   - Products provided to mailers and USPS operational facilities to enable and support the creation and processing of "automation ready" mail
   - Carrier Route Information System file
   - ZIP +4 file
   - 5-digit ZIP file
   - Additional products are produced in a variety of formats and media
6. **Mailing Customer**
   - User of AMS Product(s) to update in-house address lists and pre-sort outgoing mail to receive rate discounts and improved delivery window
7. **In-House Label/Address Process**
   - System/process used by AMS customer to generate "automation ready" mail for delivery to USPS mail processing facility
8. **USPS Mail Processing Facility**
   - Presorted mail positioned for appropriate automation process
   - Automation equipment on site
   - AMS products provide automation equipment update data
9. **Automated Mail Processing Equipment**
   - Multi-Line Optical Character Readers
   - Bar Code Sorters
   - Bar Code Readers
   - Delivery Point Bar Code Sorters
10. **Letter Carriers**
    - Receive deliverable mail for individual route sorted in delivery sequence
    - Manual sorting hours reduced

customers. Similarly, electronic imaging has permitted the use of Remote Barcode Sorting for letter mail that can not be read by the optical character scanners.

RESULTS

Developing and implementing AMS has produced dramatic improvements for the information systems function, the Postal Service's mail processing capability, and for external customers' mailing operations.

The AMS database, products, and operational support structure are now essential components of the Postal Service's operations capability. Currently, 90% of business letter mail volume is processed on mechanized or automated equipment using sort programs developed from the AMS database. This mail accounts for 70% of letter mail volume and requires less handling because it bypasses manual processing. A single piece of automated equipment using two operators can sort 30,000 letters per hour, a rate thought impossible just a few years ago. In contrast, 40 people would be required to accomplish the same task manually.

Without this critical database of addresses, the Postal Service's new state-of-the-art automation equipment could not be successfully exploited. For example, compressed AMS address directories for the Multi-Line Optical Character Reader (MLOCR) provide each MLOCR site access to all ZIP+4 national files. Use of compressed directories has reduced nonbarcoded mail by 2.5%, realizing a $50-$75 million annual savings.

Businesses benefit directly from the availability of AMS products. Timeliness of delivery is dependent on the quality of a company's mailing list, the addressing format of their mail piece, and the ability to get the mail piece to the mail carrier in the most expedient manner. Incorrect, incomplete, and "Undeliverable As Addressed" mail can drain a company's budget and impair their public image. Mailers currently spend an estimated $2 billion annually on material, preparation, and postage for mail that cannot be delivered as addressed. The USPS spends an additional $1 billion annually handling "problem" mail. Matching customers' address files to the AMS database allows identification and correction of incomplete or inaccurate addresses before they enter the mail stream.

Customers using AMS products have realized considerable postage discounts and savings. For example, Alabama Gas Company saves a quarter of a million dollars annually on postage, labor, and supplies by using AMS products to convert to delivery point barcoding. After realizing increased operational effectiveness, their President, Wm. Michael Warren, Jr., stated, "If this is a partnership that makes sense for Alabama Gas, it's the kind of partnership that makes sense for many companies…It's not just something that's valuable to the mega-company…"

Many businesses have also learned that other aspects of their business improve as a result of more efficient mailing operations. For example, Texaco, which processes over four million credit card statements a month, now realizes an annual savings of $2.4 million from postal rate discounts. As a result of improving their mail operations, they also reduced the payment and billing cycle and thereby improved the availability of funds generated from customer payments.

STEP 2: Prepare the case for class discussion.

STEP 3: Answer each of the following questions, individually or in small groups, as directed by your instructor:

Diagnosis
1. What information does the United States Postal Service (USPS) need to support its automation of mail sorting? Why is the automation of mail sorting important to the USPS?

2. What information can the USPS supply to its customers to reduce the costs of handling their mail?
3. Before the development of the Address Management System (AMS), how did the Postal Service handle its address-sorting information needs?

Evaluation
4. Was the pre-AMS system effective?
5. What systems could meet the USPS's information needs?

Design
6. Was the development of a database an appropriate solution?
7. Was the choice of a hierarchical database an appropriate choice for this application?
8. What roles should the following parties have played during the design of the AMS database: the address-management staff; the engineering staff who were responsible for the automated equipment; and the information systems staff?

Implementation
9. Has the AMS database been effective in meeting the USPS's information needs?
10. What additional benefit does the AMS provide for the USPS and its customers?

STEP 4: In small groups, with the entire class, or in written form, share your answers to the questions above. Then answer the following questions:

1. What information needs exist in this situation?
2. What systems existed to meet the needs prior to development of the AMS?
3. What deficiencies existed in these systems?
4. Was a hierarchical database an appropriate solution?
5. Was the AMS effective in meeting the USPS's needs? ●

Hisuesa (Hidroelectrica del Sur de Espana, S.A.)

STEP 1: Read the Hisuesa case. (This activity is especially suited for use in conjunction with Chapter 7 of *Information Systems*.)

Mr. Alfredo Málaga, Director of Distribution and Sales for the utility Hidroeléctrica del Sur de España, was very annoyed with the company's Data Processing Service (DPS). He let it be known to Samuel Balmes, head of Planning and Control, who was the highest-ranking manager with responsibility over the DPS in the firm. Málaga declared: "In order to resolve the problems posed by your Service in terms of writing different customer database access programs which I need to develop on a routine basis, I've had to create my own data processing center. Now, the company urgently needs a support system for its marketing activities, and the answer I get from the Data Processing Service is that they'll start analyzing the problem in 1991! This is ridiculous! Data Processing has become a giant which feeds on itself to survive. Maybe we should just leave it at Data Processing and omit the "Service" part."

HISTORY

The utility Hidroeléctrica del Sur de España is one Andalucías' foremost generators and suppliers of electrical power. The company, based in Algarinejo (Granada) has a production capacity of 1,060 mega watts (Mw) from hydroelectrical sources, 1,564 thermal Mw from coal and gas, and 820 Mw from its joint operations in three nuclear power plants. Its supply network reaches 1,450,000 customers throughout the whole "Autonomous Community" of Andalucía and has a total length of approximately 15,000 miles. In 1988, HISUESA invoiced over 120 billion pesetas. The utility has 40 branches spread out over its area of influence; personnel assigned to the branches are in charge of sales and collection activities, systems maintenance and expansion work and consumption read-out monitoring.

The utility's organization structure is shown in Exhibit 1. The Board of Directors is made up of shareholders' representatives, and an important bank is the majority owner of the utility company, and therefore designates HISUESA's president. At present, as all the country's utilities, the company is planning a restructuring which will strengthen the commercial side as opposed to the classical areas of emphasis of production and engineering.

During the 60's and—to a lesser extent—the 70's, Spanish utilities underwent tremendous expansion because of the need to provide the country with the necessary production infrastructure in order to maintain the enormous economic development during this period. However, according to the Energy Plans of recent years, no productive capacity expansion has been necessary. As a result, the industry—and HISUESA along with it—has moved to dismantle its engineering and construction departments, which have been packed with engineers specialized in the design and construction of power facilities, and instead focus on commercial and quality of service aspects. But now there are signs that indicate a future need for additional production capacity as of 1994, which may require new construction activity beginning in 1991. At any rate, due to its location in Andalucía and its fuel mix, it is highly unlikely that the government will single out HISUESA to build the new power plant.

This case was prepared by Professors Rafael Andreu, Joan E. Ricart, and Josep Valor. June 1989. Copyright © 1989, IESE. The names and figures given in this case have been altered to maintain confidentiality.

EXHIBIT 1 — Organization Structure

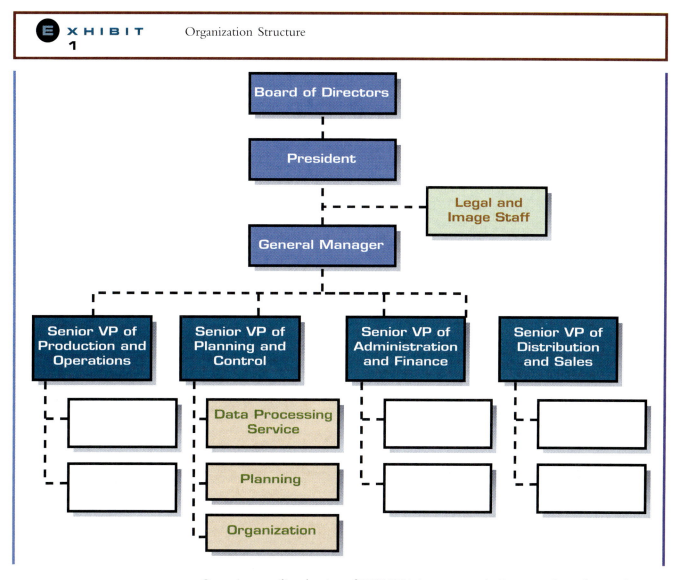

Operating a utility the size of HISUESA is no easy task. For example, each year there are some 230,000 jobs of maintenance, upgrading and extension of the medium- and low-voltage supply networks (new customer service connections, repair work, power line replacement, etc.) which involve some 2,000 utility and subcontracted workers.

A recent study by a prestigious American consulting firm established the two following basic strategic objectives for HISUESA:

1. Reduce costs, especially through (i) improving efficiency in existing power plants, (ii) reducing loss of power in medium- and low-voltage lines, and (iii) reducing the level of customer fraud.
2. Increase sales per customer, promoting the replacement of other energy forms, such as natural gas or diesel fuel, in favor of electrical power. Good sales pitches would be convenience, safety and savings in the case of installing double-rate meters and storing heat overnight in special accumulators. These sales pitches are valid for both domestic and industrial users.

However, it is obvious that in order to fulfill these objectives, it is necessary to upgrade the service quality, reducing power outages and instabilities to a minimum.

THE ELECTRICAL INDUSTRY IN SPAIN

The Spanish electrical industry is very highly regulated, both in terms of price (set by the Government) and production. In Spain, power is transported from the power plants to the transformers (high-voltage transport) using the national system owned by REDESA[1] which, in cooperation with the utilities themselves, sets production figures which must be adhered to by each of them. It is assumed that REDESA, which knows the cost variables of each power plant in Spain, as well as each water and coal supply point, makes the optimum decisions taking into account the national scene, so that any number of utilities could have several power plants shut down and distribute energy produced by other utility's plants. This is, in fact, the most general case, because one of the state-owned companies ENDESA, has no supply system and sells all of its production to the utilities, including HISUESA. There is a complicated system of economic compensation in order to offset the different cost structures and consumption levels of the various utilities.

DATA PROCESSING AT HISUESA

Exhibit 2 shows the organization structure established by HISUESA for Data Processing. It is classified as a "Service" and reports to the Senior Vice-President of Planning and Control. The head of the DP Service is Mr. Pablo Mateu, an industrial engineer specializing in computer science since graduating in 1973. He joined HISUESA as a programmer right after graduating and moved up the ladder within the Service until reaching the top post in 1981. Nobody in HISUESA would ever question Mateu's knowledge and expertise in computer science.

The organization is divided into functional areas, in such a way that maintenance is separate from new systems development. There is a group in charge of user-oriented PC-based computer applications, maintaining the utilities 126 compatible personal computers and training the users in the operating system and in the basic tools adopted by the utility, specifically DOS, Word-Star, Lotus 123 and D-Base III. In 1988, 311 HISUESA employees successfully completed the training program set up by the Data Processing Service's user support group.

At present, the Service had 104 employees, of whom 56 were technical personnel, most of them college graduates. The other 48 made up the support group: operators, administrative staff and support personnel. The Service operates 24 hours a day, 365 days a year.

The basic technology used by HISUESA's systems is IBM or compatible. The Service has three main frames: two IBM and 1 IBM-compatible, each with 16 Mb of memory and a processing capacity of 4 MIPS. Throughout the utility there are 468 terminals, in addition to the 126 PC's which have already been mentioned.

The utility has a proprietary communications network, totally independent from the national telephone company. Utilities are allowed to set up their own communications system, as they must provide a public service that depends heavily on communications and cannot be subject to the ups and downs of the state-owned telephone system.

The Data Processing Service's expenses for 1988 were approximately 1,234 million pesetas, which included hardware maintenance costs. Communications costs, however, were not included in this figure, as they are considered an expense attributable to Production and Operations.

---

[1] Red Eléctrica S.A., partially owned in conjunction by all of the utility companies, although majority ownership is in the hands of the public sector.

Industry experts in Spain considered HISUESA's computer department as fairly high-quality, although internally the service provided to the company is considered deficient.

Applications in operation are grouped into 12 large systems, which are all interconnected in some way or another. Some of them, such as Payroll or Customers, are derived from the first "programs" developed by HISUESA on punchcards in the late 60's and later put on tape in the 70's. This has lead to the coexistence in the same computers of systems whose basic technology is very outdated (assembly language and flat files), and very advanced (relational data bases and fourth-generation languages).

The situation of HISUESA's information systems is typified by the Management Control System. This System, developed in the late 70's using sequential flat file technology,[2] provides relevant information of company operations to HISUESA's top-level management. All of the utility's systems, such as Invoicing and Payroll, generate a specific communications file for the management control system every time they are executed. Once a month, the management control system reads all of the "summarized" files generated by the other systems and prints reports accordingly.

The last important system developed was the distribution support system. This system includes the control of all the resources employed: personnel, materials, equipment, etc. It was implemented in early 1988, and due to its implementation, each branch had to install a new terminal connected to the HISUESA mainframe. 45 man-years were invested in this system, developed in conjunction with an independent firm which supplied the analysts, programmers, work methods and management of large computer projects.

OPINIONS OF SEVERAL USERS

HISUESA users are dissatisfied with the service provided by Data Processing. Complaints are abundant, and the company is permeated by the sense that "Data Processing is dictatorial and inoperative," to the extent that general management and the Senior VP of Planning (who

---

[2]Sequential flat files are those which have no other logical structure than that all of the records follow the order in which they were entered into the computer; in order to access a certain record, it is necessary to read all the previous records.

EXHIBIT 2   Data Processing Service Organization Structure

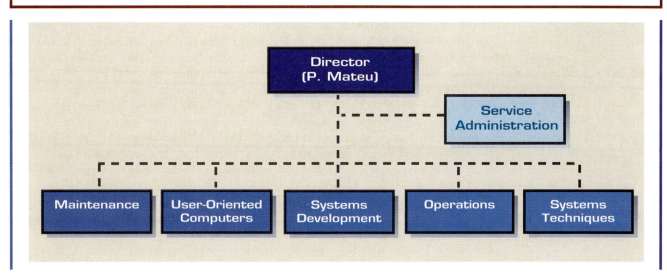

was assigned Data Processing responsibility one month before writing this case study—before that DP reported to Administration and Finance) have seriously questioned the continuity of the Data Processing management team. In following is a summary of situations of several users.

Distribution and Sales (D & S): The largest internal user. According to calculations, some 60% of the systems transactions done by Data Processing are for D & S. D & S's systems are centered on customer-based applications in which all of the information HISUESA has on its customers is collected. The application was designed to run on magnetic tape and was transferred to magnetic discs exactly in the same form. With this customer data base two basic groups of operations are carried out: routine operations and special operations.

The routine operations include meter readouts, opening and closing of accounts, invoicing, power changes in service connections, etc. For several reasons, the most common being the need to adapt to legislation in force, the systems in charge of handling the customer data base are continually modified. At present there are 5 Data Processing Service employees dedicated full-time to "customer maintenance." There are approximately 350 programs which use this database on a more or less regular basis.

Special operations, also called "non-routine operations," are those that are performed only occasionally and usually following unpredictable patterns. A typical example would be: "to make a list of customers in Jaén who have reduced energy consumption 30% or more in the past month." Every time this type of customer database access is required, a specific program (in RPG II) has to be written. Until 1987, these requests were made directly to Data Processing, which in turn put them in a maintenance "queue" until it could assign the necessary resources to fulfill the request. In some cases, this process had taken over a year to complete. In 1987, Distribution and Sales created a "Computer Operations Group (COG)," placing at the head of this new office one of the computer technicians who had an intimate knowledge of the customer system. The COG's mission was to provide specific support to D & S's management in computer-related matters. By the end of 1988, the group employed 35 people who were dedicated to fulfilling non-routine information needs. Of course, it goes without saying that the relationship between the Data Processing Service and the Computer Operations Group was not especially cordial.

A completely different problem occurs with the low voltage distribution network management group. HISUESA's distribution network is generally run down and needs a large quantity of repair work and upgrading operations. In this context, D & S had decided to replace the more than 4,000 maps and diagrams depicting the power system which had to be modified every time a small repair job was done, with a graphics-processing system which would allow quick access to any network point in the supply system, visualize both the map of the area and a diagram of the system, and enter modifications desired on-line. The system would automatically print the corresponding maps and diagrams and would emit work orders. Presently, the whole process is done manually on paper by some 10 people, 5 of them professional draftsmen.

The Computer Operations Group brought a graphics-processing work station and is beginning to experiment with the coding of some of the areas in one of the Andalucian capitals, entering information on medium- and low-voltage power lines, transformers, etc. It is thought that once the computers can cover the whole system network, the information provided on facilities will allow, together with "dispatching," a more adequate monitorization of the same, which will no doubt influence the quality of the service provided by HISUESA.

The Data Processing Service doesn't agree at all with the development of a system as important as that proposed by D & S in graphic information without them having a say in the matter, because in the future it will be important to be able to connect with this system in order to use network operation and maintenance data on a corporate level.

Administration and Finance: HISUESA's accounting system is traditional. The accounting operations are entered into the computer and each month an accounting budget is prepared, in which any deviations are calculated, etc. Its connection to the utility's other systems is not sufficiently developed. For example, there is an application of Bond and Debenture Management that control the sale of these instruments, coupon payment, etc. This application was designed so that each week it could generate a printout which was then sent to the accounting department for its further translation into accounting operations and incorporation into the accounting method. This procedure is still carried out in the same fashion, even though both applications are computerized and in the exact same computer, that is, the bond management application prints a routinely recoded summary which is re-entered into the computer, but this time within the Accounting application.

Commenting on the situation with the heads of the Data Processing Service, P. Mateu affirmed that, "it had been blown out of proportion, because it only represents a secretary's dedication of two hours a week of work."

Production and Operations: This department has practically no interaction with the Data Processing Service. This department is responsible for operating the power plants and transporting the energy to the transformer substations ("dispatching") and has large computers which work in real time to (1) follow REDESA's production orders, (2) transport the energy in the least costly fashion to places of consumption, and (3) confront multiple "incidences" that occur during the normal operation of any utility company.

The present dispatching computers are relatively old, and change is foreseen in the near future. The new equipment will be compatible with that of REDESA and will generate automatic reports on breakdowns and incidences and, consequently, help to improve service quality.

The purchases of these new dispatching computers, leaving the Data Processing Service completely out of the matter, was seen by Mateu as another potential source of problems, as when information on breakdowns and incidences was generated it had to be processed by his service's computers and consolidated with other reports on service quality. Mateu believes that the Data Processing Service should be involved in the equipment-purchasing decision in order to guarantee future compatibility.

STEP 2: Prepare the case for class discussion.

STEP 3: Answer each of the following questions, individually or in small groups, as directed by your instructor:

Diagnosis
1. What problems is Hisuesa experiencing in managing its information?
2. What systems does it currently use for data management?

Evaluation
3. How effective are the current systems?
4. What deficiencies exist in coordination of databases?
5. Does the Data Processing Service play an appropriate and useful role?
6. What systems could meet the utility's information needs?

Design
7. How should the current information systems be changed?
8. What changes should occur in the role of the Data Processing Service?

Implementation
9. What costs will result from the proposed changes?
10. Who should be involved in implementing the changes?

Step 4: In small groups, with the entire class, or in written form, share your answers to the questions above. Then answer the following questions:

1. What information needs exist in this situation?
2. What systems exist to meet the needs?
3. What deficiencies exist in these systems?
4. How should the systems be redesigned to meet the needs?
5. What issues should be considered in implementing the redesigned systems?

Activity 10: Bank Consolidates Data Processing Operations

STEP 1: Read the Bank Consolidates Data Processing Operations case. (This activity is especially suited for use in conjunction with Chapter 8 of *Information Systems.*)

The Bank of Boston, a super-regional bank holding company, has acquired banks in Rhode Island, Maine, Vermont, Connecticut, and Massachusetts. "When you attempt to merge five fairly large banks, the technology infrastructure is duplicated across all entities," says Kevin Roden, Bank of Boston's director of data processing technology. To reduce expenses and eliminate needless duplication, the bank recently launched an extensive consolidation program for its data processing operations.

"Consolidation saves systems, software, programmers, and operations personnel," Roden says. "For example, in the systems technology department, we had to make the technology meet the needs of our 'business partners'—the various business units we serve throughout the holding company—while reducing the cost of providing that service."

During the first stage of consolidation, Bank of Boston assembled teams to define corporate-wide requirements. The overall objective was to place all of the affiliate banks on a common technology platform, including common systems and similar product offerings. Using this approach, a new financial product would be applicable in all five states. Although the same products could be marketed under different names to suit local market conditions, only one development effort, instead of five, was required.

BUILDING A COMMUNICATIONS HIGHWAY

Once the bank established its equipment needs and existing product lines, the next step was to consolidate five different computer centers to provide a high-speed, reliable file-transfer network with a central data-archiving capability.

This step began with the data communications equivalent of an interstate highway system—a HYPERchannel network from Network Systems Corp. of Minneapolis, Minn. This network connects five computer centers and, within each center, links other networks as well. The result is analogous to "state highways" and "county roads" connecting the computers and peripherals.

High speed and reliability were the deciding factors in selecting HYPERchannel. According to John Osterman, Bank of Boston senior systems consultant, "There are hundreds of products that will move data. However, determining how many can do it quickly, while fitting within our existing operations and scheduling systems, was a key issue. Automation was the answer. Also, data needs to be independent of location and needs to move freely across the entire network."

Once the high-speed network was in place, Bank of Boston began removing mainframes from its data centers in Maine and Connecticut. The bank converted those sites to distribution centers that house peripherals, including laser and impact printers, tape drives, terminals, and fiche machines.

With HYPERchannel providing fast and reliable file transfer, the Bank of Boston installed USER-Access with Central Archiving, a software package from Network Systems that runs on HYPERchannel and TCP/IP networks. "USER-Access gives us a lot of flexibility," Osterman says. "For example, we can provide contingency backup for data on Tandem systems using IBM jobstreams. It solves the problem of having disparate computer systems, since we already have procedures and processes in place to manage backup and recovery in the IBM mainframe environment."

SOURCE: Bank consolidates data processing operations, *Network Management,* August 1991: 73, 74.

The Bank of Boston now has two IBM mainframes—one in the Boston location and one in Providence, R.I. The Boston mainframe supports most of the production workload for the bank, and the Providence mainframe serves as a development and contingency operation.

In addition to these systems, Tandem systems handle automated teller machine and teller transactions, and DEC VAXes handle money wire transfers, commercial loan services, treasury, trade services, purchasing and procurement, protective services, and coin room operations. The bank also has three Stratus systems and three IBM AS/400 midrange systems that handle other applications. All these systems are now part of the bank's HYPERchannel network (see Figure 1).

"Because [they] have data that is critical to the operation of the bank, these systems must be able to feed into other systems," says Roden. For example, before installing USER-Access, several manual transfers were required. "Now, USER-Access eliminates these manual transfers with its any-to-any file transfer network. Moving data can now be accomplished without risks and delays and, most importantly, we are able to retain existing operating procedures and schedules," Roden says.

AUTOMATIC ARCHIVING

Because every system holds critical information, the ability to archive computer data is a top priority in the consolidation plan. USER-Access with Central Archiving gives the bank an automated, centrally controlled backup capability to assure that all the bank's data is protected and that all information is available in the event of a disaster.

After a day's work is done, the backup of the system begins. Using the Central Archiving system, one of the IBM mainframes automatically polls the minicomputers on the network and initiates each system's backup utility to perform that day's backup. This process is completed every evening. The IBM tape drives are much faster, and the backup system is automatic. When all the data has been backed up by the system, the tapes are transferred to the Rhode Island center, where they are held for transfer to a remote archive vault.

Because archiving is controlled by the automated job scheduling system, human assistance is not required, reducing the opportunity for human error. Using Central Archiving, the IBM can back up 610 MB of Digital Equipment Corp. data in 47 minutes, while simultaneously backing up Tandem data and processing thousands of interactive transactions.

In addition to being efficient, the new system has reduced the bank's operating expenses. The system has also helped the bank's redeployment process, which ensures that employees are working on priority tasks.

"Our business partners charge us with the responsibility of providing data movement, computer power, and data security," Roden says. "We seek to meet those requirements while staying as clean and simple as possible. We employ technology that meets the needs of our business partners in the hope that it will help create a competitive advantage for Bank of Boston. USER-Access with Central Archiving is helping us to achieve this objective."

STEP 2: Prepare the case for class discussion.

STEP 3: Answer each of the following questions, individually or in small groups, as directed by your instructor.

Diagnosis

1. How did the information needs of Bank of Boston change as a result of its bank acquisitions?

Evaluation

2. What types of systems existed before the consolidation?
3. How effectively did these systems meet Bank of Boston's needs?

FIGURE 1 Bank of Boston Central Archiving Network

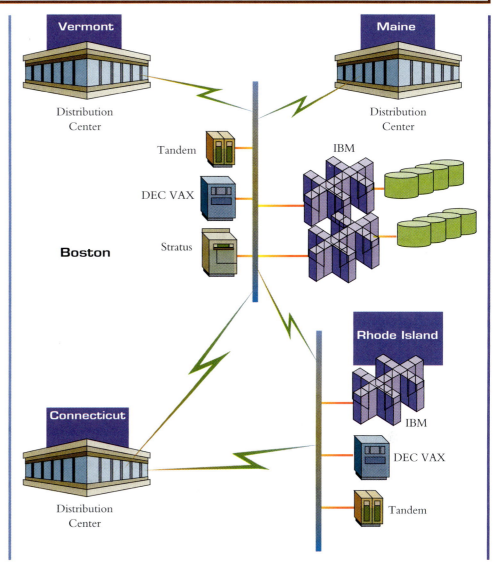

Design

4. How did Bank of Boston consolidate its communications operations?
5. Did the communications highway selected by Bank of Boston meet its needs?

Implementation

6. What issues did Bank of Boston face in implementing the new system?
7. How effectively did it handle these issues?

STEP 4: In small groups, with the entire class, or in written form, share your answers to the questions above. Then answer the following questions:

1. What impact did the acquisition of new banks have on Bank of Boston's information needs?
2. What types of hardware did Bank of Boston select to meet these needs?
3. How well does the new system meet the bank's needs?
4. How effectively did Bank of Boston handle the implementation issues it faced?

Activity 11: Airtour Vacaciones

STEP 1: Read the Airtour Vacaciones case. (This activity is especially suited for use in conjunction with Chapter 9 of *Information Systems*.)

"I think that we should start *now* to think how we are going to use information technology in this business, even before deciding our business strategy. It occurs to me that they are not two separate matters. If we really want to be innovative in this industry—if we really want to carry out those ideas which made us decide in the first place to leave those bogged-down companies because they were devoured by the day-to-day inertia, then I think we should do it by taking information technology into account from the onset. I am convinced that if we do it like this, we will find better ways of approaching the business itself. As a matter of fact, my nephew was telling me the other day about a database system…."

José Mª Echegoyen was impatient. He believed, as did his associates, that it was possible to "greatly improve" the tour-operating industry, so he was determined to establish an innovative company—AirTour Vacaciones. There was no doubt in his mind that, in time, computers would be an indispensable part of the business. His associates Alfonso Ruiz and Ricardo Palma, who were both as experienced as José Mª in the tour-operating industry, agreed with him, though less enthusiastically.

Ricardo plunged in: "Cut the sermon, José Mª. Here we go again with your love affair with technology! I am not arguing about the fact that we were going to need the computers' support, nor that when we do use it, we will use it better than what they did in our old companies (it won't be all that difficult), but I refuse to put computers before business. I want us to become outstanding tour operators who use computers creatively whenever we need them, not outstanding computer specialists who sell packaged tours because they think the business is well-adapted to the technology. We'll get to the computers, but only once we are perfectly clear about what we are going to do with the business."

The discussion wasn't new. Alfonso, always the conciliatory type, timidly stepped in. "Actually, Ricardo, I think you are exaggerating a little. My impression is that José Mª was just proposing thinking about the business and computers at the same time… I don't think it is a matter of subordinating one thing for the other. In fact, I think we should seriously consider this. . . after all it might not be such a silly thing."

"Thanks a lot, especially about it being silly," José Mª couldn't help showing his irritation. Slamming the door as he left, he shouted, "See you on Monday! I hope that you rest up this weekend and come back a little more reasonable on Monday morning!"

HISTORY

According to the founding partners, AirTour Vacaciones was to be a tour-operating firm that was "small, for now, but with a lot of ideas." "We are going to make some people in the industry look pretty bad. We are sick of obsolete procedures that impose constraints on business opportunities. AirTour will be different. We will give more service and be more efficient than the rest. It is going to be very hard for our future competitors to react; they are too big, and the years they have been following the old procedures have made them sluggish."

> This case was prepared by Professor Rafael Andreu. It is intended to be used as a basis for class discussion rather than to illustrate either effective or ineffective handling of an administrative situation. Copyright © 1989, IESE.

The 80's were just underway. José Mª, Alfonso and Ricardo had worked almost 20 years each in different tour-operating concerns and combined, their experience was tremendous in several important facets of the business: purchasing, product design, sales, reservations, management, finance, etc. Above all, they were convinced that, "the paperwork involved in this business borders on sheer lunacy; if we start from scratch, it will be relatively easy to be a lot more efficient than what is normal for this industry."

Besides being experienced professionals, the three partners were close personal friends. Despite never having worked for the same company in the past, they had often exchanged ideas and had finally decided to set up shop on their own. The main reason for doing this was to implement these ideas without having to adhere to pre-established structures that were simply out of place in the context of the 80's. For this reason, they did not want the control of the new company to get out-of-hand. Given the rather reduced availability of capital, they decided to start up with a small-scale operation.

Without the necessary resources to start up activities with a powerful infrastructure, they had decided to focus their initial activities in the Barcelona Metropolitan area, offering their products exclusively to travel agencies in this area. They thought that this could be achieved with a very small staff, starting with 6–8 people including the three partners. In addition, the initial intent was to structure their products around stays in typical tourist spots, both on a national level, especially the Balearic and Canary Islands, and some traditional international destinations, such as Greece, Egypt and Italy.

Another desired characteristic of the new company related vaguely to the concept of "quality service" towards their direct customers (travel agencies) in addition to the end-consumers of the products (tourists who bought packaged tours designed by a tour operator through one of the travel agencies). They had decided upon the name AirTour Vacaciones in an attempt to convey the idea that the supply consisted basically of packaged tours in which transport would be mainly by air (during the early 80's, this usually meant by means of charter flights, which had to be specifically contracted in advance).

THE BUSINESS

Basically, the tour-operating business consisted of combining attractive travel and lodging arrangements, describing them in a brochure with information related to dates, seasons, rates, special features of the hotels (location, services, etc.), and supplied these combinations to travel agencies, which in turn would offer them to their customers. When the travel agency's customer chooses a package from a specific operator (typically travel agencies have a selection of brochures from different tour operators), the agency contacts the tour operator in order to confirm space availability, both in transportation and in lodging arrangements. In case the specific arrangements chosen by the customer are unavailable, the tour operator offers alternatives until the travel agency finally reaches agreement with the end-customer (the traveler). Thus, the travel agencies play the role of middleman between the tour operators and the end-customers, offering a wider choice of arrangements to the latter and a sales-distribution channel to the former.

One of the most important activities in the tour operator's business process is purchasing, both of travel and lodging arrangements.

The job of designing a package on the basis of transportation and lodging pre-arrangements is also one of the basic activities in the tour-operating business. Experience played a predominant role (combining different hotels with transportation on certain dates and different lengths of stay which had proven successful in the past), as well as the ability to offer attractive prices which wouldn't dismay the customer right from the start. The process was complicated by the fact that one hotel could offer a myriad of pricing alternatives: depending on the size of the hotel room, its location (view of the sea, of the parking area, etc.), different plans (half-board, full-board), and different possibilities (additional cots for children, maximum specified and associated extras, etc.).

Although a considerable percentage of the price for the package indicated in the brochure was attributed to transportation and lodging costs, there were other important costs incurred: administrative procedures associated with reservation management and control, confection of lists for controlling aircraft boarding and room allotment procedures (for the latter, it was necessary to send a telex to each hotel with information on who was going to arrive, on what day and for how long), and the retail sales activity, i.e., the commission accorded to the travel agencies. Some of the product cost components were not completely independent: for example, providing hoteliers with precise and reliable information created an image which could lead to improved contracting arrangements over the successive seasons; similarly, a rapid and reliable reservations system could affect travel agencies' inclination to "push" a specific operator's products.

THE INDUSTRY

In the early 1980's, the relationship between travelers and travel agencies in Spain, and the relationship between the travel agencies and the tour operators as well, suffered from several inefficiencies that, in certain cases, rendered them virtually ineffective. For example, most tour operators (at least most of them with a national presence, that is, which sold vacations through travel agencies throughout the whole country) used a manual process for controlling the reservations and confirming them for the travel agents. Delays were commonplace when an agent telephoned a tour operator in order to reserve accommodations for one of its customers. The operator's response time was even lower when they had to offer alternatives due to a lack of availability of the chosen accommodations; in many cases, these delays forced the end-customer to visit the travel agency on two—and sometimes even more—occasions in order to confirm his reservations and obtain the necessary travel vouchers.

In addition to this time-consuming process, the relationship between the tour operator and the travel agency suffered from other incidences which caused inconveniences to all concerned. One of these was the common industry practice of letting the travel agencies themselves prepare the travel vouchers for their customers once the reservation was confirmed by the tour operator. This procedure, which would probably be justified in the case of travel agencies located in different cities than the tour operator, was a generally applied practice, but in fact it gave final control of the reservation to the travel agency, opening the way for possible errors in issuing a document in the tour operator's name. If, for example, one of these mistakes lead to over-booking of a hotel or of a flight, the traveler would blame the tour operator, whose name appeared in the travel documents along with—on occasion—the travel agency's name. Despite the fact that the end-customers were more customers of the travel agency than of the tour operator (by virtue of the fact that the customer usually did not specify the tour operator which would be arranging his accommodations; rather, the determining purchase factors were convenience of dates, destinations, accommodations and price), it was considered that a negative experience could, in fact, affect the customer's perception of a certain tour operator, who would thus lose the possibility of repeat purchase from that customer.

Tour operators normally invoiced travel agencies after take-off of each flight as, on many occasions, the documents needed to issue these invoices weren't freed by the manual reservations process until after the departure of the flight in question. Therefore, the invoicing was variable, because two reservations that were made a month or more apart could be invoiced at the same exact time if the same flight was used. This didn't represent a major problem for the travel agent, who usually charged cash for this type of activity; but a slight inconvenience did arise in the process of checking invoices, which was done according to flight departures, while in his file they were usually filed according to the date of the reservation. Travel agency personnel would check the tour operator's invoices during low periods of sales activity. For the tour operator, this process often meant delays in payment and made cash discounts almost impossible. Exhibit 1 shows a schematic summary of the process structure followed by the industry in the relationship among tour operators, travel agencies, and end customers.

The manual process of reservations control, which was highly labor-intensive, had several other inconveniences apart from the slowness of confirmations and invoicing. In effect, maintaining an ongoing control of sales per flight was very complicated because it interfered with the sales and reservations process. However, this control was very important for the tour operator, who had contracted a charter flight and would lose any forthcoming revenues by unoccupied seats. The possibility of offering package discounts, which increased as the departure date neared, was seriously hindered by this circumstance. The same problem, although with less ill-fated circumstances, occurred in hotel sales control because of the number of hotel rooms secured before the season, a certain proportion of which could be cancelled with sufficient advance notice; at any rate, these cancellations brought on complications with the hotel trade.

As already mentioned, during the period we are referring to, a great majority of air transportation contracted by tour operators was in the form of chartered flights, which had to be contracted in full and in advance. There was a very limited supply of charter flights and very little price difference among the suppliers. It was possible to secure part of a passenger capacity from other tour operators that had previously contracted the whole flight, but that obviously lead to more costly flight arrangements and the possibility of not having guaranteed availability of seats.

Hotel rooms also had to be secured in advance, usually at the beginning of each season and specifying the days and numbers of rooms. Obviously, the supply was much more abundant, although the system by which rooms were contracted was virtually standard for the whole industry. This system consisted of contracting beforehand a certain number of rooms which could be "released" for a set date; the period in which the pre-reservation could be cancelled was called the "release period," which had to be negotiated on an individual basis with each hotel for each season. Practically none of the industry participants negotiated hotel reservations without this release clause, due to the risk involved in making a firm reservation before the beginning of the season. Although this could feasibly mean reducing costs, very few tour operators considered the extra risks worthwhile. However, it often occurred that after cancelling pre-reserved rooms within the period established by the release conditions, many tour operators were forced to contract rooms on an as-needs basis as a result of requests for reservations in certain hotels which, for one reason or another, were successful or popular among the clientele. It was very difficult to predict the hotels for which this would be necessary, so the tour operators would forego firm reservations and would accept the price increase which would surely accompany a last-minute reservation. Besides, this could give a sense of improvising which, as almost always happened, would soon enough be known by travel agencies and even by the end-customers.

In the early 80's, there were very few tour operators in Spain which operated on a national level; most of them had local operations, mainly within the larger cities' spheres of influence.

THE FUTURE

The next Monday, the three partners were once again trying to figure out the most appropriate business profile for AirTour Vacaciones. Over the weekend, Ricardo had decided to make a few treasury and balance sheet forecasts which encompassed the next three years and were based on fairly conservative sales and purchasing estimates. The results were not brilliant, but they weren't completely discouraging either.

A-56 Activities and Readings in Information Systems

EXHIBIT 1 Basic Structure of Industry Procedures

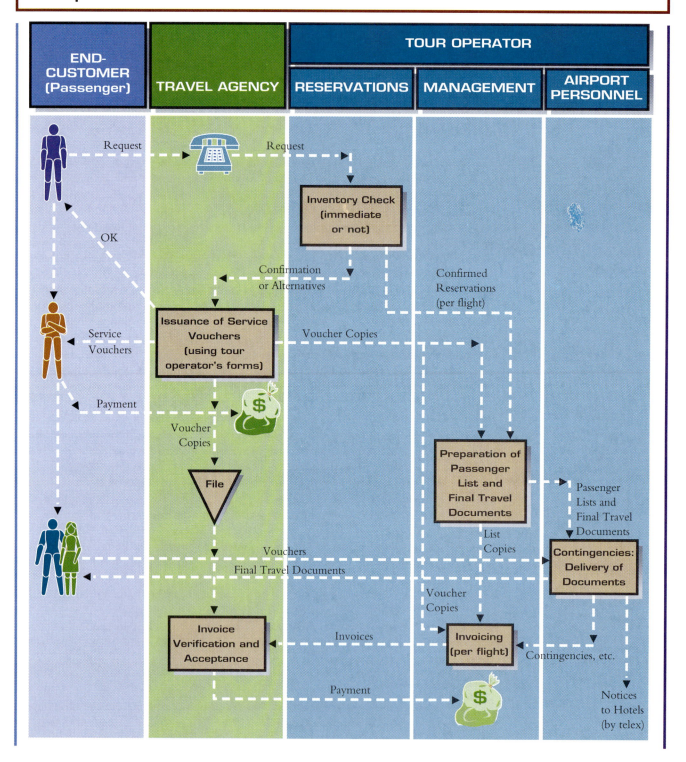

"One thing is for sure, we are going to have cash problems at the beginning. The bad thing is that I haven't been able to isolate one sole cause for it. It looks like there are a bunch of little problems that have gotten together to ruin our predictions. I spent all Sunday testing different scenarios with the help of this damned spreadsheet and I always come up with one financial black-hole or another. Do we really want to be independent? We could fix it all up with a venture capitalist."

José Mª and Alfonso reacted almost simultaneously. "Of course we want to be independent! We have talked about this over and over, Ricardo. We don't want anyone telling us what we have to do just because they are the ones that have the money. If we are convinced of our approach, we have to take the chance all by ourselves. If not, it isn't worth the hassle. I understand that after one weekend of working alone, the situation might begin to lose its perspective . . . Let's focus on this again."

"Alright. Let me tell you both about a little of what I've done and why I'm so worried. The first difficulty I have come up against is the problem of securing aircraft space. Either way, whether we buy whole flights or just a few seats from another tour operator, the problem is that you have to pay up front. And this is even before we start generating sales, which in this industry comes later. On top of that, if we purchase seats from a competitor, it will come out more expensive. It is a different story, though, with the hotels. You can pay late; hotels invoice you late for real occupation, because in the middle of high season, when they are up to the rafters in tourists, they don't have time to take care of administrative matters until the season is almost over. I'd still like to know what would happen if we could negotiate other payment conditions . . . although, how are we going to pay if we get paid so late?"

Alfonso joined in the discussion: "Well, couldn't we discuss ways of changing all that? If we are going to innovate, this is as good a place as any to start. Couldn't we get the travel agents to pay us earlier?"

Ricardo didn't think matters were so clear. "How are you going to make the travel agents pay earlier? Nobody likes doing that! Unless you offer something in exchange . . . The first thing that comes to mind is that we could offer cash discounts, something that nobody has ever offered in this industry . . . But how credible will that be, coming from the newest and youngest members on the scene? Besides, in order to do that, you have to invoice earlier too. The invoicing is done after the flight because, if not, it could create a big mess in the reservations activity. And don't forget, reservations are our sales activity! If we mess up the reservations side of the business, we'll find ourselves pushing up the daisies."

José Mª couldn't hold back any longer. "And what about the computer aspect? Are computers going to help us or not? This is exactly what I wanted to say last Friday! After all, maybe starting out small could give us some kind of advantage. I think a good reservations system wouldn't be that difficult to set up if we are just going to operate in Barcelona. As I was telling you the other day, they are coming out with database systems even for small computers . . . And with a good database, developing a satisfactory reservations system can be relatively easy."

"Don't start up with that again, José Mª," Ricardo said in a less belligerent tone than the Friday before. "You are getting me nervous with all this computer business. Maybe you are right, but I don't understand the first thing about computers! What the hell is a database system? Is it a fast reservations system? Or is it just something which will let us have a reservations system if we use it correctly? If it all boils down to that, I don't trust it. The truth of the matter is that I have seen too many of these schemes fail utterly."

Once again, Alfonso intervened to avoid what looked like a possible outbreak of hostilities. "Well, as long as we are supposed to be creative, I have some other ideas. For example, why don't we do something in the line of welcoming arrangements? We could charge cash on the spot for that and maybe that way, cover up some of the holes in Ricardo's estimates."

"Hey, that's not such a bad idea. I'm sure we can't just start off doing that, but I suppose that we could take it into account in the future. At any rate, I still think that we need something a little more radical. For instance, we need to grow very quickly. We need to be able to contract full flights as soon as possible. I know it is risky, but at least we can save ourselves the extra charge if we have to go to our competitors for seats. Besides, I really don't think they would respect their contracts with us if they suddenly got more demand for a certain flight. If we could contract whole flights, we wouldn't have to face that risk."

"I'm sorry to have to insist, but I think it is my duty. If we can set up a reasonable reservations system, I think we could probably consider opening up in Madrid pretty soon. We could even do it initially by 'postal express' or something of the sort, simultaneously centralizing reservations management in Barcelona."

"I think we should deal with all this a lot more in depth and do it from a cohesive and global standpoint. Maybe you are right after all. Maybe it is true that this damned computer business can open up ways out of this impasse that we're up against. If we are able to break the vicious circle of 'small—high cost—unattractive pricing—growth problems—small,' which is really what is behind our difficulties, maybe we can finally take off and do what we've always said we wanted to do."

"Well, Ricardo. You really flatter me! I never thought I would be able to convince you. Let's get to work! Look, I think that a quick and efficient reservations system is just the beginning. The efficiency itself will help us in terms of cost, but we'll also be able to do more. This morning we haven't spoken about hotel contracts. I'm sure that we could do something interesting in that field if we have computer capacity. After all, our sales are part of their reservations! And what about the end-customers? Don't you think that the image of a young, technologically advanced firm with computerized documentation, etc., would help us to attract more customers? And what about the travel agents? A good reservations system is almost as important for them as it is for us. Maybe by doing this we could convince them to work with us before going to the others. Ricardo, let's see that spreadsheet! We have to take a look at your forecasts! With computers, we'll sell more, we'll be more efficient and instead of having 'black-holes' we'll have . . . What do you call them? Buffers? Yeah, that's right, a financial buffer!"

Ricardo, desperate, sunk back down into his chair.

STEP 2: Prepare the case for class discussion.

STEP 3: Answer each of the following questions, individually or in small groups, as directed by your instructor.

Diagnosis
1. What information needs does AirTour Vacaciones demonstrate?
2. What types of problems does such a company typically encounter?

Evaluation
3. How can the company use information technology to address these problems?
4. How can AirTour Vacaciones use information technology to support its business strategy and make the business more competitive?
5. What aspects of the business should be automated?

Design
6. What would be the components of an automated system for this company?
7. What types of hardware and software would support such automation?

Implementation
8. What issues must the owners consider in automating their company?

STEP 4: In small groups, with the entire class, or in written form, share your answers to the questions above. Then answer the following questions:

1. What information needs does AirTour Vacaciones have?
2. How can automation address these needs?
3. How would an automated system look?
4. What issues should be considered in implementing the system?

Shorko Films SA[1]

STEP 1: Read the Shorko Films SA case[1] (This activity is especially suited for use in conjunction with Chapter 9 of *Information Systems*.)

"Computerized process control was all upside down for us, with no downside. It was an investment which gave us a chance—it meant change but it was a symbol of the future." Christian de Pierrefeu, General Manager of Shorko Films SA, was reviewing the last two years' experience of introducing a distributed process control system to his packaging film factory. "We had our backs to the wall in 1987 and there was no alternative—it was a marvelous opportunity. The plant is now profitable. But this is only part of the achievement. Process Control is a starting point; it changes your thinking—you look at quality, consider customer service, change your methods . . . rethink competitive strategy." Bernard Delannoy, Information Technology Manager, reflected on Process Control a little differently. "When you've tasted it, just like wine, you realize it is rather good."

COMPANY HISTORY AND BACKGROUND

Shorko Films SA is located at Mantes-la-Ville, northwest of Paris, by the River Seine. It is the second European manufacturing plant of Shorko Films, one of 30 "Full Reporting Businesses" which make up the UK chemicals and textiles corporation, Courtaulds Plc. The sister production site and Shorko headquarters is at Swindon, England, which also provides common services such as financial management, gross production scheduling, marketing and information technology support. Within Courtaulds and Shorko, the two sites are usually referred to as Swindon and Mantes.

Mantes, prior to 1984, belonged to Rhone Poulenc. The plant had been losing money steadily since 1974 and annual losses had increased in 1982. Shorko Films, in contrast, had shown consistent profits over the same period in spite of operational problems. Through the acquisition in 1984, Shorko gained European market share in its sole product, OPP (oriented polypropylene) coextruded film, and prevented capacity falling into competitors' hands in a growth market.

Principal rivals included Mobil, ICI, Kalle, Wolff and Moplefan. Courtaulds paid nothing for the fixed assets, but provided, £1.9 million of working capital. They paid a somewhat larger sum for goodwill, for both the OPP and cellophane product lines, the latter being increasingly substituted by the former in the packaging industry. There also was an understanding that Mantes would be kept at least until the end of 1986 and that Shorko would assume responsibility for any redundancy costs.

By 1988 the Shorko division's total sales were £65 million, yielding a return on sales of roughly 13% (Appendix 1). Mantes contributed profits of £2 million. Shorko occupied second position in the European OPP market behind Mobil.

OPP film resembles cellophane in many ways and is used primarily in the food packaging industry. By the mid 1980s OPP had overtaken cellophane in terms of market tonnage. OPP is cheaper by between 25% and 35%, not least because it is not so dense, producing 30% more

---

[1] This case was prepared as a basis for class discussion rather than to illustrate either effective or ineffective handling of an administrative situation.

Reprinted from *Strategic Information Systems: A European Perspective.* Edited by C. Ciborra and T. Jelassi © 1994 John Wiley & Sons Ltd.

film for an equivalent weight of cellophane. Other comparative advantages include appearance, machinability, heatsealing properties, gauge thinness, finishes and printing capabilities.

During the early 1980s, the OPP market grew at 15% per annum, slowing down to about 7% in the latter half of the decade. Finished rolls of OPP are either taken by end-users or further processed by "converters"—usually involving printing or meeting other special customer requirements—before delivery to the end customer. Courtaulds owns some converter businesses.

MANUFACTURING PROCESS

All OPP film is based on the homopolymer of propylene. Polypropylene is a thermoplastic resin supplied to film manufacturers as granules. The resin is melted, stirred to ensure homogeneity and filtered for purity before extrusion through a horizontal slit to form a thick band about 0.5–2 cm thick and up to 1 metre wide. Plain film is then formed by stretching the thick band both lengthways and sideways under carefully controlled conditions (biaxial orientation). Orientation gives the film its stiffness and clarity. For heatseal applications, each side of the film has to be given a thin layer of material, with a lower melting point so that seal can be formed without distortion of the base. As well as imparting heatseal properties, the outer layers can be formulated to give optical properties such as sparkle, and handling properties such as slip and crackle.

Manufacturers have a choice of technical methods both for adding the outer layers to the base film and for the orientation process. Heatsealable layers can be added to the film by either coating or coextrusion. Orientation is achieved by either a stenter or a tubular method. Shorko pioneered the coextrusion method, against early industry skepticism, and uses the stenter process. Coextruded films are, in effect, three-ply laminates comprising a central layer of homopolymer and two outer layers of copolymer. By varying the thickness of each layer and the type of copolymers used in the outer layers, the properties of the finished product can be extensively varied to suit specific customer or market requirements.

A schematic of the Mantes manufacturing process is shown in Appendix 3. Raw materials in the form of polymer chips and special additives (plus scrap) are fed into hoppers which feed three extruders. The main extruder produces the central homopolymer layer of film and two satellite extruders each produce a melt which passes through a filter and then a slot die to form a single three-ply web of film. This web is then chilled and drawn through a system of rollers which reheats and stretches it to a specified ratio. The stretched web is then fed into a stenter which stretches the web in the transverse direction to yield a film up to 4.5 metres wide.

Passing through the stenter, the web is thermo-fixed to enable it to withstand normal conversion and end-use temperatures. It then cools and passes through an electrostatic treatment process which allows the film to accept print or additional coating by third party converters. The treated film web is then wound onto a mill roll which is removed, stored as work-in-progress and eventually moved to the rewinding machine. Coating has turned out to be the costlier process. It requires an extra operation, the prices of coating materials have risen faster than for copolymers, and coated film scrap cannot be recycled.

Three basic film types are produced by Shorko: transparent, pearlized and metalized. Film rolls finally undergo a slitting process to provide the sizes the converters require. Typical users of OPP are wrappings and seal packaging of biscuits, confectionery, potato crisps and cigarettes by companies such as United Biscuits, Nabisco, and Rowntree Mackintosh.

At Mantes, there are two film production lines. Line 1 can produce 4600 tons per annum of 4 m wide film while Line 2 produces 6500 tons per annum of 4.4m width. The main film processing variables which can be controlled are line tension, speed, pressure and film gauge. The lines at Swindon are newer and faster than those at Mantes. Swindon had three lines in early 1989, with a fourth being installed. Their existing three lines could produce 25,000 gross tonnes per annum. Shorko's strategy has been to become the lowest cost producer of OPP, to build market share, and to extend the product range (thereby reducing the reliance on commodity product-markets). This strategy often has led to high volume, easy to make product types being scheduled on Swindon's bigger, faster lines. One consequence was recent investment in an automated warehouse at Swindon in order to stock the output of longer runs and be able to offer more immediate response to commodity film customers.

TURNAROUND

Since 1984, Shorko's strategy assumed that Mantes would be closed down at some point. Retention of the two sites was seen to prejudice the low cost manufacturing strategy and it had been planned that Mantes would cease to operate in 1988. However, considerations of avoiding single plant exposures, maximizing continental market share, and smoothly managing expansion at Swindon persuaded Shorko's management to retain the Mantes capability until market growth declined—despite its inherited higher labour, energy and tax costs.

"When I arrived in 1985, the future of Mantes was limited," explained Christian de Pierrefeu, "unless we made drastic changes. The factory capacity was 6000 tons per annum, employing 210 people. There were too many Chiefs and not enough Indians. The management system was loose. Under Rhone Poulenc, the decline of cellophane put Mantes into the red. There had been strikes and general discontent. Given Shorko's declared strategy, I had to persuade the management team to take its own action to survive." A rationalization plan resulted including a first reduction of fixed costs, shedding labour, introducing more flexible working, finding more volume and specializing in certain qualities of film in agreement with Swindon, in order to create longer runs. The outcome was a profit of £1.1 million in 1985 on 7000 tonnes.

"Early on we reduced the workforce by 10%. We had to perform to get any investment whereas Swindon, because of the strategy, was getting, almost automatically, new lines," explained de Pierrefeu. "Then at the same time that the go-ahead was given for the fourth line at Swindon, the Board approved our investment in Process Control. It was probably a psychological move that some investment went to Mantes to show faith in the future."

De Pierrefeu attributes the idea to the former Managing Director of Shorko, Chris Matthews. The IT Executive for all Courtaulds Films and Packaging businesses, Bill Hedley, confirmed this. "When Chris first looked at Swindon lines, he said they were ten years behind in electronics. He concluded that the existing engineering and research experience in Courtaulds was very limited in this area. He then visited Mantes and reckoned the management team had the motivation and capability to implement state of the art Process Control." The Mantes General Manager agreed. "I saw Process Control as a good opportunity to expand. Nobody else would have helped us bring in new technology except Chris Matthews. He understood Process Control and he knew the supplier we chose, Valmet. Introduction of new technology gave us the chance to change the organization, tackle problems, look at jobs—it was a tool for new systems and a new organization. I had no better alternative."

Shorko Films SA signed a contract to supply a Valmet "dramatic classic" distributed process control system, with ACV, using local Valmet agents, at the end of March 1987. The system was to be installed on both lines. The following benefits were identified:

- Labour reduction and optimization.
- Reduction of mechanical and electrical failures.

- Speed optimization leading to increased production.
- Faster start up times.

The system was successfully commissioned in August 1987 and was in full use for day and night working two months later.

"From an IT perspective," commented Bill Hedley, "the project has several interesting aspects. First, leading edge technology was introduced into Mantes without the drive or assistance of the group's Research, Engineering or IT functions. What do we learn from this? Second, the General Manager took Mantes' new IT Manager away from the division's programme of implementing a package-based set of integrated basic business systems in order to concentrate on the Valmet system. Fortunately, Bernard Delannoy is an electrical engineer by background with both computing and engineering experience. It has been helpful to have one person responsible for both factory systems and commercial data processing. Then before long we have to decide how to interface the process control data and computing with the Trifid package of business systems running on the McDonnell Douglas computer. This will be essential for both process improvement work and management information."

DISTRIBUTED PROCESS CONTROL

"Basically," explained Jean-Claude Caillaud, the Production Director, "the Valmet system comprises hundreds of sensors or nodes reading or acting on all the variables in the process. There are 1000 nodes on each line and 500 in the reclaim area. The sensors record temperature, pressure, speed, air velocity, time, length, gauge, tension, voltage and similar parameters all wired up to the HP computers in the control room."

The distributed process network acquires and processes measurement data, monitors processes, controls valves and motors, generates alarms, executes mathematical expressions and conducts logic operations. In the control room are two screens for each line. The operators can see synoptics, change control parameters, examine recent process histories and analyse trends on speed, temperature, recipes and other key variables. Alarms on key parameters and parts of the line also show up on the screens and ring bells.

Many of the benefits are those which come from any automation. Jean-Claude Caillaud graphically described one impact. "A change of recipe takes 20 minutes now instead of 2 hours to 2 days previously. This is possible because all the parameters are in the system memory and the computer does all the necessary changes. When it was manual, we always forgot one parameter."

In the Mantes system, the control room (Appendix 4) was made the centrepiece of the factory. The VDU screens replaced three large control panels on the shop floor which previously had partially controlled separate sections of the lines. The Mantes management team decided to have the control room as big as possible to create enough space for the technology, provide an organized atmosphere, and provide a conducive environment for the operators. The intention was to reinforce the notion that the process control system was integral with the factory—the two were interdependent. Thus, everything electronic is connected to it and all control activities are directed from it. Plant meetings are held there, the shift manager's office is in the rear and the quality control laboratory is to one side. Finally, all the processing, switching and memory units are housed in the control room. In late 1988, a new HP 9000 computer was ordered to add 800 Mb of memory in order to store one year's data for analysis. Without this, only 32 hours' process data could be stored.

Valmet, the system supplier, is a Finnish corporation. The Damatic Processing Automation System was the first system ever to integrate logic, motor and sequence controls into one single system with regulatory control functions.[2] Major adopters have been pulp and paper mills and subsequently chemical and petrochemical plants.

SYSTEM INSTALLATION

"It was important that we used our own team for specifying the system and defining the parameters, rather than relying on external advisers," explained François Gaillard, the Management Accountant. "For our part, we knew nothing about process control and for their part, Valmet knew nothing about our process." A team of four Mantes personnel and four Valmet specialists jointly built the software, customizing the Damatic system to fit the Mantes process, lines and practice. This took three months. The Mantes members comprised the Information Technology Manager, an electrician and two foremen. In addition, shop floor representatives were appointed to help communicate the system to the shop floor, to contribute their process knowledge and line experience, and to specify screen contents and formats.

Simultaneously, Valmet built the control hardware. The whole team was then transferred to Finland to progress the hardware and software integration. The technical room was built in May and June, the hardware installed in July, and the control room built in the first three weeks of August. Total commissioning time was four months. Line 1 started up under the new system on 21 August.

"Back in March I explained the project to the workforce and emphasized it meant organizational change," recalled Jean Claude Caillaud. "We took key people to a small factory in Paris who had installed a process control system. The aim was to demystify the project." In May, 24 operators had two days' on-site training on process control, cabling and computing provided by the local Valmet agency, ACV. "Employees had to learn to control the process from a keyboard instead of by hand," commented de Pierrefeu. "They had to define parameters on-line rather than apply screwdrivers and turn valves. Now everything is visualized. They get a view of what is happening from graphics and synoptics. They see all the automatic adjustments happen in the right order, compared with the old days of going to all the sensors and controls and forgetting one." In July the head of each line was able to see the screens and work the test system. In August the wiring was done during the factory shutdown, helped by 15 operators who took no holiday.

"Between August and November," commented Caillaud, "we did automatic start ups and then gradually improved start ups, closures and restarts. We worked to improve everything we could on the line—downtime, manning, changes. We set targets for the operators with bonus payments if the process control system achieved previous performance. It did."

Throughout this period and for six months after installation, Valmet supplied a Project Manager. His task was to analyse and understand the plant, create a document and drawings and oversee the software development back in Finland. He worked on site and according to Caillaud was "key to our success and a very good technologist."

Christian de Pierrefeu was clear about the scale of change being demanded. "I explained to everybody what the challenge was. I spent a lot of time on this. I spent week after week explaining what we were doing and why. I stressed that we were fighting for survival. Process Control changes everything. I discussed the project with the trade unions and explained that everything would change. Process Control imposes a different approach to manufacturing. Before, your management of the process was as good as the best foreman's experience. Afterwards, it is a question of what is the best way, because you specify the parameters from the best knowledge of everybody and codify it into the software. So people must act as a team and follow the system. Mantes employees didn't like it at first but now they are convinced

---
[2] As claimed in the Valmet product brochure.

it is better. They see the system as a summation of all the best people's knowledge and experience. Now our people could not work, and would not work, without the Valmet system."

"The biggest change," de Pierrefeu observed, "is we now have employees not workers. This change of status is the crunch. We have given the operators responsibility. If they are not on the line, they are working somewhere else, perhaps in packaging, or on the grinder. Once the system is running correctly, people must accept flexibility. Their jobs are automated and in previous terms there is nothing for them to do. But now with Process Control you need flexible working. If something goes wrong on one line, you move people from another. If the screen tells you a motor is heating up, you send a commando team to sort it out wherever they are. Before, if one line performed better due to its engineering, or because of the grade it was making, the line workers would say 'we are better than the others.' They all have to work together now."

Jean Claude Caillaud confirmed this experience. "We used to have three operators per line and five shifts. Now we have five operators, often only four, on both lines and they can all work the system. Their flexibility agreement includes checking, feeding the masher, grinding, attending to problems and doing lab tests. The shift foreman runs the plant but now he is operating the system, looking at system problems. The foremen have become 'managers'."

EVALUATION

The initial capital cost for the Valmet system was £700,000 and the predicted payback was two years. Payback was seen as the key financial criterion for two reasons. The lines were old and the future of Mantes was uncertain. Valmet said the system would perform better than the expectations built into the capital proposal. A novel agreement was made. The turnkey contract was priced at a 20% discount. However, if results exceeded expectations the full cost of FF1 117,920 would be paid by Mantes in the last term of payment in 1989. This agreement is reproduced in Appendix 5.

When asked why Valmet was chosen as the supplier the General Manager replied, "Chris Matthews said Valmet was best from day one and he was proved right."

In early 1989, a post audit suggested that most of the operational goals were being met. Operators had been reduced by five. Mechanical and electrical failures had not really reduced, because maintenance had increased as the lines aged. Speed optimization exceeded expectations on both lines. Downtime had reduced on Line 1 from 6.9% to 5.8% and on Line 2 from 6.3% to 5.8%. Likewise start up time after filter changes had improved by approximately 30%. Job changes on average had been reduced from 100 minutes to 57 minutes on Line 1, and from 100 minutes to 64 minutes on Line 2.

These operational gains translated into financial benefits in excess of the original payback calculations. Christian de Pierrefeu believed the Process Control investment had been a major contributor to increased profitability at Mantes. In three years return on sales had risen from 2.24% to 9.53% and return on investment from 19.56% to 34.1%. Tonnage had increased by 3000 tons, of which 1000 tons was attributed to the impact of the new system in 1988. De Pierrefeu added, "We really invested because our back was to the wall. We were not afraid to change organization, practices and philosophy. It has been a very deep change."

"Yes, the big change from the production viewpoint," commented Caillaud, "was not technological but human. You can't invest in technologies if you don't invest in people, especially in training. Otherwise you get problems very quickly. We had two motivation factors which helped though. First, it was a matter of survival. Second the fact that we had an investment project was a plus."

"We also managed the project as a team," noted de Pierrefeu. "I spent about one-third of my time on it because it was a key project with big issues. I went to Finland and took the team to get them to believe in it. I had to be convinced to get them convinced." Caillaud commented that gaining belief and commitment is easier when the management team is small. "The intensive timeframe also provided a good challenge. And maybe it helps to be a foreign subsidiary." François Gaillard agreed. "If performance is bad, it is no problem for a foreign parent to close the factory. Therefore we just had to improve our profitability."

NEXT STEPS

"The Valmet system soon showed us we didn't know enough about the process. Process control raises questions and you must improve knowledge of the system." Christian de Pierrefeu went on, "The next change is to drive the system and not be driven by it. Having got people to work the system, the next stage is to change the direction of dominance. It has taken one year to learn how to work the system. Now we must close the loop."

The General Manager described three investment phases. Computer process control of the two lines was the first phase. "Next we started to say how can we improve quality? Valmet had a Canadian subsidiary who had developed a gauge control system for paper mills which guaranteed a constant gauge overall. We asked them to apply the same idea to film to link the extrusion die to the film end to achieve autocorrection." This was installed in Mantes in September 1988 and quality improvements of 20% had been recorded. The slit yield on Line 2 was reaching nearly 90%. This was due to producing more flat film and losing less edge trim. Improved yield and fewer customer complaints had resulted in a paycheck of less than three months.

Phase three is investment in a process management system (PMS). This is seen as the means of learning how to drive Process Control rather than be driven by it. PMS allows analysis of historical data and process simulation to learn more about the process. "We are not necessarily sure what is, say, the correct temperature for a grade or what are the tolerances," explained de Pierrefeu. "We need PMS to help us improve the whole line and understand and optimize all the parameters. In two weeks' time I am taking the team to a paper mill to see PMS in operation."

The Mantes team were planning for PMS. In October 1988 operators had begun four weeks of post-implementation training. Each operator had to attend a local technical college to acquire new knowledge and skills before they installed PMS. The course required mathematics, physics, polymer science, extrusion technology, laboratory measurement and microcomputing. The aim was to get everybody to a best and common level before the PMS arrived.

"Our next problem," noted Bernard Delannoy, "is not only developing PMS on top of the Valmet system but how to link it to the McDonnell Douglas computer for storage, analysis and management information reporting." It had been made a requirement by Chris Matthews and Bill Hedley early on that Valmet's technology would be compatible with plans for developing basic business systems and MIS.

Christian de Pierrefeu, however, was considering the next opportunity. "After PMS," he commented, "and with our experience of running an automatic plant, Mantes would like to have Shorko's next new line. I want to make Mantes the specialty films plant for Shorko. We can't beat the 300 metres per minute and 8 metres per width line at Swindon. We realized all along that we couldn't match them for speed or width on any of their lines. Thus we have decided to go for specialty films which attract higher prices and earn more profit. Process Control has given us the capability—we can produce smaller quantities and more product lines and still achieve a good slit to sale efficiency. We can change from grade to grade now because of Process Control. So we don't want a faster or wider line but one designed for reliability and flexibility. With computerization we now have a systems approach not a 'fix it' mentality and we can get the specialized film business."

APPENDIX 1   Courtaulds Films and Packaging, Shorko SA, Mantes. Profit and Loss Account (1988)

1. Volume	
Production:	
Standard	10,404 tonnes
Sub-standard	418 tonnes
Total:	10,822 tonnes
Sales:	
Standard	11,727 tonnes
Sub-standard	529 tonnes
Total	12,256 tonnes
2. Financial	**£000s**
Sales	21,303
Raw materials and variable production costs	12,869
Gross margin	8,434
Fixed costs:	
Production	4,828
Selling and marketing	947
Finance and administration	679
Total:	6,454
Trading profit	1,980

APPENDIX 2: Shorko Films SA—Management Organization Chart

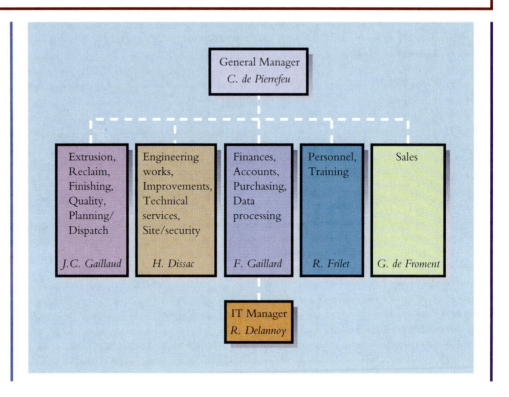

APPENDIX 3: Schematic of OPP Process

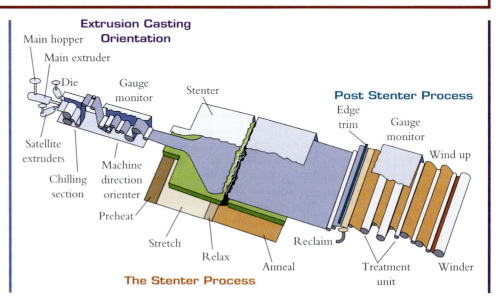

APPENDIX 4 Process Control Room

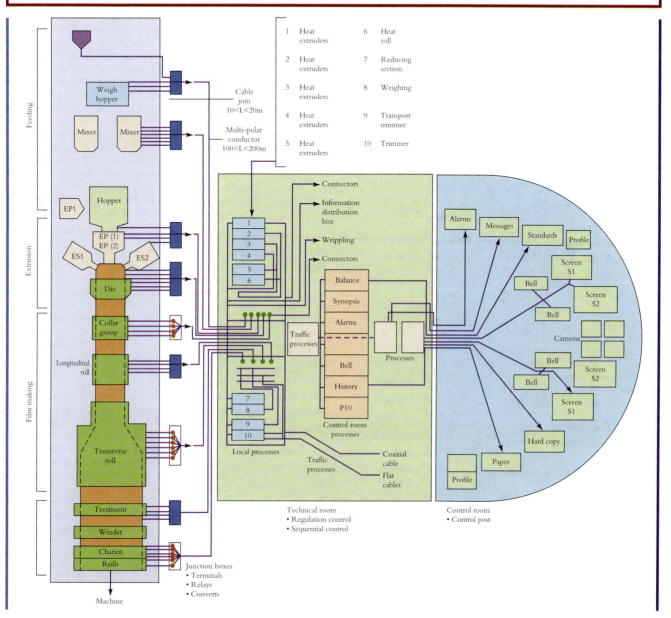

APPENDIX 5: Agreement with ACV

			Amount of Savings
1	Labour reduction: 5 operators less	PDS	75,000.00
2	Reduction of mechanical/electrical failures 1.30 h production/month	PDS	25,000.00
3	Speed optimisation +0.5% on S1 +2% on S2 increase production: 130 t	PDS	90,000.00
4	Production downtime/film break 5.3% to 3.8% on S1 and S2: 140 t	PDS	100,000.00
5	Improved start-up time after filters change and reduction of lost time after shut down: 45 t	PDS	30,000.00
6	Job changes for S1 and S2 4 h reduced to 2 h on basis 3 per month on S1 7 per month on S2 i.e.: 185 t production increase 500 t	PDS	130,000.00
			TOTAL SAVINGS PDS 450,000.00

"After analysis of the goals to be reached in Mantes with a DAMATIC distributed control system, we have the pleasure to inform you that we accept to bind the settlement of the last term of payment to a performance guarantee on the following basis:

- Principle of bonus for AVC is accepted if the guarantee results are better than expected.
- Maximum value of penalty of bonus: 20% of the total value of our turn-key offer, i.e. : FF 1,117,920.00
- Period of evaluation: 12 months: from January 88 to December 88.
- Saving objectives are based on a 500 t/y production increase. This production increase together with labour reduction will cause a GBP 450,000 savings (rate of exchange and film cost price: Jan. 87).
- Savings costs are as follows:
- Variations on the several saving points will be accepted as long as the total amounts remain unchanged
- Penalty or bonus calculation:
  At the end of the evaluation period, SHORKO or ACV will have 4 week time to prove respectively that:
    - the objective has not been reached. SHORKO will bring elements to prove its claim,
    - the objective has been exceeded: ACV will bring elements to prove its claim.

Then, the companies will have 4 weeks to settle the matter. If SHORKO makes no claim, the last term will be settled as agreed.

STEP 2: Prepare the case for class discussion.

STEP 3: Answer each of the following questions, individually or in small groups, as directed by your instructor.

Diagnosis

1. Why, when he arrived in 1985, did Christian de Pierrefeu feel that the future of Shorko's Mantes plant was limited?

Evaluation

2. Why did Chris Matthews suggest the idea of automated process control?
3. What benefits did de Pierrefeu expect to achieve from automation?
4. What was the attitude of the machine operators to the proposal for process automation? How did de Pierrefeu and Jean-Claude Caillaud manage their expectations?

Design

5. What types of information does the automated system need to collect in order to properly control the machinery at Mantes?
6. What was the role of the managers at Mantes in the design of the automated systems?
7. What was the role of the machine operators in the design of the automated system?
8. How effectively did the management team and its contractors address the opportunity to design the system to collect information that could be used to further improve process management?

Implementation

9. How effective was the automation system in achieving its design objectives?
10. What was the impact of automation on the machine operators? What was its impact on the managers?
11. What should de Pierrefeu do next?

STEP 4: In small groups, with the entire class, or in written form, share your answers to the questions above. Then answer the following questions:

1. What were the objectives of automation at the Mantes plant?
2. How well did the Valmet system meet these objectives?
3. What additional changes are possible to increase the value of the automated system?
4. How did implementation of the system change the roles and perspectives of operators and managers? ●

Activity 13: Benetton SpA

STEP 1: Read the "Fashion Success Story of the 1980s: Benetton SpA" case. (This activity is especially suited for use in conjunction with Chapter 10 of *Information Systems*.)

> One reason why the Roman Empire grew so large and survived so long—a prodigious feat of management—is that there was no railway, car, airplane, radio, paper, or telephone. Above all, no telephone. And therefore you could not maintain any illusion of direct control over a general or provincial governor, you could not feel at the back of your mind that you could ring him up, or that he could ring you, if a situation cropped up which was too much for him, or that he could fly over and sort things out if they started to get in a mess. You appointed him, you watched his baggage train disappear over the hill in a cloud of dust and that was that. There was, therefore, no question of appointing a man that was not fully trained, or not quite up to the job; you knew that everything depended upon his being the best man for the job before he set off. And so you took great care in selecting him; but more than that you made sure that he knew all about Roman government and the Roman army before he went out.
>
> Antony Jay[1]

THE WORLDWIDE TRANSACTION SYSTEM

"We want to provide our agents with the information they need to control their own sales and account receivables," said Bruno Zuccaro, Director of Information Systems at Benetton SpA in Treviso, Italy, as he explained the Worldwide Transaction System (WTS). At Benetton, the WTS represented the latest effort to formalize the company's unusual business system, developed over several years and highly dependent on informal and implicit policies. Although the WTS was not out of character for a company which prided itself on the use of information technology (IT), Bruno worried that its introduction would not preserve Benetton's culture based on informality and trust.

"To work for Benetton, Luciano says, you have to be a little crazy. Let me explain," Bruno said, as he proceeded to describe some of Benetton's informal business policies:

- Being crazy is having originality in solving problems, imagination in design, creativity in management, vision of the business, no fear of making mistakes, because there are very few guidelines.
- Second, the important things are few; in whatever you do, start by making things simple. Don't complicate matters, reduce them to their essentials. There are no complicated rules in the Benetton system. For example, we never intended to install our Point of Sale (POS)[2] system to control our agents, quite the contrary, we wanted to give maximum support to the company's agents, our *Centurioni*.
- Third, it is important to be ready. Try to anticipate what is happening, and use your imagination to identify and adapt to the new situation. For example, we have two fashion seasons a year and by the time you get feedback from the market, you are already working

> This case was prepared by Research Associate Robert C. Howard, under the supervision of Professor Werner Ketelhöhn, as a basis for class discussion rather than to illustrate either effective or ineffective handling of a business situation. Copyright © 1990 by IMEDE, Lausanne, Switzerland.

[1] *Management and Machiavelli,* Hutchinson Business, London 1987.
[2] Luciano Benetton wanted a system which could register information at the point of sale (POS) and transmit that information at the end of the day during the first two weeks of the season.

for the next season. In 1989 this meant 2,000 items every six months. The problem here is to anticipate the market, not to follow the market.

Giovanni Cantagalli, Vice President of Operations, underscored Bruno's comments regarding the flexible atmosphere at Benetton.

> This company is a miracle: there is no organization chart; it isn't clear who does what. It was created on a non-industrial framework. Compared to the experiences that I've had in other more structured companies, it seems everything holds together by chance, and yet we turn over more than L 1,600 billion a year.

In referring to POS, Bruno was hinting at a previous problem created by the careless introduction of information technology to the Benetton culture.

> There were a number of managers who saw POS as an opportunity to control and monitor our agents and shopowners. Where Luciano emphasized maximum support to the agent, one can understand why he was opposed to installing POS in a way that might undermine the relationship between himself and his Centurioni. In fact, the reason we wanted to install POS was to monitor the market, not to monitor the agents or control the shops. It supported the reassortment process which had become a whole new business—a task which had become increasingly complex with the growth of Benetton in recent years. POS was simply a tool to keep the company from becoming too complicated.

Unlike POS, however, the WTS was a far more sophisticated tool for information management and formalizing company rules. That is, where POS served as a "market thermometer" providing the latest sales information on fashion trends, WTS would go one step further and enable agents to manage their accounts more closely without having to resolve problems through Treviso. Nonetheless, what was intended to serve as a decentralizing tool, to move the responsibility of shop coordination from Benetton headquarters in Treviso to the agents in their respective areas, could be viewed by some agents as a supervisory tool, thus threatening to undermine the company's implicit policies and working procedures. "Based on the POS experience, is it possible to introduce the more complex WTS without damaging the entrepreneurial flare and informal atmosphere so fundamental to our success?" asked Bruno.

THE BENETTON SYSTEM IN 1989

Under the leadership of Luciano Benetton, he and his three siblings—Guiliana, Carlo, and Gilberto—had, in the course of 25 years, created the classic American rags to riches story, albeit in remote Northeast Italy. By 1989, the world-renowned industrial fashion company had an annual turnover of $1 billion generated by over 5,000 shops worldwide, supplied primarily by Italian manufacturing facilities.[3] The company, however, had not attained this position without growing pains and, by the end of the 1980s, the management of Benetton looked back on several growth phases. Toward the end of each phase, management had been inclined to review the company's business system and consider the best way to introduce information technology while preserving the company's success.

Design

Though outside designers had been used since the company's beginning, by 1988 their length of stay was limited to a maximum of six seasons (three years) to guarantee a regular supply of innovative ideas. In addition to outsiders, Benetton had a series of design teams for each of its clothing themes. Aside from the company's main theme—*The United Colors of Benet-*

---

[3] For a more thorough discussion of the company's history, see IMD case *Building the Benetton System*.

ton—some of the more recent themes included: "Anthology" which featured United States clothing styles of the 1950s; "Marina" with a nautical emphasis; and "Type de Nimes" dedicated to denim garments. For each of these themes, design teams completed or adapted product ideas within given cost boundaries. Given this variety of themes, the company's designers rarely set a fashion trend but, given the conservative styling policy, they rarely missed one either. "Benetton is not fashion. Ralph Lauren, Yves St. Laurent, and Chanel are fashion and we respect them, but we're a whole other world," said one Benetton executive in charge of corporate communications. "We don't challenge people to buy our latest ideas, we find out their ideas and desires, and provide them," he added.

Cut, Make and Trim (CMT)

In the apparel industry, raw material sourcing and manufacturing were highly dependent upon the fashion cycle. Aldo Palmeri, Chief Executive Officer (CEO) of Benetton Group SpA, described his company's fashion cycle.

> We show two major fashion collections a year, 12 months in advance of the sales season. For example, for Autumn/Winter 1989, we began to show our collection in November 1988, and we started to order raw materials at the same time. We go long, according to prices and ranges, but we buy less than half our total needs at this stage. We complete our purchases only when we have firm orders from our store owners at the beginning of January (refer to Exhibit 1).
>
> The production cycle, starting between November and January, is divided between functions undertaken at Benetton and those subcontracted out. We start to deliver the products at the end of April, but the starting point for credit to shopowners is September 1; that's when the clock starts ticking. Payments are due at 30-, 60-, and 90-day intervals. In other words, the first payment is due at the end of September, the second at the end of October and the third at the end of November. This means that the peak of indebtedness at Benetton is when we've completed production and delivered the goods, but haven't yet been paid by our customers. That's between May and the end of September for the Autumn/Winter collection.

Specifically, Benetton took 90–120 days to pay its suppliers, whereas it took only 30 days to pay its subcontractors. "The subcontractors can't handle the strain of extended credit, but the raw material suppliers can," added Palmeri. Furthermore, since raw material suppliers benefitted from guaranteed volumes, they were asked in return to take charge of the inventories, and be flexible and responsive to Benetton's needs.

By the end of the 1980s, the production process at Benetton had evolved towards internal and external locations. Internal production concentrated on capital intensive steps of the business system such as raw material sourcing, cutting, dyeing and distribution. External production, on the other hand, focused on labor intensive steps in the business system, including sewing and 99% of the wool knitting (refer to Exhibit 2). Knitting facilities, or laboratories as they were called within Benetton, invested in their own equipment and owned 12 machines on average, of up to six different types. Also, Benetton kept track of which laboratories owned what equipment, in order to send each laboratory the appropriate type and amount of work. Specifically, subcontractors' resources were optimized by limiting their involvement to one or two production stages while guaranteeing them a 10% profit margin on cost. In addition, company policy kept investment costs down by adapting old machinery to new tasks instead of replacing it.

Benetton Group SpA was sensitive to the needs of its external subcontractors and attempted to keep them busy year round—except during Benetton's August vacation. In addition, Benetton assisted these laboratories financially. That is, in arm's length competition, one typically paid subcontractors as little as possible. Benetton, on the other hand, tried to pay the right price, defined as the time for operations, the cost of manpower and a plant

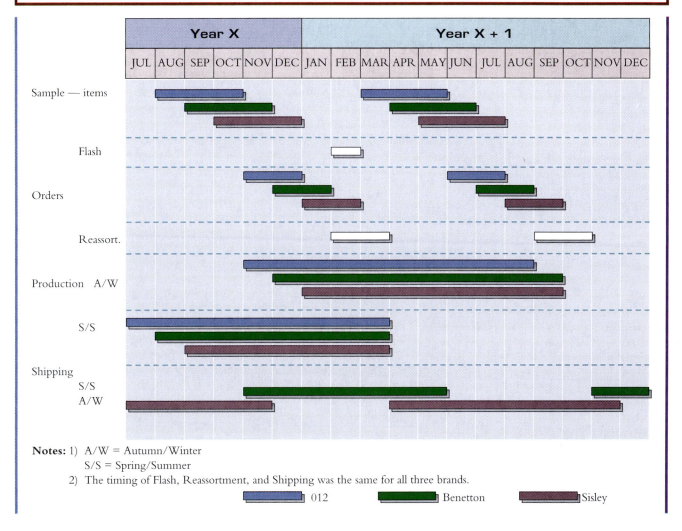

Notes: 1) A/W = Autumn/Winter
S/S = Spring/Summer
2) The timing of Flash, Reassortment, and Shipping was the same for all three brands.

fee. Moreover, Benetton sometimes helped subcontractors upgrade their machinery in line with fashion trends by buying the old equipment. As a second alternative, the company allowed subcontractors wide margins on some orders, thereby freeing up the capital to invest in new machinery. Still, where subcontractors had difficulties in purchasing their equipment, Benetton provided lease arrangements.

In addition to the financial support and guaranteed work at full capacity, subcontractors lowered social costs[4] and corporate overhead yet, as owners, closely supervised operations. Moreover, subcontractors benefitted from small sales, marketing, and accounting departments and thus concentrated on manufacturing and making one invoice per month. This system,

---

[4] In Italy, companies with more than 15 employees were subject to union and state control, and paid 49% of workers' salaries in social costs. Thus, subcontractors lowered their social costs by limiting employees in their family enterprises to fewer than 15 people.

> **EXHIBIT 2** Flow of Materials

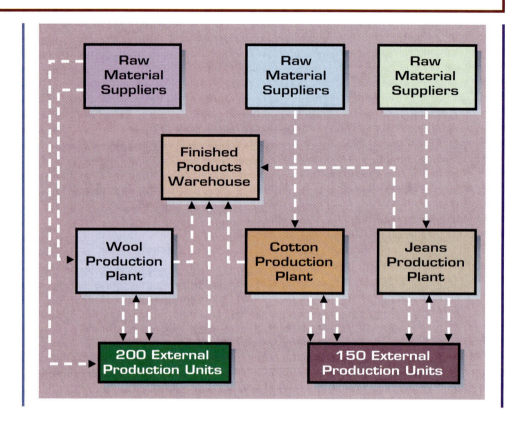

Luciano believed, encouraged people to work exclusively for Benetton—even on weekends if necessary—and reinvest their profits in the business.

The CMT cycle, therefore, particularly the eight months between order taking and delivery, provided Benetton time to adjust the level of its external resources. To summarize, Benetton purchased raw materials and, after inspection at Benetton plants, sent them to subcontractors before bringing the semi-finished products back to its own plants for completion. Knitting or non-knitted materials requiring cutting with the latest computerized technology, for example, were performed at Benetton with capital intensive equipment.

Once knitted, sweater parts were sent out and assembled in laboratories. Thereafter, some assembled garments were returned to Benetton for the capital intensive dyeing phase, a process which some executives believed accounted for 90% of the perceived quality image in Benetton's distinctly colored sweaters. In the finishing stage, which included inspection, pressing, folding, bagging and packing, garments were again sent to subcontractors, before being shipped to warehouses.

As a rule, Luciano tried to reproduce this system when moving into new markets and did not manufacture outside Italy unless required by local conditions. Two examples were Brazil, which was closed to imports, and Spain, where cotton imports were controlled. Local conditions aside, the internationalization of manufacturing provided a degree of protection from exchange rate fluctuations. In the early 1980s, Benetton established production facilities in France and Scotland; Spain in 1985, and Rocky Mount, North Carolina, in the US in 1986. Though small in volume, these foreign facilities complemented Benetton's Italian manufacturing capabilities. For example, high value added cashmere garments were produced in Scotland, woolen garments in France, and cotton articles in the US.

Excluding the US articles, the French and Scottish products represented less than 5% of Benetton's total sales. Moreover, products manufactured at these sites had limited distribution. Specifically, in France, only woolen garments were produced and distributed to a portion of the French retail stores. The cashmere garments produced in Scotland, on the other hand, were distributed primarily in Japan, France and Belgium through normal department stores that had no association with the Benetton name.

Distribution

By the late 1980s, distribution became the most automated function at Benetton. Aside from distributing goods automatically, the system reduced the average delivery time and improved the level of service. For example, all merchandise was bar-coded in local currencies and could be processed electronically at the point of sale. Furthermore, the company tried to get 60% of a season's order to each shop at the start of the season. As Giancarlo Chiodini, Director of Logistics, said, "We have succeeded in linking the shop and the factory floor, eliminating everything in between. Our physical distribution and manufacturing system is completely in phase with commercial realities in the store." (Refer to Exhibit 3.)

Informally, Carlo Benetton oversaw production, subcontracting, and distribution. Generally speaking, the role of manufacturing had changed substantially in recent years and, by 1989, a strong emphasis was placed on innovation and cost reduction. As part of their responsibilities, plant managers had to coordinate the manufacturing details of all production facilities, and plan and control quality. Moreover, a plant manager's success depended on securing the trust of Carlo, who maintained informal relations with long time and trusted subcontractor-employees. In other words, to become a Benetton partner-subcontractor, good relationships with Carlo were a necessity. Then, too, if an employee left the company, he could continue to subcontract or, alternatively, lose his guaranteed business with Benetton—it all depended on Carlo. As a result of this uncertainty, there was a great incentive to stay in the company and continue earning money as a subcontractor.

Distribution Network

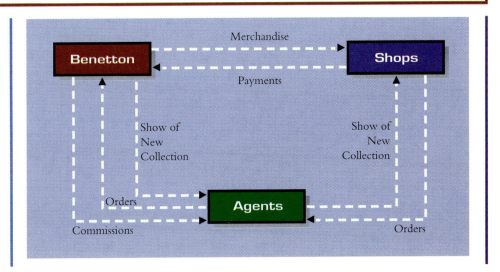

Agents

Mainly through verbal agreements, company agents were assigned large territories which they sought to populate with Benetton shops. These verbal agreements were managed primarily on the basis of trust, and it was not until the early 1980s that formal contracts began to be written between Benetton SpA and the agents. Shopowners themselves kept a close eye on the market, constantly passing on information and suggestions. "We are one with the commercial department of Benetton," asserted Paolo Panizzo, Benetton's agent in London and owner of five shops. When each new collection was ready, agents took about 30 days to present the sample collection to each shopowner and helped the owner in selecting his order; at the end of the day the order was sent to Benetton. As no inventory was to be left in the shops at the end of a season, the agents, who were ultimately responsible for inventory, shifted it to other stores to minimize inventory losses. At the end of a season, any remaining inventory was turned over to a specialized organization which distributed it in third world countries, outside Benetton markets.

By using self-employed agents who promoted and supervised their territories with the rigor of actual owners, Luciano encouraged entrepreneurial energy in the business and fast expansion in the number of shops. The agents' major incentive and source of income came from the high risk, high reward opportunity to invest in the prime-sited shops they oversaw. Thus, agents could move items between stores if the owners agreed; they also monitored markdowns and were expected to maintain contacts with the final consumer. Manlio Tonolo, agent for Northeast Italy, who owned 40 of the 200 shops he supervised, said, "It's important to be able to read the culture of young people; an agent who has nothing to say about customer trends is of no further use to the company. My clients can learn from my shops and vice versa. The company's basic needs have not changed, it still needs a certain level of craziness." Normally, agents had a small organization to perform their multiple activities; they hired young assistants who controlled the shops' overall image and problems on a weekly basis. In addition, assistants helped the agent to monitor new trends in young people's culture by visiting bars, discotheques, etc. to observe behavior and fashion trends.

Agents were formally coordinated by eight area managers, most of whom had been hired since 1984, to choose new agents, open new markets, monitor sales and payments, and follow item movements. In other words, the area managers' job was operational in that they supported the agents in the merchandising task; a service aimed at maintaining clean, well managed shops—essential for a quality image. Furthermore, area managers collected the Basic and Reassortment orders from the agents, checked windows, and conducted market research by opening up a shop. As a norm, however, area managers did not own shops themselves, which built a potential motivational problem into Benetton's formal structure. For example, Ricardo Weiss, who was the area manager for the US, Canada, Japan and some other countries, supervised 25 agents and was responsible for 1,000 shops. In other words, area managers were employees of the corporation and were paid employee salaries. Agents, on the other hand, were impresarios in nature and earned a lot more money than area managers—sometimes creating a difficult relationship.

Under Luciano, the commercial director and the area managers were the marketing department. Nearly all the members of the commercial department were Italian, had been hired by Luciano, and were accustomed to working directly for him. Franco Furno, Head of Organization and Development, commented on the informal versus formal reporting relationships at Benetton.

> Informally, the real marketing manager at Benetton is Luciano. He has three people reporting to him: Venturato, mainly for Europe; Weiss, for the Far East; and Martinuzzo, for Africa and the Middle East. Formally, however, these three persons report to Cantagalli.

Although the commercial directors acted as staff for Luciano, they were not told what had to be done, as Luciano expected employees to understand what was needed. Aldo Palmeri explained in an interview in February 1989:

> Luciano Benetton has created a breed of new entrepreneurs among our agents and shopkeepers. The most important agents now fly their own private aircraft. They're people who were not necessarily in the commercial field before Benetton came into their lives. Luciano wanted people without the pre-fixed ideas of conventional agents in the fashion field. He wanted young, enterprising energetic people who, with proper motivation, would be sympathetic to Benetton's way of doing business and would give their maximum.

Luciano had rarely replaced an agent for failure to meet expectations. Similar to Europe, the marketing organization for America was split into regions, each of which was supervised by an agent.

Retailing

Though Luciano selected shop locations at first, by 1989 locations were also chosen by agents. Each store had standard fixtures such as open shelves and could accommodate about one-third of a season's sales. Also, the shops' window displays, developed by Tobia Scarpa, changed each week and started new trends. Displays, which reinforced ongoing advertising campaigns, were set up by store managers trained by Benetton agents. Typically, the clothes were placed near the window to create a cumulative attraction.

Shopowners were obliged to buy only Benetton clothes, achieve minimum sales levels, follow guidelines for price mark-ups, adopt the standard shop layouts designed by Tobia Scarpa,[5] pay on schedule, and allow for agent-partners. Generally, a shopowner had five shops and did not have to accept returned goods sold by another outlet. Likewise, they could not return merchandise and had to pay for whatever they ordered. Prices, which were set by Benetton, tried to provide 50% gross margins.

Affiliates invested about $70,000 per shop, providing Benetton with a captive distribution network without financial commitments, expensive staff or the need to oversee day-to-day performance. Furthermore, Benetton controlled markdowns, stockouts, and inventory risk while enjoying a costless source for financing retail growth. "The classic shopkeeper had to be killed and we killed him. The real strength of our company is that a whole group has accepted the same policies for production and sales," declared Luciano. In 1989, fewer than 10 Benetton stores were owned and operated by the company, and turnover among shopowners was low. For example, of the 200 stores supervised by Manlio Tonolo, only five shopowners had been replaced during the last 10 years.

Promotion

At Benetton, approximately 4% of sales was spent on direct advertising. Television campaigns concentrated on Benetton's young and sporty image, while magazine advertisements depicted color and lifestyle images. In addition, the company sponsored sports events reflecting the interests of the family. Since the early 1980s, the switch away from country campaigns stressed Benetton's image as a worldwide company with a single theme and position—an infinite variety of color possibilities. In 1983, Benetton launched a global advertising campaign showing interracial crowds of children wearing Benetton clothes and the flags of various countries. Using slogans such as "Benetton—All the Colors of the World" and "United Colors

---

[5]Tobia and Afra Scarpa were both natives of the Veneto area where the Benetton story began. After designing the first Benetton factory in 1965, the Scarpas became close friends of the Benettons. Therafter, Tobia Scarpa designed all Benetton shops, starting with the first shop in Belluno in 1967.

of Benetton," the campaign sought to convey the message that Benetton products had no frontiers. The latter slogan proved so successful that, at the end of 1989, the management agreed to make it the new logo.

THE INCREASING ROLE OF INFORMATION TECHNOLOGY

With the advent of computer-aided design (CAD) at the Ponzano factory, Benetton used computers capable of developing complex stitching in 256 basic colors, or 17 million shades. And, five kilometers away at Villorba, CMT underwent a revolution with the introduction of computer-aided manufacturing (CAM). Thus, from the early 1980s on, raw materials were fed into preprogrammed machines which cut 15,000 garments every eight hours. The combined impact of CAD/CAM on CMT shortened the time span between design approval and manufacture, significantly reducing material waste.

In 1986, Benetton completed its famous automated warehouse in Treviso with the expectation that it would suffice for 20 years. However, within a year and a half after completion, the company's turnover began to test the 300,000 box per day limit of the facility. In 1989, the facility was run by a handful of technicians and had a top operating capacity of 18,000 packages per day. Among its automated features were robots that slid silently between storage racks, programmed to handle cartons of garments. In turn, cartons were moved along by a series of belts, chutes, and cranes under the guidance of a sophisticated computer system.

Aside from revolutionizing a number of tasks within each step of the business system, the information age also brought those steps closer together. For example, CAD and CAM together made it economically feasible to design and manufacture 2,000 products each season, appealing to a host of narrow market segments. In other words, Benetton's integrated distribution, sales and communication systems had effectively removed much of the inventory risk from its business system. (Refer to Exhibit 4 for Benetton's information systems organization.)

Using advanced telecommunications, Benetton received data on sales trends around the world 24 hours a day, every day of the year. Daily updates on sales and inventory were transmitted to Ponzano, where they were analyzed and passed on to the relevant departments. "This technology has brought us closer to the consumer, to eliminate all the filters between the factory and the man who buys," said Giancarlo Chiodini, Director of Logistics, in 1987. "In this way, we have been able to become a global operation with a global vision," he added.

Benetton committed itself to using the best information systems available and, because of the company's fast growth, systems were constantly being restructured. On average, Benetton spent about 1.2% of its annual turnover on hardware, software and computer personnel. In 1985, for example, as part of its ongoing commitment to IT, the company bought a 5% participation in the Italian subsidiary of Nolan Norton, a leading United States information systems consulting firm. In summary, information technology served as the bridge between the manufacturing companies and the market, provided the programming and control of all the external production units, managed centralized distribution around the world, and supported the centralized management of financial flows.

At Benetton, the most important information system was that which connected agents to the firm. Originally, Benetton used a network system consisting of dedicated minicomputers, in seven European cities, connected to mainframes in Italy. With growth, this network became too expensive and, by the end of 1987, agents were connected to the Mark III General Electric Information System's value added network. Available round the clock in 750 cities in 25 countries, Mark III provided network access to customer data such as order-entry, confirmations, color instructions, which orders were sent to which plants, and which orders were transferred among plants. Furthermore, Mark III used General Electric's telecommunications satellite, thus eliminating long distance, transcontinental telephone charges for

EXHIBIT 4 — Information Systems Organization

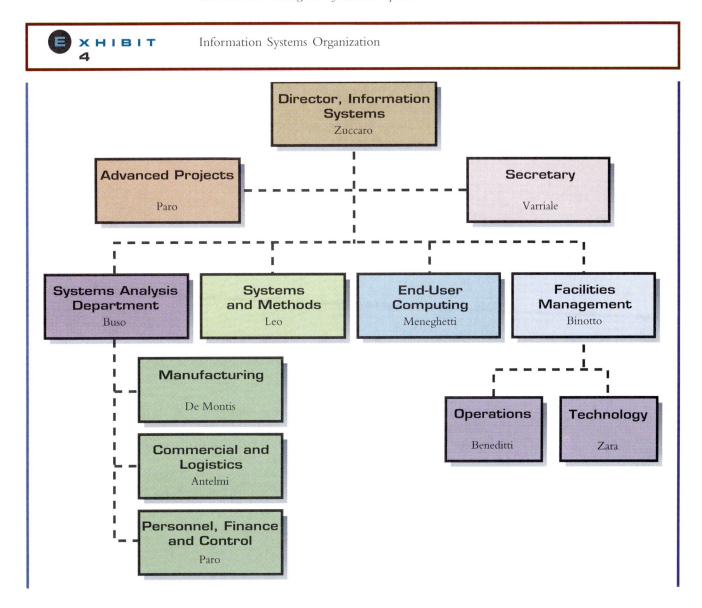

data transmissions as well as for the company's 24-hour Information System Center at headquarters.

Mark III proved to be indispensable for managing Benetton's large database from one computer and at a low cost. During reassortment, for example, shop orders forwarded by agents were collected twice a day through the Mark III network and stored in a central order portfolio. Thereafter, agents were informed on the status of their orders; the plants and the forwarding department were informed of orders as soon as they were collected; plants received finishing and packing instructions each morning; and the forwarding department was informed about the estimated arrival times from plants. "All this," explained Bruno, "would not be possible without a sophisticated information system."

EVALUATING THE BUSINESS SYSTEM

Aldo Palmeri attributed Benetton's success to its entrepreneurial culture in distribution; its philosophy of laying off risk in production, and its highly developed customer-led marketing.

Setting up a classic direct sales network is often weakened by people being paid to be bureaucrats. Intermediaries tend to dominate such a structure and take the benefits from people at the sharp end. What we've done at Benetton is strip down the distribution network to the essentials; we've cut out the middlemen—the wholesalers in our fashion business and the intermediaries in the financial services field—and created dynamic sales forces in each business.

In 1989, Benetton SpA was run by only 30 executives; the company itself employed about 1,500 people, but provided employment for some 10,000 people altogether.

In the past, the system succeeded because all the partners in the chain—the Benetton family, agents, and subcontractors—enjoyed good profits. Moreover, the Benetton family took a lead role in reinvesting those profits and, thus, set an example for their agent and subcontractor partners. In brief, profits provided the financial muscle for growth and were reinvested into shops, laboratories and the high technology needed to support a growing business. In the early 1980s, analysts estimated that Benetton's productivity was on a par with that of producers from Asia. "It's not difficult to have speed and flexibility when you're small. It's harder when you're big. Having more than 5,000 sales points gives us that dimension," Luciano said in early 1989.

POS FOR REASSORTMENT

At Benetton, shopowners had three opportunities to adjust their orders. Using the Spring/Summer season as an example, agents could specify—from August to December—the color of up to 30% of previously ordered woven items held *in greggio*.[6] Later, a "Flash" collection, based on early customer requests, added about 50 new items to the basic product line. Thirdly, the reassortment process allowed shopowners to reorder the 30–50 items they expected to be the most successful in the ongoing season. It was then Benetton's responsibility to produce and ship those items as soon as possible.

For a given product portfolio in a season, prices at Benetton declined over time. That is, Benetton products were sold at their full price for three months, then at 70% for 30 days, and finally at 50% of full price. In volume terms, shops sold 70% of their offering at full price. Thus, missing a popular selling item at the beginning of the season strongly affected the profitability of the shops, because of missed sales at full margins. With this in mind, Luciano saw an opportunity to get early feedback on the style and colors that would be popular in the season. With that information, the 50 bestselling items could be identified and included in production at the start of the season.

However, in obtaining that feedback, Luciano sought objective information which avoided the bias of shopowners' opinions. Furthermore, that information had to be provided quickly and far enough in advance to meet Production's five weeks' lead time. Most importantly, that information had to provide a service to the agents. To perform the task, a $5,000 POS system was chosen, consisting of a cash register and microcomputer. Typically, each installed system captured and processed the price, style, color and size of about 30 items per day.

At the time of its introduction, there was no intention to install POS in all 4,000 shops; only a selected sample of 100 shops would use POS to determine early trends in the marketplace. Specifically, POS served as a market thermometer by providing advance planning notice for the reassortment business by identifying the 12 bestselling items, colors and styles at the beginning of the season. Thereafter, orders were put into production under the constraints of available lab capacity, types of machines that could be reprogrammed, and availability of raw materials. The season's production schedule was adapted as much as possible, without creating bigger costs by disrupting the manufacturing plan. However, if an agent

---

[6]"Greggio" was the Italian word for unbleached. At Benetton, holding items "in greggio" meant leaving them undyed.

demanded a big enough order, and the capacity was there, Benetton SpA would also put it into production, consulting other agents on the same items.

POS created the reassortment business by telling the stores what they should reassort—shopowners did not get a chance to order what they thought the market wanted. Quite the contrary—agents told them what POS's sample said the market wanted. That is, the whole technique was essentially a statistical polling problem. Over time, reassortment changed significantly and grew to become 10% of the business. In other words, POS was a tremendous success and, by 1989, every agent in the world had information on what would be available at Benetton factories. Agents then proceeded to sell these products to their shops. In summary, POS supported the Benetton belief that information about customer needs was inherent in the marketplace; it was only a matter of keeping in touch with the market to translate these needs into garments.

FORMALIZING ENTREPRENEURIAL POLICIES

Benetton Group SpA, which in 1989 included over 5,000 stores around the world, needed to create as homogeneous a behavior as possible among its 80 agents. Yet, because of the company's growth, the standardization of procedures had become increasingly dependent on information technology like POS, designed to support the agents. For example, from 1982 to 1989, the average number of shops coordinated by an agent had increased from 25 to 60, respectively.

About 2,000 administrative clients owning more than one shop were having problems with blocked shipments because of their credit rating. In fact, by the late 1980s, area managers were spending up to 35% of their time following up on payment problems. Bruno explained:

> The following situation often happens. The shop calls the agent complaining, "I'm not receiving the items." The agent calls the warehouse saying, "Why don't you send the items?" Then, the warehouse calls the commercial people asking, "Why do you block his credit?" and so on. So the agents call Luciano and complain about bureaucracy! "My clients will not pay until they receive their merchandise!"

One executive added a bit more insight on the scenario by describing the sequence of shipping activities. Once finished, goods were shipped directly from the central warehouse to the shop; there were no warehouses in foreign countries. In turn, the company billed clients with no billing to companies in between. In other words, customers received bills from Benetton, Atlanta, Columbia, etc. Thus, to receive quick payments, with no costs attached, information on customer payments was needed. Otherwise, shipments could not be made if payment of previous shipments had not been received. This scenario, he added, was why the company needed a Worldwide Transaction System (WTS)—purely for business reasons.

By the same token, Luciano Benetton believed in providing the agents with easier access to shop information; agents should decide the shipment priority of the stores within their territories. Bruno explained:

> The agents should see the situation at the customer level (shops). What was ordered, what was in possession, what was in the warehouse, and what was shipped. Then, they should also get information on credit maturity so that in the future, the agents will make the decisions (directly through computers) on what is shipped to whom, and when. If part of the items are blocked, it will be the agents' decision and responsibility, not Benetton's.

Bruno went on:

> The WTS was meant to help the agents, but these people are supermen, fantastic promoters and salesmen, and you cannot believe everything they say. Objective information and service to the

EXHIBIT 5 Commercial Organization Benetton Group as of January 1990

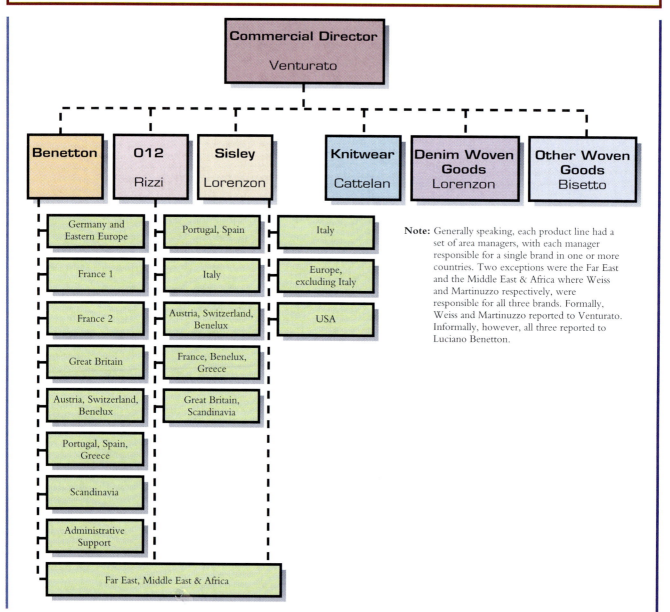

business is the main objective of our computer systems. Luciano says, maximum support to the agents, our Centurioni. When I arrived in 1985, my predecessors were fired because they tried to develop POS as a system to control the shops and agents; the would have destroyed the Benetton system. Luciano does not give precise instructions, only vague guidelines. If you interpret them well, you are OK. It is not enough to simply say "I understand." Also, Luciano is a promoter, salesman, and entrepreneur. You cannot believe everything Luciano says either, you have to interpret what he needs.

A number of agents were concerned that the Worldwide Transaction System might be used to monitor their performance. In that case, what guarantee was there that agents would use the system or the information it would provide? "Creativity is born of the people around you, and we have many who contribute to our success," said Luciano Benetton. "We are only one part of a large clan," he added. Bruno was concerned that, in the process of installing the new system, there could be a repeat of the "POS experience" on a far greater scale. In an organization where some of the most important policies were implicit, Bruno wondered if he could introduce the new system without disrupting the company's proven strategy.

Bibliography

Signorelli, Sergio and Heskett, James L., Benetton (A) & (B), ISTUD and Harvard Business School, 1984/85.
Lee, Andrea, "Profiles: Being Everywhere," *The New Yorker,* November 10, 1986.
Vitale, Michael, Benetton SpA: Industrial Fashion (A), Harvard Business School, 1987.
Bruce, Leigh, "The Bright New Worlds of Benetton," *International Management,* November 1987.
Finnerty, Anne, "The Internationalization of Benetton," *Textile Outlook International,* November 1987.
Ketelhohn, Werner, The European Women's Outerwear Industry in 1987, IMEDE, 1988.
Jarillo, Carlos and Martinez, Jon I., Benetton SpA, Harvard Business School, 1988.
Lorenyoni, Gianni, Benetton, London Business School, 1988.
Barry, Mary E. and Warfield, Carol L., "The Gloabalization of Retailing," *Textile Outlook International,* January 1988.
"Benetton Learns to Darn," *Forbes,* October 3, 1988.
"From Fabrics to Finance," *The Banker,* February 1989.

STEP 2: Prepare the case for class discussion.

STEP 3: Answer each of the following questions, individually or in small groups, as directed by your instructor.

Diagnosis
1. Why did Luciano Benetton want a POS system?
2. What types of information does Benetton's POS system collect?
3. What types of information do shopowners and agents require?

Evaluation
4. What benefits does the POS system provide for Benetton's shopowners, agents, area managers, and headquarter managers?
5. What evidence exists to indicate that the system has improved productivity at Benetton?
6. What problems does the existing POS system fail to address?

Design
7. What changes should be made in the transaction processing system to address the shipment-blocking problems at Benetton?
8. What types of hardware and software are needed to support such changes?

Implementation
9. What problems did Benetton experience during the initial roll-out of the POS system?
10. What problems do Bruno and some of the agents anticipate if a new system were to be built to address the deficiencies in the existing POS system?
11. What benefits would such a system provide?
12. How should Benetton proceed?

STEP 4: In small groups, with the entire class, or in written form, share your answers to the questions above. Then answer the following questions:

1. What information needs do Benetton, its agents, and its shopowners have?
2. How effectively does the current POS system address these needs?
3. What changes would allow the company to have its information needs met more effectively?
4. What issues should be considered in upgrading the system?

Acme Engineering

STEP 1: Read the Acme Engineering case. (This activity is especially suited for use in conjunction with Chapter 10 of *Information Systems*.)

COMPANY BACKGROUND

Mr. John D. Smith is the chief accountant at the Acme Engineering Co. in Christchurch, New Zealand. Mr. Smith reports to the company CEO, Mr. J.F. Acme (as do all other top departmental managers). The company manufactures large metal fabrication equipment on special order from customers. The industry of which it is a part is highly competitive and this has put increasing strain upon corporate finances through depressed profit levels. Since the company is family owned change has come slowly. The company has yet to adopt many of the newer methods for controlling:

- costs
- project tracking
- inventory level management
- cash flow control

Unfortunately the competitors have not been standing still and as a result of their implementing innovative control procedures they have seriously eroded Acme market share. Over the past 5 years Acme's share of this market has slipped from 23% to 14% of total industry sales. However the market has been growing and as a result sales over this period have increased from 3.2 million dollars to 4.7 million dollars per year.

The company currently has 120 employees in total.

ABOUT ACME OPERATIONS

The machines that are used in manufacturing are high precision multi-process metal forming and handling equipment. There are typically 50 orders or so in the shop at one time with average manufacturing duration of 3 to 4 months. The typical machine requires 120 unique operations (with an average duration of 1 to 3 hours per operation) to be performed in its manufacture at different points along the production schedule.

An additional indication of the complexity of the products that are produced is the inventory of parts that must be maintained for making Acme's product range. Currently held in stock are 8200 unique parts with an average item turnover of 6 months. Unfortunately there is no formal reporting system to determine turnover or demand for particular items in the existing inventory system.

Purchasing is generally notified by the inventory control department using a purchase requisition when a part is out-of-stock, but there is no specific system for determining when a part is low in stock. A card file is maintained which records when an item was last purchased, purchase price, description, part number and quantity purchased.

This case was made possible by the co-operation of an organisation which wishes to remain anonymous so the names of people have been disguised. It was written by John Vargo, Department of Accountancy, University of Canterbury, Christchurch, New Zealand. This material should be useful for class discussion or as an outside project. Copyright © 1990 Vargo and Associates Ltd., Christchurch, New Zealand.

The Problem

Low profitability has triggered much concern on the part of the family members, who are the primary shareholders. This brought about the employment of a number of new top level managers. These were hired for the express purpose of straightening out the existing information systems and management procedures, and implementing, if feasible, changes to the existing systems.

In discussions with the current management team a number of problems have been discovered. It has been reported that many employees are dissatisfied with current working conditions and this has affected productivity. There are also customer complaints that delivery of their ordered machines are usually overdue, often by as much as 30 to 60 days. Industry averages and statistics also show the following anomalies:

	Industry Average	Company Average
Inventory Turnover per year	4.1	2.5
Rate of Return on Total Assets	12.3%	4.6%
Avg. time to deliver an order	102.0 days	143.0 days
Average staff seniority	14.8 years	15.4 years

Other key company figures for the most recent year include:

Total Assets	$5,000,000
Total Inventory	$1,540,000
Total Sales	$4,750,000
Total Cost of Sales	$3,980,000

At the current rate of decline the profitability of the company is likely to go negative during the next twelve months and the owners have decreed that there shall be a solution preventing such an occurrence. Given the current technological changes in Acme's industry it also is becoming imperative that investment be made in a number of new and rather expensive manufacturing machines. Unfortunately at this point there is insufficient information available from the current information systems to do any sort of Return On Investment (ROI) calculations for current machines or new acquisitions. As a result the owners are understandably hesitant to invest more funds in new equipment until this lack of information is rectified.

ORDER ENTRY

Interviews have been conducted with a number of management staff; the responses to these interviews are presented in the following pages. One of the first interviews was with Lou Ming, order entry supervisor (reporting to the Marketing manager). Lou was asked about which areas he felt needed improvement.

> **Lou:** "The starting point for all activity here is at the point of order entry. When a firm order is received it starts the ball rolling for everyone else. Upon receipt of an order, purchasing must buy any special items required to manufacture the machine. Naturally this means the stock control clerk must determine if the necessary parts are already in stock and notify the purchasing department of out-of-stock items. In parallel with this the production control department schedules the new order into the production area, queuing behind all previously entered jobs, unless of course it is a priority job, and which ones aren't? There are a lot of politics played by the sales reps trying to fulfill promises they have made to customers regarding prompt delivery dates."

Interviewer: "Does this encompass the full chain of events as you see it?"

Lou: He paused, and then replied, "No, a number of other factors come into the picture as well. For example the customer credit status must be checked by Customer Service and the order approved. This is supposed to be done before the order is entered for scheduling, but more often than not we discover after the fact that this has not been done. This usually occurs because the salesperson was under pressure from marketing to meet the monthly quota, which has become harder and harder to achieve over the last year or two."

INVENTORY CONTROL AND PURCHASING

Interviews were next conducted with Maxwell Lu (inventory control manager) and Rita Nair (purchasing manager) both of whom report to the manufacturing manager.

Interviewer: "Maxwell, what is the condition of the inventory control system?"

Maxwell: "We run reasonably smooth most of the time, but there is the occasional hiccup when a new order enters the system since each machine we make is specially manufactured. As a result we often do not have in stock all of the parts needed to manufacture the entire machine. The order entry department sends to us a copy of the engineering specification which includes a parts list for the order. It is on the basis of this list that we determine if all parts and materials are in stock. For the parts we are missing a purchase requisition is prepared, which is given to the purchasing department."

Rita: "The only problem is that the purchase requisition doesn't usually include all of the items that are needed, and later on when the delivery date for the job has become critical, we usually receive an urgent request for the missing parts. Naturally we try to honour these requests, but inevitably it takes longer than we would like to procure the needed parts. Often we end up paying a premium for the parts due to the "rush order" nature of the request."

Maxwell: "This does happen occasionally, but it is just part of the complexity of the business environment and level of technological innovation in which we work."

Interviewer: "How often would you estimate this occurs?"

Maxwell: "Oh, perhaps two or three times a month, and we send through four purchase requisitions for each job that comes in."

Rita: "Bunk!! We must receive at least 10 or 12 such special requests per month which would be concerned with half of Acme's total active job orders at any given time!"

Interviewer: "Do either of you have any records dealing with this question of urgent requests?"

Rita: "I thought you would never ask! I maintain a log of all purchase requisitions coming through Acme's office and I annotate the log with the nature of the request. I go through and tabulate the categories monthly and I have the results of that tabulation with me. As you can see here, over the last six months the range of urgent requests has varied from eight in November to 14 in January."

Maxwell: "Well it isn't my fault, I just send on requests coming from production control. They are the ones who are supposed to get the list right in the first place."

PROJECT CONTROL

The next interview was with Jo Napp, the manager of production control, (responsible to the Manufacturing Manager).

Things in production control were pretty tense at the time; the following interview reveals a great deal of that tension.

Interviewer: "Well Jo how are you today? Got everything under control?" (making a little pun to put Jo at ease which he obviously was not when the interview began. Unfortunately he did not take it very well).

Jo: "What is that supposed to mean? Do you think you could do a better job controlling such high technology manufacturing? I want you to know I have been on the job here at Acme for over twenty years and every year we have turned a profit! Could you do better?"

Interviewer: "I was only making a small pun, not commenting on your competency. Now relax, I didn't come down to argue with you, just to have an open talk about how we can work together to overcome the problems the firm is facing. Now honestly Jo, what do you see as the primary problems in your department?"

Jo: "That is what I keep saying, the problem is not in this department, it is the bloody incompetents in engineering who keep messing up our schedules, and giving us incomplete data!"

Interviewer: "Easy now, instead of pointing the finger at engineering, let's just work together to solve our mutual problems. Now what exactly is the trouble, without hammering engineering please, just tell me your point of view."

Jo: "Nearly every new contract that comes in initially looks fine. The project file appears complete and suggested manufacturing operation duration times and parts lists look reasonable. But no sooner do we get a detailed schedule for the project worked out, printed and in the file, then the salesman and engineer come in with some changes. The next week there are more bloody changes, and on she goes ad infinitum! How on earth are we supposed to keep to schedule if they keep changing the requirements? To compound the problem purchasing offers us a bundle of useless excuses about suppliers being on strike, material shortages and out-of-stock conditions. To top it off the INVENTORY control department doesn't know the meaning of the word control! They have tons of parts for machines we manufacture rarely, and are constantly out of stock on the materials we use most."

Interviewer: "But we do live in a rapidly changing environment, surely we can expect some changes and have to learn to live with them?"

Jo: "Well I suppose some changes are reasonable, but every week? Besides it takes days to set up a decent schedule for these projects given the ten manufacturing stations we are trying to control with up to 50 projects being in the shop at one time. We cannot possibly maintain accurate schedules for all those projects with constant changes. We don't have enough clerks, and they cannot write up and coordinate the changes quickly enough to provide useful information. Besides that inventory control tells us one thing and does another. Max Lu often claims that we have parts in stock. Then later on when the parts are actually required in Manufacturing we discover that his records were wrong and the parts are not actually there. Naturally then we have to issue a rush request for parts. So don't blame me if things are all fouled up, what do you expect me to do, smart guy?"

Interviewer: "Well thank you for giving me your point of view, you have certainly given me much to think about, I'll be in contact in the near future."

RESOURCE SCHEDULING

The manufacturing department was next on the list, in order to discover their view regarding schedules and optimum equipment usage. Frank Tate was the manufacturing manager and known for being very competent.

Interviewer: "Everything running smoothly today Frank?"

Frank: "Yes, things seem to be going well, aside from the usual hiccups due to lack of parts, or Marketing climbing on our backs to shorten delivery times. But all in all we run as smoothly as can be expected."

Interviewer: "What do you attribute the smooth running of the manufacturing area to?"

Frank: "The team of workmen under me are all well trained and enjoy their work. Generally speaking, we have the latest in equipment and a good maintenance crew. This all keeps the jobs flowing through as well as possible given the difficulties with scheduling."

Interviewer: "Excuse me, but could you tell me more about the difficulties with scheduling, exactly what problems have you noticed?"

Frank: "Well, there seem to be a number of perspectives to be considered. From our point of view we work most efficiently when the jobs are scheduled into our ten workstations in such a way as to avoid long queues of jobs. But we often have times when one machine workstation will have five or six jobs waiting and other stations will be standing idle. This creates obvious inefficiencies both in terms of equipment usage and manpower utilization. The problem seems to be that the original scheduling of jobs is done by Production Control based on what they believe is the availability of time on the workstations and the delivery time promised by Marketing. Unfortunately their information is rarely up-to-date. In addition the parts required to manufacture the machine are not always in stock, and any delays in one job can affect other jobs that are in the queue behind it. To compound the problem the Marketing department together with Engineering often put pressure on us through Production Control to change the schedule of a particular job, because the customer is screaming."

"Naturally we try to accommodate Production Control's subsequent changes, but it does throw off the other scheduled jobs. Although we may get that particular job out in record time, it just passes the problem down the line so that the next week there may be one or two other jobs on the "critical" list with necessary queue jumping changes in the schedule."

Interviewer: "Overall how does that affect your productivity?"

Frank: "It certainly doesn't help. The owners want increased efficiency, but given the constraints from Marketing and Engineering it has been very difficult to make much improvement. We have 10 basic resources (workstations) to schedule, at present our average utilization is about 52%. And Marketing keeps bringing in more jobs on the over-utilized machines while some of our best equipment stands idle. To be honest with you this really irritates me! Why can't they sell some products which would soak up a bit of our excess capacity?"

Interviewer: "Do they know which workstations have excess capacity at particular times so they could concentrate on selling related products?"

Frank: "Well … in all fairness the idle workstations do vary a bit. Because of the fluctuations in the scheduling of jobs I'm not always sure where our idle capacity is located in terms of workstations and time periods. This problem of resource scheduling is a tough one and I'm not really sure how to solve it."

Interviewer: "Do you know what sort of information you would like to get out of a resource scheduling system if there were such a thing?"

Frank: "If someone wanted to design a resource scheduling system I could certainly tell them what I would need in terms of reports for myself, and I also have a few ideas as to what Production Control and Marketing could use in the way of information!!"

MARKETING

Steve Thompson (Marketing Manager) had worked hard trying to maintain the company's market share, but the market pressures and his reaction to them had painted him as the villain in a number of earlier interviews.

Interviewer: "Have a seat Steve."

Steve: "I do not have a lot of time to spare, I'm a busy man you know."

Interviewer: "The reason I rang you Steve was to discuss your information needs as marketing manager and look at some potential solutions to the problems that are facing the company. What are the biggest problems facing you and your department?"

Steve: "Primarily we face a very competitive market where price and timely delivery are the main factors. Both of these seem to be a problem here at Acme."

Interviewer: "I understand that you very often rush through "priority jobs" for key customers?"

Steve: "Yes that is right, and all Acme customers are 'key customers.'"

Interviewer: "What information would be most useful to you to avoid the need for 'rush orders' and allow you timely delivery?"

Steve: "If I knew what Acme manufacturing resource availability was, projected over the coming 2-3 months I would know what equipment to promote through our sales force. This factor together with up-to-date projected delivery times for jobs that are in the manufacturing process currently would allow me a much more accurate projection of delivery times. Naturally this would increase our esteem and integrity in the eyes of Acme customers. Cost is also a factor that has plagued us. To compete we have to keep our prices in line, but with our cost structure some sales actually lose us money. At least if we knew what our costs were going to be for a particular job we could decide whether to take the contract or not. As it stands however it is usually weeks after the tenders are due that we finally discover what cost on the job will be, and even that is usually a bit of a wild guess!"

MEETING OF POTENTIAL USERS

After interviews with department heads it was decided to call a meeting of potential users and top management to discuss the prospective information system. Included in the group which met were managers from:

- Marketing
- Order Entry
- Manufacturing
- Purchasing
- Production Control
- Inventory Control
- Engineering
- Customer Service

This group decided to form a Steering Committee for this Systems Development project. It was agreed that the first task was to discuss and enumerate the problems and develop a list of users needs and requirements for such a potential system. Some of the basic facts that came out in these early discussions including advice from consultants are included in the following information.

BASIC SYSTEM REQUIREMENTS

It is estimated that initially six VDU's will be required if a computerized installation were used, with possibilities for adding another 6 to 8 VDU's over the next five years. Only one new employee would be required, an experienced computer operator who could also do some light programming. All data entry operators would be retrained from current clerical positions and remain attached to their current user departments. Each user department would require their own dual purpose (draft quality and letter quality) high speed (200+ cps) dot matrix printer for producing reports, invoices, purchase orders etc.

Given the probable complexity of the software for the applications being considered and the need for on-line access at all times by purchasing, inventory control, marketing, and manufacturing, it is estimated that at least 6 megabytes of RAM will be required initially in any computer that might be considered. Hard disc storage capacity has yet to be estimated.

ADDITIONAL INFORMATION

The following additional points arose in these early discussions and are based on the assumption that satisfactory systems can be installed on a timely basis to overcome the basic information systems problems.

- The expected useful life of the new system is five years with salvage value estimated at 20% of initial hardware cost at the end of that period.
- Estimated cost of data conversion is based on 120 characters per minute (verified) being keyed into the database.
- Insurance is estimated to be 1.3% per year of the estimated replacement cost.
- Estimated cost of hiring a new employee is 50% of first year salary, and cost of retraining existing clericals to become data entry operators is two months salary each.
- "Off the shelf" software could be found to handle most applications but some applications would require extensive modification.
- It is believed that utilization of manufacturing equipment could be increased from the current level of 52% to 68%.
- 5% of the current cost of sales is due to the "rush" nature of many orders.
- Turnover rates could be brought into line with industry averages.
- Data Information:
    - Individual order = Prox. 400 char.
    - Engineering Specs for indiv. order = Prox. 80 char. per operation per order.
    - Individual Item of stock = Prox. 240 char.
    - Scheduling record = Prox. 160 char. per operation per order.
    - Purchase requisition = Prox. 320 char.
    - Master workstation record = 240 char. (1 for each workstation)
- Only information for the current year's orders need be "on-line" at a given time, since all data for completed orders from prior years could be loaded on to tape for storage.

STEP 2: Prepare the case for class discussion.

STEP 3: Answer each of the following questions, individually or in small groups, as directed by your instructor.

Diagnosis
1. What concerns did low profitability trigger?
2. How effective are the company's control procedures?
3. What types of information does Acme Engineering require?

Evaluation
4. What types of transaction processing systems does Acme Engineering currently use?
5. How effective are the order entry, inventory control, purchasing, project control, and resource scheduling systems?
6. How effectively do these systems interface?

Design
7. What changes should be made in the transactions processing systems at Acme Engineering?
8. What types of hardware and software would support such systems?

Implementation
9. What issues must the owners consider in upgrading the transaction processing systems?
10. What are the likely costs and benefits of such improvements?

STEP 4: In small groups, with the entire class, or in written form, share your answers to the questions above. Then answer the following questions:

1. What information need does Acme Engineering have?
2. How effectively do current systems address these needs?
3. What changes would allow the company to have its information needs met more effectively?
4. What issues should be considered in upgrading the system? ●

Activity 15: Norman Furniture Generation Ltd.

STEP 1: Read the Norman Furniture Generation Ltd. case. (This activity is especially suited for use in conjunction with Chapter 11 of *Information Systems*.)

1.0 A Depressing Meeting

Brian Robertson was far from happy and was in the process of telling the directors of Norman Furniture Generation Limited the reason for his current state of depression.

Mr. Robertson had in front of him the half-yearly financial report for NFG Ltd. (Appendix 1) and it was the contents of this which was the main contributor to his feelings.

Addressing the Financial Director, Mr. O'Connor, he said, "Peter, these are the worst figures I've ever seen. O.K. I know all about the recession but these figures reek of disaster. We're really missing the boat somewhere. If these figures don't improve by the next shareholders meeting then heads are going to roll."

Peter O'Connor had expected just such a reaction when he had prepared the interim financial report but then, as now, he felt very much at a loss as to the prime cause.

"I've been over the report Brian and hate to say it, but they all point to the recession as the reasons for our poor performance, maybe we could tighten up on costs but other than that. . . ." "That's just a poor excuse for a poor performance," replied Brian Robertson, "We have everything on our side, new factory, new machinery, good industrial relations and a damn good product range, if we can't make this work then there's no hope for any of us. As for costs that new computer of yours should be able to keep a tight enough rein on those!"

The other board members were Jim Allyn, Production Manager, Otto Gustaf, Chief Designer, Liam Murphy, Marketing, and John Butler, Personnel. Liam Murphy spoke next, "The product might be a good one but it's becoming near impossible to get retailers interested. It's not that our prices aren't competitive but that our competitors' products are simply more popular."

"Then it is to me that you place the blame!" snapped Otto Gustaf, "I design a superb product range; your salesmen just can't sell."

"Let's not start blaming each other, that's a sure road to bankruptcy. I know that in Production I have reported inability to complete some specialised orders in order to maintain capacity on our standard product range. That's been a policy adopted from our parent but maybe we need to change our thinking."

Brian Robertson had cooled off somewhat but listening to his directors he didn't like what he was hearing.

"Gentlemen," interceded Brian Robertson, "I am getting the impression that none of you know what the rest are doing. Two years ago we spent a small fortune introducing an information system and you Peter (Finance) were placed in charge of the computer. It seems to me that the one thing we don't have is an information system. If that piece of electronic junk can't do its job then we'd better get a system that can! I want an appraisal of your individual information needs by the next meeting in one month's time."

The rest of the meeting was uneventful but the directors all left with a gloomy feeling and some reservations about their own future with NFG Ltd.

This case study was compiled by T.J. Young of Sligo R.T.C. based on general experience in the problems of M.I.S. development and computerisation. All personnel are fictitious. Copyright © 1983 T.J. Young

2.0 COMPANY BACKGROUND

Norman Furniture Generation Ltd. had been set up in Ireland three years ago as a result of pioneering work by the Industrial Development Authority (IDA) to attract wood processing companies to the West of Ireland. The parent company is Norman Wood Products Limited, a hugh establishment with its head office and main processing plant in Cleveland, Ohio. The Great Lakes provided a ready made shipping outlet as did the railway to New York. The vast forest of both hard- and softwoods to the west of the Appalachian Mountains provided an almost endless supply of raw material.

The "sell" to Norman Wood Products had been relatively easy. Along with the tax incentives, the IDA was able to offer an advanced factory, large areas of maturing forest and an attractive set of demographic statistics regarding population growth. Norman Wood Products were also committed to a move establishing manufacturing in Europe, and Ireland became a natural choice.

Norman Wood Products is an old established company set up from an amalgamation of lumbering companies of the late 19th century. It became a public concern in 1910 and was one of the largest existing wood processing concerns. Initially the work undertaken was straight lumbering and sawing but during the late twenties expanded into the area of furniture manufacture. This was achieved by the setting up of a subsidiary company, Prime Furniture Limited, of which the parent held 51% of all shares. The policy was to leave the subsidiary company to its own devices. Basically, Norman Wood Products acted simply as supplier of the wood for the furniture making company. The post war boom years of the 1950s and 1960s saw a vast expansion of Norman Wood Products with the establishment of furniture manufacturing, paper making and wood processing companies throughout North America. The policy of ownership and noninterference became a matter of course.

These policies were taken to Ireland, although Norman Furniture Generation Ltd. not only designed and manufactured its own products, but also sawed its own wood supplied by the Forestry Commission. In addition, wood not available locally was imported from Europe rather than the United States. It was up to Norman Furniture Generation to design its own products, primarily with a view to supplying the Irish market but with plans for expansion to export into Britain and the European mainland. These longer term objectives would involve expansion in size and further investment by the parent company.

2.1 Setting Up NFG Ltd.

Brian Robertson was given full autonomy for this and was moved from the board of the parent company to become Managing Director of NFG Ltd. Much of the initial planning took place in the States and consequently the advance factory at Shannon became operational within six months of Brian Robertson stepping off the plane. Local labour was readily available and only one member of the board, Otto Gustaf, had to be consulted.

The initial work involved sawing and planing timber and manufacturing chipboard and hardboard sheets. A year after this work began the first furniture products rolled off the production lines.

The current operations may be summarised as follows:

a) Sawing and planing softwood timber supplied locally.
b) Manufacturing chipboard and hardboard from "sawing waste."
c) Domestic furniture production. (See Appendix 2 for product range and description.)

2.2 Data Processing

The parent company had computerised its data processing in 1962 with a relative degree of success and Brian Robertson, a graduate of M.I.T., was familiar with the advantages of computerisation although he had not been directly involved with either the design or running of an information system. An enthusiasm for M.I.S. was brought to Ireland by Brian Robertson and consequently he had felt ready to commit NFG Ltd. to computerisation at a very early stage.

The initial production and operations of NFG had not involved a heavy D.P. burden and all functions had been manual for the first year of operation. The functions in the early days had involved payroll, purchasing, budgeting and stock control. Since the early operation did not involve customer supply but simply to stock-pile seasoning timber and chipboard, no order processing departments had been necessary. Liam Murphy had dealt with early inquiries and as furniture products became available for sale an assistant to Liam Murphy, dealing with order processing, was recruited. Effectively no order processing had been carried out on a manual basis, since the computer had been installed ready for this function.

Six months prior to the commencement of furniture manufacture, Brian Robertson had introduced the concepts of computerisation to the board. His enthusiasm influenced the other board members and generated a high level of commitment from the functional heads to EDP. The tender for the computer was won by IBM. Peter O'Connor, a qualified Chartered Accountant, was sent to England for an intensive two week course provided by IBM. Upon his return the "computer project" was handed to him by Brian Robertson, who then himself took little interest. The traditional accountancy view of Peter O'Connor, with an emphasis on budgeting and cost control, was built into the D.P. system. The administrative functions were computerised in rapid succession by the use of standard software packages. The computer, an IBM System 38 has now been installed for two years. Details of the computer system are given in Appendix 3.

3.0 PRESENT COMPANY OPERATIONS

3.1 Finance and Accounting

Peter O'Connor is the Finance Director. He is a fully qualified chartered accountant of fifteen years standing and is now forty years of age. Prior to his appointment to NFG Ltd., he had worked for an accountancy and auditing company in Galway.

He had extensive knowledge of auditing and had learnt from his dealings as an external auditor that if the costs are controlled then "the rest of the company will look after itself." Consequently, he kept tight control over budgeting and insisted on weekly expenditure breakdowns from the other departments. The ability of the computer to analyse these reports and produce a mass of financial control information had impressed him. He confessed, however, that he rarely has time to read all of the reports he receives but is confident that his Budget Controller, Frank Henry, utilises these reports within his department. A typical Department Performance Summary Report is shown in Figure 1.

3.1.1 Budgeting and Costing

Working primarily from computer reports the department is concerned with appraising the performance on a weekly basis of the individual departments and the company as a whole.

Frank Henry explains, "We are primarily concerned with negative variances. I produce a report outlining these from the computer printouts and feed the figures to Peter. In this way we can react quickly to large variances or continuing negative trends. It seems that the discrepancies in some areas are getting larger, especially those for Marketing and Sales while Production's variances are improving, if anything. I'm not sure that the budgets are in line any more but Peter is not the sort of bloke you could tell that to. You see the budgets for next year are based on an increase based on the previous year's average lending rate, plus a proportional increase, which is pretty conservative to allow for increased turnover."

```
              NORMAN FURNITURE GENERATION LTD.
       ----------------------------------------------

                   DEPARTMENT PERFORMANCE SUMMARY

      Date .........................................

      Department ...................................

              Current Week                                    Year to Date

      Budget Actual Variance       Cost Category         Budget Actual Variance
                                   Materials
                                   Direct Labour
                                   Supplies
                                   Indirect Labour
                                   Taxes
                                   Insurance
                                   Depreciation
                                   Equipment
                                   Building
                                   Department Total
```

3.1.2 Purchasing

A daily computer produced stock for re-order report is simply matched to a preferred vendor file and orders placed accordingly. A weekly stock ledger is received and, providing there is available time, a member of the purchasing staff carries out a physical walk through and spot check. This occurs maybe 25% of the time. Twice yearly, a full inventory check takes place in order to identify discrepancies. Where they occur, the book value is adjusted manually and the EDP department notified. These adjustments are typically of the order of $+/-5\%$ of average stock held.

3.2 Production

The three main departments of sawing, chipboard manufacture and furniture manufacture are essentially independent. Where possible the timber sawing and chipboard manufacturing act as suppliers for furniture production but all of the furniture departments' needs are not met in this way, nor are all of the other departments' products totally absorbed by NFG Ltd.

The surplus sawn timber and manufactured chipboard is sold at a relatively high profit.

The policy of Norman Wood Products was always one of "push the standard lines" and this was pretty well adhered to by NFG Ltd. It was felt that this helped Marketing. In the entire operational life of NFG only a dozen or so complaints had been received regarding faulty products. In general, the products were regarded as being well designed and of high quality.

APPENDIX 1 Half-Yearly Interim Reports

(A) Trading and Profit and Loss Account

June of Current Year—6 Month Report

Opening Stock	200,000		
Add Purchases	622,000	**Sales**	
Closing Stock	244,000	Sawn Timber	100,000
Cost of Sales	578,000	Chipboard & Hardboard	300,000
Gross Profit	522,000	Furniture —	
Salaries	400,000	Bedroom	400,000
Rates	5,000	Other	300,000
Insurance	10,000	TOTAL	1,100,000
Computer-			
Rent	14,000		
Main	8,000		
Media	10,000		
Marketing	80,000		
Other Expenses	60,000		
Profit	(65,000)		
Tax	—		
Net Profit	(65,000)		

Balance Sheet

June of Current Year

Owner's Capital		Fixed Assets	
Owner Equity	1,000.000	Building	400,000
Retained Profit	20,000	Other	300,000
		Depreciation	(28,000)
			672,000

Current Liability		Current Assets		Inventory	
Tax		—			
Creditors		120,000			
				Timber	100,000
				Sawn Trees	50,000
				Chipboard	50,000
				Other	44,000
					244,000
				Debtors	200,000
				Cash	24,000
		1,140,000			1,140,000

The only complaint from Jim Allyn was regarding special orders, "I'd like to be able to tout for jobbing orders, say a specialist product range to equip an hotel, but we're so wrapped up in standard products that there's no chance of that. Mind you, with all the paperwork for budgeting control and inventory, there isn't much time either. Still, I've got faith in the marketing guys; there are some damn good area reps employed here."

3.3 Marketing

Liam Murphy had a reputation as a task master who expected results and usually said exactly how he felt about matters. As a Manager, he was pretty well-liked, or at least respected, and the sales team was well-organised and coordinated. In Liam Murphy's own words, the Marketing Department . . . "is there to sell products. We make or break a company and if we can't sell, then we all go under. I've negotiated good rates of commission for the salesmen and as long as they reach their quotas I'm happy. Things have been difficult with the recession, almost as hard to sell as to fill out Peter's quota and budget forms! It just means we'll have to push a bit harder."

Liam also insisted on professionally produced product brochures and good advertising campaigns. These were carried out by the Marketing Services Department who also handled customer enquiries.

APPENDIX 2 Sales Graph—6 Monthly Figures

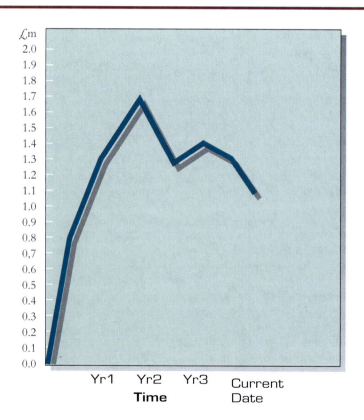

APPENDIX 3 Computer System

C.P.U.:	IBM System 38, 2MBytes Memory
Disks:	Fixed Disks with 258MBytes
Tape Drives:	4 Units; 60 I.P.S. Read
V.D.U.:	6 Units
Lineprinter:	1 Unit: 300 L.P.M.
Software:	RFG II, COBOL
Database:	Facility Part of CPU Architecture

APPENDIX 4 Report Analysis

Report	Frequency	For	Inputs	Files
Budget Variance	Weekly	Costing	–Actual Costs	–Dept. Costs File
Payroll Suite	Weekly	Wages	–Clock Cards –Overtime Slips	–Wages Master
Stock Ledger	Weekly	Production	–GRN Issues Returns	–Stock Master
Stock for Reorder	Weekly	Purchasing/Supplier	–Issues Returns GRN	–Stock Master –Vendor File –Open Order File
Invoices	Weekly	Finance/Customer	Orders	–Cust. M.F. –Finished Goods
Delivery Report	Weekly	Distribution/Customer	–Orders	–Cust. M.F. –Finished Goods
Statements	Monthly	Finance/Customer	–Orders –Cheques –Returns	–Cust. M.F.
Back Order Analysis	Monthly	Production	–Stock for Reorder –Delivery Report	–Stock Master
Bad Debts	6 Monthly	Finance	–Statements –Invoices –Cheques	–Cust. M.F.
Production Schedule	Monthly	Production	–Finished Goods –Delivery Report Summary	–Finished Goods
Sales Performance	Weekly	Finance	–Sales	–Cust. M.F.
Sales/Area	Monthly	Marketing	–Sales	–Cust. M.F.

STEP 2: Prepare the case for class discussion.

STEP 3: Answer each of the following questions, individually or in small groups, as directed by your instructor.

Diagnosis

1. What information needs do the managers of finance and accounting, production, and marketing have in this company?
2. What computer systems exist to meet these needs?

Evalaution

3. What objectives should the computer system have for each functional area?
4. How well do the existing systems meet the managers' and the organization's needs?
5. Does the existing system have the characteristics of a state-of-the-art decision support system?

Design

6. What changes should be made in the existing system?
7. What reports should the new system provide?

Implementation

8. What are the likely costs and benefits of these changes?
9. Offer a schedule for implementing the changes.

STEP 4: In small groups, with the entire class, or in written form, share your answers to the questions above. Then answer the following questions:

1. What information needs exist at Norman Furniture?
2. What types of systems exist to meet these needs?
3. What changes would you propose in the system to better meet these needs?
4. What are the costs and benefits of implementing these changes? ●

Activity 16: Pinsos Galofré, S.A.

STEP 1: Read the Pinsos Galofré, S.A. case. (This activity is especially suited for use in conjunction with Chapter 11 of *Information Systems*.)

THE USE OF A DECISION SUPPORT SYSTEM IN A NEW FIELD

The chief financial officer of Pinsos Galofré S.A., Josep Cortada, was sitting behind his desk reflecting over what Fernando Vallvé, product manager in the industrial division, had just told him on the phone. They had been talking about the success their recent decision support system for animal feeding was having in the field. The latest release had now been used in the field for some time and seemd to be working well. The dealer network, althought initially very skeptical, was now using the system more and more and was even suggesting modifications to be made to the system.

Josep Cortada could still remember the day when he first became involved in the project. It had been while he was temporarily responsible for the Formulation group, which formed part of the Research and Development Department. (See Exhibit 1 for an outline of the organization.)

Quite by chance while walking about the offices one day, the general manager and himself ran across a student from the local university who was working at the company during his summer job. The student explained that he was in the finishing stages of writing a decision support program for the Sales Department. He went further to explain that some people from that Department had expressed a need for a tool to help them calculate the "ideal" food rationing for animals in farms where there was already animal food available, resulting, as byproduct, of normal farm operation.

The request had been for a program that would take into consideration the nutritional value of the products that the farmers already had, and compute the best product mix of Pinsos Galofré products to supplement those. The idea behind the request was very much in line with the overall business focus of the company, which emphasized trying to provide a total service to customers, not just selling animal food products.

It took the general manager and himself about 10 minutes to understand the problem, then he told the student: "Isn't this problem a rationing problem? In that case, why don't you use linear programming, which is what we use in the formulation processes that we run here every day?"

BACKGROUND INFORMATION

Pinsos Galofré S.A. has existed for 21 years, and has grown continuously over this period. Sales in 1985 exceeded 20,000 million pesetas.

The company consists of two operative divisions as shown in Exhibit 1. The Consumer Goods division produces and sells pet foods, while the Chow division produces and sells animal food to farmers. There are two corporate staff functions; Finance and Administration, and Research and Development.

SOURCE: Copyright © 1989 by IESE.

Exhibit 1 Organizational Outline

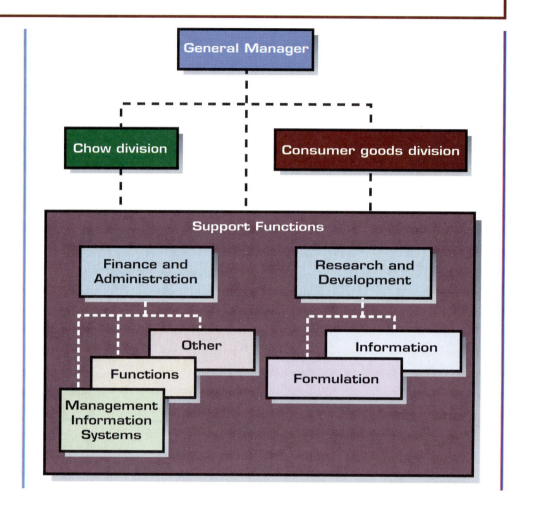

The main customers in the milk production sector of the Chow division are small to medium size farmers, although not many of them have less than 10 cows. (For an estimate of the structure of Spanish dairy farms, see Exhibit 2.) These farmers are generally too small to be able to support by themselves the services and technology that Pinsos Galofré can.

Pinsos Galofré's products are manufactured in seven factories located throughout Spain, and they are sold through a network of 500 independent dealers. The dealers can sell other products in the agricultural sector but, in virtue of an explicit agreement, not any product competing directly with those of Pinsos Galofré. This dealer network gives the company practically 100% market coverage in Spain.

From a very general standpoint, the chow or animal food business involves the following activities: buying/importing raw materials, mixing them, adding some other components, pelleting, and finally sending the products to the dealers for selling. One of the key steps in the process is the so-called "formulating" step, in which the mixings to be performed are designed. In this step, linear programming is used to a very great extent.

Estimated Structure of Spanish Dairy Farms in 1984

No. of cows/farm		No. of farms	Mean no. of cows	Total no. of cows
1 to	2	50,000	1.5	75,000
3 to	4	60,000	3.5	210,000
5 to	9	100,000	7	700,000
10 to	25	40,000	15	600,000
25 to	50	18,000	30	240,000
50 to	100	1,700	70	120,000
More than	100	300	133	40,000
Total		260,000	7.6	1,985,000

THE DEVELOPMENT PROCESS

In fact, the idea for the tool that the Sales Department was requesting had originated as a consequence of the good working relationship existing between the Marketing department and the Research and Development department within the Chow Products division. This was in turn due to the fact that there was a lot of interaction between the two groups. It was well understood that Marketing being directly in touch with the market, it could sense the needs there and ask for support from Research and Development, which then would come up with proposals for solutions to whatever problems were identified.

Josep Cortada explained how they had gone about developing the program package:

> The first attempt to give an answer to the problem was done back in 1984 by a student working here during the summer. He used some kind of a "rule of thumb"—heuristic—approach, which produced reasonable but unequal results. The problem with such an approach was that it could not assure an optimal solution. This led to a search for better procedures, which in turn resulted in a process of continuously adding new heuristic rules to the algorithms employed. As a consequence, the corresponding computer program was growing and growing and nobody seemed able to anticipate "how near" it was from definitive.
>
> When I first heard about the project, it struck my mind that this would be a perfect application for Linear Programming (L.P.), which is a nice tool for solving exactly these kind of problems. I had spent several years of my earlier career working in an Operations Research group in an oil company, where I was heavily involved in the development of L.P. models. Besides being a nice tool for solving the problem, linear programming would also identify an optimal solution. It was my personal opinion that a solution which was good, but not optimal—so that the farmer might be able to come up with a better one himself—would be a somewhat dangerous solution. It would never get much credibility.

He continued:

> The first thing we did after we decided to try a linear programming approach, was to experiment with an old package that I had in one of my files. Since it seemed to work, we then spent some 5 to 6 months, a few hours during the day, some evenings, and some weekends, trying to develop a prototype tool using linear programming. The most challenging aspect of this work was working out and testing the appropriate L.P. constraints. We worked with Fernando Vallvé, a product manager who used to do the hand calculations, coherently with his theoretical knowledge of nutritional constraints and the needs of the animals. Converting these rules into valid formulas that could be used in the linear programming model did not turn out to be all that easy, however. I suppose that his lack of knowledge about programming and modelling, and our lack of

knowledge about his field made it difficult for us to communicate effectively. Eventually, however, we did manage to come up with some 10–12 valid constraints that worked well.

Some of those constraints were not at all obvious. For example we had to introduce the concept of the animals' stomach, which is affected by both food weight and volume. Although these can be linked by taking into consideration the concept of food density, and this seemed to introduce non-linearities in the model. Eventually we were able to remove them, after some algebraic manipulations. This process shows, in my opinion, the importance of being able to combine biological and modelling expertise in order to be successful in this kind of work.

The next step in the development was to "commercialize" the product. To make it suited for the field, a user interface had to be added, as well as reporting and recovery facilities, etc. This work took about another year to be completed, and the program was introduced in the field late in 1985.

The introduction into the field was not totally without problems. Most farmers, as well as many of the dealers, had never touched a computer before. When they were told that a "hi-tech" product like this computer package was going to be used as a tool to solve their day to day practical problems, their response was only: "You can't be serious!" It took some time to sell the idea to the people in the field, and a lot of effort had to be put into training both salespeople and the dealers.

The second version of the program, which was released about half a year later, included a post optimal analysis facility, which allowed users to perform sensitivity analyses. More specifically, it would show by how much some characteristics of a critical component would have to change in order to trigger its inclusion (or exclusion) from the optimal blend, and it could also provide answers to the question of why a specific component was not included in the optimal blend. The program package used two data files, one specifying the different Pinsos Galofré products, and the other defining the different by-products that the farmers might have. In the latest version of the package, each different customer could be represented in this second file with his own products.

Regarding the experience after having completed the project, Josep Cortada commented:

> In order to succeed in a development process like this, certain conditions need to be fulfilled. You normally need to have experts in different fields who are able to communicate and work well together. In addition, you also need to have some "generalist" who can see the project as a whole, and be able to lead it in the right direction. We were lucky to have all these criteria reasonably fulfilled.

There have been requests to extend the package so that it can better fulfill its users' needs. For example, somebody who has different types of cattle, for milk and meat production, wanted the program extended so that it would be capable of taking both categories into consideration. However, these types of requests turn out to require integer programming, and thus have not been attended yet.

WHY A DECISION SUPPORT SYSTEM?

Fernando Vallvé, product manager, commented on why the decision support system was introduced:

> First of all it was the natural thing to do, given our business approach. Our dealers are trained to give the farmers a good service. The farmers have different products and by-products on their farms which combined with our products can give complete nutrition for their animals. We wanted to introduce the concept of total cost for the farmer. To obtain this, we needed to identify a balanced diet. An unbalanced diet contains a surplus of certain components, which are thus wasted. What our dealers needed was a powerful tool to analyze what would be the cheapest and best way to combine the different nutritional components available. Since we had the appropriate tool within the company, namely linear programming, and also had the technical

skills required in form of the vets and technicians, the whole thing seemed only natural. Combining these factors with the aid of a PC, we could provide the powerful tool required. Chow or animal food is to a very great extent a commodity business. By introducing this decision support system, we differentiated ourselves from our competitors, introducing higher efficiency and quality. It improved our image and built confidence amongst our customers.

Josep Cortada added:

You might say that the introduction of this decision support system in a field where this technology until then had been very little used, was a strategic one. Strategic in the sense that we wanted to use this technology to provide better service, and by this we believed that we would gain competitive advantage. Personally, I believe that computer systems today should be used as much as possible to move the decision support systems closer to the field.

After the start-up difficulties—train people in the use of the package, etc.—were circumvented, the system was an immediate success. Dealers and customers were very pleased with the service it provided. There were several "success stories" and the program turned out to be quite "creative" in the sense that it came up with feasible solutions that nobody had thought of before. Like one farmer put it: "I'd never thought that a cow could eat this much of this by-product and still produce the normal amount of milk!"

In some cases, the Pinsos Galofré representative believed that the genetic capacity of the animals had been underestimated. By providing a better balanced feeding plan using the package, the production of these animals had indeed been improved. The program was used a lot and the dealers said that they were able to sell more because of this improved service. Specific sales increases were difficult to measure though, since sales were very dependent on what the farmers were growing themselves, which in turn depended, amongst other things, on the weather.

Overall, however, customers were very pleased, since they could now go to the dealer, run the program in less than ten minutes, try several options, etc., and thus use the package as a tool for themselves to arrange the optimal feeding plan for their animals. They were also in this way able to include their by-products in their feeding plans. In addition, if the nutritional contents of a farm by-product is unknown, Pinsos Galofré can also offer analysis services to establish this with accuracy.

About advantages of the decision support package the Chief Financial Officer comments:

One PC can easily handle many products, which means that we can become more flexible, and be able to supply more "customized" products. The package can also be used to indicate what kind of products we should sell in different regions, and thus it can help us in this context to make product decisions which eventually will make us more competitive. By designing products "customized" for a specific region, we will be able to sell a blend that together with the farmers' components will make a very cheap total package for the farmers. In this way we will be able to adapt our product offer to the characteristics of different regions. Eventually, both the farmers and ourselves will be better off by this; the farmer getting cheap feeding and we getting competitive advantage. There is also another important factor in the feeding of cows in which the program can be of help. The production of the cows may, to a certain degree, vary between a maximum and a minimum depending on how they are fed. This fact can be used by the program to suggest different feeding programs for different market situations.

THE SITUATION IN JUNE 1986

On the question of how we viewed the situation in June 1986, Josep Cortada answered:

We're quite content with the situation as it is right now. We have improved our customer service, and we are now ahead of our competitors in the use of this kind of new technology in our field. However, we cannot expect this situation to last forever. There are already some software companies delivering similar, although not comparable, packages, and we must of course expect some kind of reaction from the competition. There are limitations to what we can do to stay ahead of the competition, since we don't feel we have the resources to keep a person working full time on the use of information technology in this area. Today some 200 of our 500 dealers have installed a PC and are using this package regularly.

After his very optimistic conversation with the product manager, Josep Cortada was wondering what the future would bring in relation to the advantages they could gain from the use of this software package....

Some three years had passed since the introduction of the last version of the decision support system for feeding of animals. Thinking back on what had happened over those years, Josep Cortada thought that most of it had been inevitable.

First of all, their major competitors had come up with similar packages. There were several software packages in the market which could do similar things, although they were not as complete as Pinsos Galofré's system. In addition, some local public institutions in Catalonia and Navarra had started projects to develop similar tools for the farmers, which would be offered for free, as a means to support growth in the farming sector. In this respect it seemed that the kind of computer tool that Purina had developed some years earlier was turning into an almost commonplace product. However, the "Galofré System" still had some advantages. Josep Cortada explained:

> In our system we have a file including all our products, and we can run the program and test against all these specific products to find the optimum solution. Other programs will be a lot more difficult to use in this respect. For instance, the programs provided so far are very general, and try to take all possibilities into consideration. There is also the problem related to the constraints that have to be specified in the program. We spent a lot of time and effort working out the different constraints, and I know that we have some constraints included in our program which are not present in some of the other similar packages. These constraints are of prime importance to the "goodness" of the program. Our program is also very user friendly and oriented towards the specific task it is supposed to solve. Take for example the way we solved the rounding problem. In the field you cannot operate with 10.0035 kilograms of grass. Therefore our program rounds these numbers off and tells how this affects the constraints given. Some other software packages just leave the decimals in, leaving the farmer with an impossible mixing and measuring job, without saying anything about what will happen if the blend doesn't come out exactly as prescribed.

In addition to the advantages of a good software package, Pinsos Galofré had an advantage of having a good dealer network. In the chow business the most important measure of quality is the "guaranteed quality" offered at any time. The customers know they can rely on Purina to support all their needs; they have tried the package and know that it works. As a consequence, the customers will be reluctant to change to somebody else's software packages and products.

Purina is currently the market leader in its field in Spain. Fernando Vallvé, the product manager of Pinsos Galofré, was wondering what, if anything, he should do to keep the competitive edge the company had in the market. Should he look into new ways to get competitive advantage? If so, how? Would an extended use of information systems be a proper way to go to try and achieve this competitive advantage?

STEP 2: Prepare the case for class discussion.

STEP 3: Answer each of the following questions, individually or in small groups, as directed by your instructor.

Diagnosis
1. What information needs was the decision support system designed to meet?

Evaluation

2. How well does the existing system meet the managers' and the organization's needs?
3. What factors influenced the components of the decision support system?
4. Does the existing system have the characteristics of a state-of-the-art decision support system?
5. What has been the impact of the existing system?

Design

6. Should any changes be made in the existing system?

Implementation

7. How should changes be made?

STEP 4: In small groups, with the entire class, or in written form, share your answers to the questions above. Then answer the following questions:

1. What information needs exist at Pinsos Galofré?
2. What types of systems exist to meet these needs?
3. What changes would you propose in the systems to better meet these needs?
4. What are the costs and benefits of implementing these changes?

Activity 17: Executive Information System Design for Frito Lay

STEP 1: Read the following scenario. (This activity is especially suited for use in conjunction with Chapter 11 of *Information Systems*.)

Back in 1930, our founder, Herman Lay, did everything. He bought and cooked the potatoes, packaged the chips and put them in his truck, brought them to the stores, and sold them. He did his own quality control: if people yelled at him when he went back the next day, he knew his chips didn't taste good. He had his accounts payable in one pocket and his accounts receivable in the other, and he could tell just by patting his pockets if he could afford to buy a few more potatoes or maybe a newer, bigger truck.

Herman was in constant touch with the marketplace. And so the company grew, took in partners, and built a group of strong regional companies, each of which put out products different from all of the others.

And then, in the 1960s, things began to change. Frito Lay merged with PepsiCo and, like other large companies at the time, emphasized its size and scale. It entered the era of national products, TV commercials, and professional management.

Built on functional excellence and high productivity, supported by national consumer polls, the company prospered. But, in the early 1980s, the competitive environment changed again. Small, regional companies geared to local tastes began to emerge, and large companies, especially those that could not move quickly, began to have problems. Because their frame of reference was national, the large companies were not focused on regional marketplaces and on the delivery outlets, or channels, for their products.

But advances in technology now make it possible for large companies like Frito Lay to return to the regional approach, to be in close touch with their customers, and to let people at every level of their organizations understand the dynamics of what they do and how what they do affects their companies' balance sheets. And they are able to do this while maintaining consistency in the quality of their products and the marketing leverage of well-known brand names.

Here's how we're doing it at Frito Lay.

BUSINESS VOLUME AND VELOCITY

One of the two most critical aspects of Frito Lay's business is volume. We sell four to five billion bags of our various products each year and move them from 40 plants through 10,000 salespeople into 400,000 stores. We had to master volume early on.

The second element critical to our business is velocity. Since we sell impulse items, we need very high service levels and penetration. If you walk by a shelf and our product is there, you'll buy it. But if it's not there, you won't go elsewhere and look for it. Furthermore, our product has a shelf life of 35 days, so we build very small warehouses. We invented "just-in-time" manufacturing because, if nothing left the warehouses for three days, our storage facilities would be full. At the other extreme, if production were to stop, the entire system would be empty in 10 days.

Excerpted and reprinted with permission from Charles S. Feld, Directed decentralization: The Frito Lay story, *Financial Executive*, November/December, 1990, pp. 22–25.

COMPLEXITY

Up to the early 1980s, our business wasn't very complex. We had national patterns. We were predictable. A bag of Doritos bought in New York tasted exactly the same as a bag of Doritos in California. We had an orderly process of building and implementing our annual plan, measuring its results, analyzing what worked and what didn't, and making the requisite changes. We had 10,000 employees in 40 plants who did their jobs very well.

Then the world changed, and, as our regional competitors got stronger, we kept introducing new marketing programs in the belief that we had to become less predictable if we were to be competitive. The problem was, as we became less predictable to our competitors, we also became less predictable to our own plants and sales force. So we had lots of short runs, shipped product by air quite often, and ran promotions on Thursday for a product that didn't arrive until the following Monday. As we shrank our cycle time, our business system became increasingly dysfunctional.

SYSTEMATIC CHANGES

To become flexible and sensitive to the local marketplaces while continuing to maintain national standards of quality and service meant we had to make changes to our business culture, organization, and infrastructure. We had to get off all paper systems, off the functional orientation, off the annual planning cycle. We needed to be a "short-cycle" company, and so we embarked on a seven-year program to completely rewire our information system. And, because our budget was essentially flat, we had to fund this project largely through the greater efficiency it produced.

We decided to build our new information system around three major frameworks: a planning and analysis system, an operational transactional system, and an executive decision support system.

THE PLANNING AND ANALYSIS SYSTEM

The planning system is really a system for measurement. These measurements give us the chance to think about our company as sales, the same way small regional companies think about their businesses.

The planning system contains detailed data from each locality: its P&L, products, and promotion and pricing proposals. We also buy sales records from supermarket scanners, which contain information about our own products as well as those of our competitors. With this information, we can spot trends; we can begin to plan.

These data can be recalled by locality, by brand, or by distribution channel. All our field, brand, and channel managers have instant access to these data; if the competition appears to be gaining ground, our managers can immediately plan the appropriate promotion or pricing strategies. And, because the system tells everyone what is going on, our people in purchasing, manufacturing, and logistics can speedily implement any such plan.

In order to facilitate all this interaction, we built a lot of different technologies into the system so that users don't have to hunt for product codes or location numbers; nor do they need more than basic computer skills.

THE TRANSACTIONAL SYSTEM

With our regional products, specialty brands, and the promotions we run at different times in different cities, our business has become very complex. If sales and operations are not in sync with each other, the plants will overship or undership products because they have to guess about demand, and then they end up airshipping or sending trucks out half empty. But because every one of our 10,000 salespeople has a hand-held computer through which he or she processes orders, we are able to coordinate sales and production effectively.

The goal of the transactional system is a constantly updated database that covers every inventory point. It will show what shipments left the plants yesterday and that today's shipments will be delivered tomorrow. Everyone who needs to, knows exactly where every bag of Doritos is. In due course, we will try to tie our suppliers into this network also.

Despite our short cycle time, this network of databases will allow us to anticipate sales and to meet our sales orders 99.5 percent of the time without having to do short runs at the plants. An additional benefit of the system is that all the actuals get posted into each region, channel, and brand where they belong—every bag, every check request, every gallon of gas that comes through the operational systems. Having these data in one place, rather than scattered throughout the company, gives us an immediate readout, allowing us to build forecasts.

THE EXECUTIVE DECISION SUPPORT SYSTEM

It's not unusual these days for a large company to install an executive support system. Usually, such a system is available only to the 20 or so top executives. What is unusual about our system is its pervasiveness throughout the company.

In this, the fourth year of our systems project, 120 people are linked through PCs, but we expect to reach our intended total of 600 in a year or so—our senior staff and field managers at all levels nationwide. We call it directed decentralization, where decisions at every level can be made quickly and from a well-informed perspective. Everybody sees immediately where he or she stands.

Much of the project so far has been involved in getting our measurement system in place, which we have done. With our old system, we used to spend our time measuring things, but we didn't have time to analyze our findings. Now our measurement is done in a day and we have the time to find out what all this information means. Why are we losing market share? Where did our plans go off, by how much, and why?

The system has also shown us how to eliminate unproductive effort. We haven't been forced to lay off people; rather, we have converted unproductivity into value-added activity.

We are also building analytical capability into the system, such as the set of rules that watches the competitive data. Our system software can, for example, examine the data loaded into our system from the supermarket scanners and send off an alarm when it picks up a new product. If the system picks up a new product in, for instance, St. Louis, it alerts our division manager in St. Louis, the brand manager of our competing product, and our senior staff. We track the success of the new product, and we can begin to develop our own new product if we feel it's necessary.

And so we're back to Herman Lay again. He knew about a change in his market as soon as it happened. With our new system, so do we. Information quickly moves up in the organization, and just as quickly down. Clear and immediate information is available at every level, and communication is constant and continuous. The world will never be simple again. Nor will it be predictable.

STEP 2: Individually or in small groups, develop a proposal for the contents of an executive information system for Frito Lay. The proposal should identify the needs of the president and CEO at Frito Lay, the objectives of the EIS, its components, and its outputs.

FIGURE 1   Directed Decentralization: How It Works

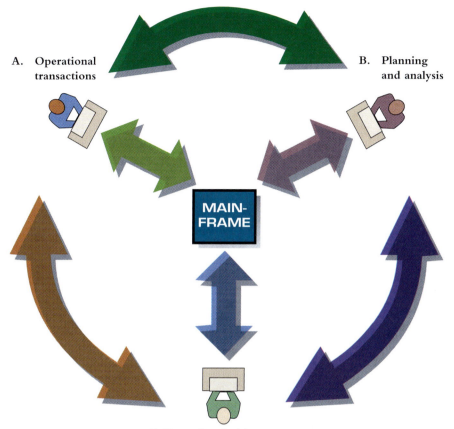

A. Operational transactions

B. Planning and analysis

C. Executive decision support

Frito Lay's system is built on a relational database. Any information entered into the system is immediately accessible to all users:

A. A salesman processes an order on his hand-held computer. The purchasing, manufacturing, and logistics facilities are notified immediately and begin processing the order. Each successive transaction is entered as it occurs; that is, the company can track where the order is in manufacturing, when it left the plant, and when it will be delivered.

B. At the same time, this information is available to the planning and analysis system. This allows the brand manager, the channel manager and the area manager to spot trends in consumption. Competitive information from supermarket scanners is also fed into the mix, enabling managers to see their markets in wider perspective and to develop appropriate strategies to respond to market needs.

C. This information, broader and more general in scope, becomes instantly available to top management. This allows managers to understand what is going on throughout the company, where the firm is losing market share, and why. This in turn allows the executive process to enter the picture sooner and with greater impact.

STEP 3: In small groups or with the entire class, share your proposals. Then answer the following questions:

1. What are the top executives' needs at Frito Lay?
2. What elements should be included in the EIS?
3. What issues should be considered in designing an EIS?

Activity 18: Implementing Business Process Reengineering: A Case Study

STEP 1: Read "Implementing Business Process Reengineering: A Case Study." (This activity is especially suited for use in conjunction with Chapter 12 of *Information Systems*.)

PAYOFF IDEA. A business process reengineering project at Blue Cross and Blue Shield of Massachusetts illustrates the fundamental precept of empowering employees to act on their own. Information technology, including a departmental LAN and client-server enabled the business change. This article describes both the organizational and IT shift needed to support the new business concepts. The IS department's role (and its failings) offers lessons for IS managers seeking greater involvement in line management–directed business reengineering.

INTRODUCTION

Health care and health care costs have become a national priority. The current economic environment, an aging population, and the advances in extensive and expensive medical treatment are having a revolutionary impact on companies in the health insurance field. There are many more options, choices, and combination packages as well as ever-changing government and state regulations and programs. Like many industries, the health insurance field is going through a volatile deregulation phase.

The 1990 annual report of Massachusetts Blue Cross and Blue Shield set the stage for a business process reengineering effort to create a new company, one that is open to change, able to react quickly and aggressively, able to offer an integrated line of health plans in a coordinated manner, and competitive in both benefit costs and administrative costs. This case study describes how information technology was used in the company's effort to reengineer its organization and, in particular, its approach to marketing. The experience draws lessons for the IS department and its involvement in business process reengineering programs initiated by business management.

COMPANY BACKGROUND

Massachusetts Blue Cross and Blue Shield is an old-line company in the health care field. It offers health maintenance organization (HMO) plans, preferred provider organization (PPO) plans, and traditional health plans. Premiums earned in 1990, when the reengineering program began, were in excess of $3 billion. The company employs some 6,000 people.

Starting out in a highly regulated portion of the industry, the company operates in a rapidly changing environment with new competitors, new products and services, and ever-increasing demands from its customers. In addition to such broad-based competitors as Aetna, John Hancock, Prudential, and various HMOs, there are niche players, including organizations that assume benefit management for a company and provide other services. The companies they service expect a reduced rate from their insurers.

Massachusetts Blue Cross was experiencing an eroding market, declining sales, and strained service levels. It had a high cost structure and an organization that reflected a traditional

Source: Written by Fay Donohue-Rolfe, Vice-President, Plan Initiatives, Massachusetts Blue Cross and Blue Shield, Boston, MA; Jerome Kanter, Director, Center for Information Management Studies, Babson College, Babson Park, MA; Mark C. Kelley, Vice-President, Small Business and Select Markets Division, Massachusetts Blue Cross and Blue Shield, Boston, MA. Auerbach Publications, © 1993 Warren Gorham Lamont

hierarchical business with multiple layers of management. The combination of a heightened competitive structure and reduced sales effectiveness because of an inability to reach new markets was having a marked business impact. The company was losing members within its accounts as well as entire accounts.

The Marketing Organization

The marketing organization was based on geographical territory within Massachusetts. A salesperson might have 300 accounts ranging from companies having 1 to 4 members, to small businesses with 5 to 24 members, to larger accounts. The salespeople had complete cognizance over their territories, servicing accounts, acquiring new business, and retaining existing business. Customer contact has traditionally been through the salespeople, who make frequent calls and handle all questions and matters of their clients either in person, over the phone, or in writing.

At the start of 1990, there were 140 salespeople and a support staff of more than 300. The marketing organization was organized into seven regional sales offices ranging from 15 to 60 employees, with several levels of management. A sales office handled multibillion-dollar high-technology companies as well as local business that fell into its territory. The seven regional offices were organized strictly by geographic territory. The other groups with direct sales responsibilities were the national accounts sales office, which sold to certain large and designated Massachusetts corporations, and separate offices for two extremely large accounts, General Electric and NYNEX. Four other groups—marketing communications, advertising, sales and service training, and marketing information systems—provided support to the sales offices.

The IT Support Infrastructure

The technical computer infrastructure that supported the sales offices was a carryforward from the traditional centralized mainframe environment (see Exhibit 1a). In the case of Massachusetts Blue Cross Blue Shield (BC/BS), there were two incompatible mainframes and two incompatible minicomputers. One mainframe housed the master data base for companies, institutions, and individual members. This system was used to calculate rates, enroll and bill new and current customers, and process renewals of existing customers. The other mainframe processed claims from groups, individuals, doctors, and hospitals. One of the minicomputers was installed to handle the new HMO and PPO insurance while the other was used for accessing marketing data bases and prospect information (a system known as Marketrieve).

These systems progressed over the years from primarily a batch COBOL orientation to an online mode with terminals (not personal computers) installed in the sales offices. The terminals connected to the claims mainframe were on each desk, but there were only one or two terminals per office connected to the group data mainframe. There were even fewer terminals for the HMO processor. The different security access codes and protocols for the mainframes and minicomputers resulted in a specialization among the office staff.

Questions concerning claims, membership, enrollments, and rates were routed to the sales office handling the account. As might be expected, in this technical environment, few, if any, calls can be answered on the spot if access to one or more mainframes is required. If a particular salesperson or administrator is not available, the call must be returned later. Processing a service call can require multiple hand-offs to different administrators. In essence, although the systems have online terminals, the process is still essentially batch oriented. A major effort has been under way by the central IS department to replace the two mainframes with a single unit that would handle both group data and claims processing, but this has proved difficult and costly to implement.

EXHIBIT 1   IT Support Infrastructure Before and After Reengineering

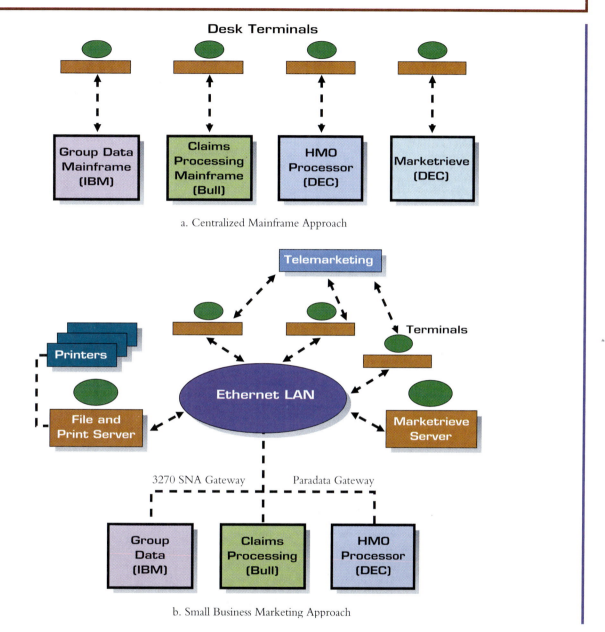

a. Centralized Mainframe Approach

b. Small Business Marketing Approach

The Small Business Marketing Group

An initial study area in the change initiative was the small business market segment, defined as companies with 5 to 24 employees. Small account losses had been averaging 14% a year. Senior management realized that new business practices were a necessity for survival. The need was compelling and changes had to be made quickly, according to the findings of an in-depth consultant study done at the end of the previous year.

THE DECISION TO REENGINEER

External pressures drove the small business marketing project. First, the consultants had senior management attention. By mid-1990, the marketing vice-president knew that January 1991 would be a high renewal month and crucial period for sales. Presentations of 1990 results were scheduled to be made to senior management and the board of directors at year's end. Marketing wanted a success story to tell by that time. The marketing VP evaluated options and decided to spin off small business accounts to a separate sales force that would use telemarketing techniques.

This change involved breaking several deep-seated corporate tenets. Telemarketing and teleservicing were culturally unacceptable to Massachusetts Blue Cross. The strong assumptions were that health insurance is too complex to sell over the phone and relationship selling is essential. A key ingredient was a sales force dedicated to a specific market segment, breaking down the long-standing geographic territory concept for new business sales. A crucial part of the new strategy was a customer focus; indeed "customer driven" became the battle cry throughout the project.

From the start, the project was business driven. Marketing took the initiative, conducting customer and prospect surveys that showed that a direct sales force was not needed if policy information was available on an accurate and timely basis by telephone. The marketers knew enough about telemarketing to realize it could be the technological enabler; however, the change required a major organizational shift as well as a major information technology shift to support the new business concepts.

REENGINEERING THE ORGANIZATION

The decision to proceed was made by July 1990 and was quickly followed by a $2 million budget (indicating the project had senior-level support). The time frame was seven weeks for the new department to become operational. The marketing director was appointed director for the project. The project director had a solid grasp of the conceptual, strategic, and practical elements of the program and the ability to implement plans. The seven-week time period was a significant constraint in initiating the project.

The Self-Managed Work Team Model

Exhibit 2 represents the new sales department organization with the spin off of the small business marketing office. The small business office was originally given responsibility for sales and support to small companies having 5 to 24 people, but this was later expanded to include companies with 1 to 4 people and extended to companies with 25 employees. The remaining accounts were organized into five regional offices; national accounts were combined in a single unit, as were the four support units. Not only were the direct reports to the VP of marketing reduced to four, but the organization levels within the units were reduced and simplified. Five levels of management were truncated into two.

By September, 20 people were hired for the new department. Four team leaders were designated. The project director delegated the recruitment and hiring of the people so that the project director only reviewed finalists after they had been screened. The people were chosen on the basis of their sales abilities (not necessarily insurance) and their experience with telemarketing. The stated objective was to hire and train leaders, not managers, who could facilitate self-managed work teams. The goals were to reengineer people, systems, and attitudes to empower people to act, and to provide the technology base they needed. The 20 people started a six-week training program, focusing on product, process, and the information systems that would play a vital role in the new marketing approach.

Senior management made a substantial investment to accommodate the major cultural change by providing an extensive education program, both up front and continuing. Cur-

The Reengineered Marketing Organization

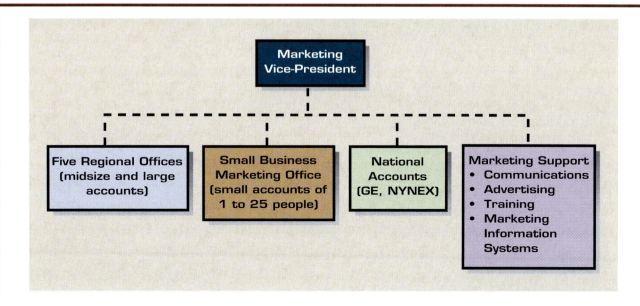

rently, the department allocates one day a week after-hours time for a training session. Team communication and team building, which promotes the individual review of one another's work while suggesting alternate ways of accomplishing work, are important elements of the new organization. Work and results are shared. On the sales floor, for example, graphs of performance versus quota and other key indicators of group performance are displayed. In addition, the first-ever incentive system has been established.

REENGINEERING THE TECHNOLOGY

In concert with the staff, the project director, who before the program started had never used a personal computer, created the systems requirements. The project director assigned an internal IS specialist who had been a member of an experimental four-person telemarketing unit that was eventually disbanded. However, the IS specialist's experience was limited to spreadsheet and word processing software.

The small business marketing group gave its requirements to several outside vendors who were hands-on implementers, rather than to the traditional planners and consultants. The official in-house IS response was to develop an RFP, but this would take too long. The IS department worked with the project director on the evaluation and selection of the vendor; from that point on, it was a team proposition.

Line Management Leadership

The project director relied on IS because of the complex interconnections that the new system would have with the existing data bases. The real challenge was to have a single IBM-compatible terminal with a Windows interface capable of tapping into the available information from the two disparate mainframes and the two minicomputer systems. In addition, the 20 telemarketers needed to be linked by a local area network (LAN) to share current information on a client-server type architecture. The project director selected the graphical interface Windows as the common interface (at the consultant's recommendation) rather than opening up the decision on interface selection, because that would potentially jeopardize the deadline. The new system was scheduled to be in operation by the end of October 1990.

The systems designer assigned to assist and provide the central IS resources needed by the small business group expressed concern at the beginning and skepticism that the project could be carried out. At first, the support from the IS group was limited because it already had a sizable work backlog. The central IS group had been working on a multiyear, $50 million project to combine the two mainframe systems onto a single integrated platform, and to completely realign IT to the business. Five years later and many million dollars over budget, the project was still far from completion. With this history, it was difficult for the system designer to believe that a project directed by department people with scant computer background and involving several technologies new to the company could meet successful completion within seven weeks.

IS acknowledged, however, the benefits of the system, both from what the application could do from a business standpoint and also from a pure IS cost perspective. Replacing four terminals with one would have a significant impact on hardware and software costs, training, and support. However, numerous problems occurred during the course of the implementation.

The Reengineered Systems

An Ethernet LAN was installed that allowed direct linkage using Windows 3.0 into both the group data mainframe and claims mainframe (See Exhibit 1b) and the HMO minicomputer (implemented subsequent to the October 1990 start-up). In addition, the Marketrieve system, which was acquired from a software company, was modified from its previous use and was connected to the LAN. The files are tailored for Massachusetts businesses. All sales representatives use this file and add their notes on individual prospects to afford continuity for themselves and their colleagues as the sales campaign unfolds. These files are accessible by anyone on the LAN and have been instrumental in the highly successful new business sales produced by the small business marketing group.

In addition to accessing the two mainframes and the minicomputer, the group has its own client-server that allows the sharing of five laser printers and other resources, including E-mail, word processing, spreadsheets, and data bases. Because of the instant access from the desk workstation to the various remote data bases and to notes that have been appended to the individual account file from previous calls and contacts, any of the sales and support people can handle an inquiry. If everyone is on the phone at a particular time, the caller has the option of waiting or leaving a voice message.

Exhibit 1b appears more complex than the original architecture (Exhibit 1a), but to the user, a transformation has occurred in simplicity and ease of use. The complex interconnectivity is transparent to the user.

PROJECT OUTCOME: GREATER EFFECTIVENESS AT LOWER COST

The results of the new dedicated telemarketing sales team with rapid access to account information have been impressive. Previously, an inquiry may have gone through six people before a response was made. Now one person handles the inquiry and in a far more expeditious manner.

By the end of 1990, according to the annual report, the small business group made almost 13,000 prospect calls. Sales totaled 73 new medical groups and 13 new dental groups, representing a total of 1,001 members. The unit established itself as an important contributor to the company's future success.

Results continue to be impressive, both on the qualitative side and the quantitative side. A year later, in the small business market there was a cost saving of $4.7 million (costs of running the old process less cost of the reengineered process), or 62%, a sales increase of 24%, a sales-retention increase of 6%, with total additional revenue of $22 million. The group made 86,000 prospect calls in 1991, a figure equal to the previous five years. Quality of service has also improved. Calls are recorded and timed. No caller waits longer than 45 seconds and 90% of the inquiries are resolved in one call of five to eight minutes. Those calls that require correspondence are handled in less than five days.

Organizational and Operational Results

A walk through the 15th floor of the Massachusetts BC/BS building, where the small business marketing group operates, reveals an open office environment with individual cubicles for managers, team leaders, and customer service representatives. There is little to distinguish who is who, based on office size or location. There are no technicians or IT professionals on site, although the LAN network is quite complex. One of the team leaders acts as the IT liaison and local network manager. All network or technical questions go to this individual, who now handles about 80% of the problems. Other problems are routed to another IT liaison in the personal computer applications area, situated on another floor.

The horizon of the small business marketing group keeps expanding and the entrepreneurial spirit has become more pervasive. The group continually searches for opportunities to improve its existing business and for new areas to apply telemarketing/teleservicing skills. It is a classic case of what can happen when the individual is empowered.

Technically, the group is in the process of installing fax capability at the workstation to reduce the time away from the phone. Another development is to enhance the client-server to have more of the customer data available locally instead of having to access the mainframe. However, the accomplishments made in such a short period are a strong motivator to the small business marketing group that these extensions will materialize.

LESSONS LEARNED FOR THE INFORMATION SYSTEMS ORGANIZATION

It is interesting to review the role of IS (or its lack of a role) in this example of business process reengineering. Although there is a large central IS organization at Massachusetts Blue Cross/Blue Shield, there was scant participation by IS professionals in the implementation. The central IS group was preoccupied with a major conversion of its old legacy systems into a new hardware/software platform. The impetus for reengineering was initiated and led by the functional department, in this case, the small business marketing group.

Business Goals Drive IS Development

The first lesson learned is that the leadership for reengineering must come from those closest to the business process affected. The marketing group dealt directly with outside consultants and software developers; there was only one central IS participant in the project. In retrospect, greater IS involvement would have alleviated problems that later arose in connecting to the central system. In this case, IS missed the opportunity to recognize the scope and importance of the new approach and to become more actively involved.

The driving force in this example, as it is in most cases, is the need to become business competitive. Information technology is the enabler, not the driver. The technology used need not be the most advanced technology on the market; many successful users of IT apply common technology uncommonly well. This is not a case study about technology: it is about business change in the way a company markets its product. Information technology has enabled the company to tap into systems that were 20 years old and to use telemarketing, which, though common in the overall industry, represented a major cultural business change to Massachusetts Blue Cross.

Timely Delivery

Another lesson learned is that line departments often set goals that seem impossible to meet, yet somehow the job gets done. Often this means arranging alliances with third parties using rapid application development approaches. Business and competitive pressures require that product cycle times be reduced. If American businesses have learned anything from the Japanese business model and from total quality management (TQM), it is that the design-to-delivery cycle of products must be compressed. This holds for IS products, particularly as information technology becomes more embedded in the business.

Redefining the IS Role

Though applications can be implemented by line departments quickly and often effectively, there is still a valuable role that IS must play. Rapidly produced programs often lack the industrial-strength qualities needed when the application moves into mainstream operation. Security, backup, documentation to incorporate the inevitable changes that occur, linkage with other systems, and error controls are just a few of these elements. Massachusetts Blue Cross/Blue Shield found that many of these problems did arise and could have been avoided with IS involvement.

Another important lesson is for IS to build an architecture that can respond to changing business needs, exemplified by the small business marketing group. The original system could not incorporate the changes necessitated by the switch to telemarketing. It was built on separate and disparate data bases. A major outside effort was required, and even then the user interface was not a completely smooth or transparent one. A future architecture must have the flexibility to easily adapt to changing business conditions and demands.

The key to success is increasingly built around alliances: alliances with outsourcers, software developers, and consultants outside the company, and alliances with operating departments and business units within the company. IS can no longer be a back-office superstructure.

The small business marketing group typifies business departments that are accomplishing work that sometimes IS claims is impossible. Technologies such as client-servers, graphical user interfaces, and a plethora of improving application software packages have become the enablers. Business managers want to see immediate response to their problems and they seek control of the resources necessary to see it happen. Whereas the central IS group may experience a priority problem, a line department does not.

CONCLUSION

This article gives an example of a company taking a high-risk course of action that it thought the business environment and the changing competitive dynamics warranted. The company proceeded to break with tradition and to reengineer the organization and its approach to marketing. One of the most important changes was the fundamental precept of empowering people to act on their own.

Information technology enabled the change. The implementation involved the installation of a department client-server, which together with a department LAN and the use of telemarketing and teleservicing, gave salespeople shared access to relevant and current information about their customers and prospects. Included in the rapid formation of a new department and a new approach to doing business was a time frame and schedule that demanded action and decision. It is a classic example of a line department–led transformation that was supported and enabled by a transformation in the use of technology. This case study illustrates that a solid business technology partnership can reengineer a company to improve its competitive position.

STEP 2: Prepare the case for class discussion.

STEP 3: Answer each of the following questions, individually or in small groups, as directed by your instructor.

Diagnosis
1. Why did Massachusetts Blue Cross and Blue Shield believe that it needed to reengineer the activities of its small business marketing group?
2. What did the new sales department organization look like?
3. What were the information needs of the new sales department?

Evaluation
4. What information technology infrastructure existed before the reengineering?
5. How well did the IT infrastructure meet the needs of the new sales department?

Design
6. What changes were proposed for the IT infrastructure?
7. How well did the new infrastructure meet the information needs of the new sales department?
8. What, if any, changes are still required?

Implementation
9. What steps were included in the implementation of the new systems?
10. What role did the IS organization play in the implementation?
11. What role did the line management play in the implementation?
12. How effective was the implementation?

STEP 4: In small groups, with the entire class, or in written form, share your answers to the questions above. Then answer the following questions:

1. What prompted the reengineering at Massachusetts Blue Cross and Blue Shield?
2. What information needs did the business process redesign create?
3. How effectively did existing information systems meet these needs?
4. How effectively did the new information systems meet these needs?
5. Was the implementation of the new information systems effective? ●

Staying at the Top with Otis Elevator

INTRODUCTION

Otis has been the leader in the elevator industry in France for more than a century. In fall 1991, about six months before the scheduled implementation of SAFRAN-O, the last of five information technology (IT) applications resulting from the new Master Plan launched in 1986, Bruno Grob, CEO of Otis France, wondered how and to what extent IT had contributed to sustain this unique market position, as well as if and how it could do so in the future.

> "The competitive advantage doesn't come from the tool [the computer system]. The tool is a tool, and the tool will remain a tool.... The tool should be served by a strategy, by a human resource, training, motivation, and anything else."

OTIS WORLDWIDE (OVERVIEW)

Otis Elevator was founded by Elisha Otis in 1853. Over the last 150 years, it has been one of the world leaders in the manufacture, sales, and service of elevators and related products. It is renowned for its long standing tradition of quality products and dependable customer service. Since Otis Elevator is perceived to be the best, its products and services are sold for a premium price. Otis especially dominates the markets for the sales and maintenance of elevators for large projects. It specializes in customized elevators. During the last five years it has increasingly turned into a service company, whose main business is "to transport people, not to manufacture lifts." (Pierre Istace—Quality, Marketing, and Communication Manager at Otis France).[1]

In 1975, Otis Elevator became a subsidiary of United Technologies Corporation (UTC), one of the fifty largest industrial companies in the world. UTC owned 100% of the stock of Otis New Jersey (ONJ), which is the parent company of Otis. (For the legal structure of Otis see Exhibit 1.) This affiliation opened the door to massive research resources for Otis. Through collaboration with the United Technologies Research Center, Otis developed electronic elevators and increased its efficiency in installing elevators.

> "Being part of a $19.8 billion corporation gives us a stature in global markets we would not enjoy standing alone."
>
> Karl Krapek
> Former President of Otis

Otis Elevator with its four geographical divisions, North American Operations, Latin American Operations, Pacific Area Operations, and European Transcontinental Operations (ETO) was the only elevator company with a strong presence in every continent.[2] It maintains offices in 45 countries. About 46,000 Otis employees work out of approximately 570 headquarters and district and branch offices around the globe. Otis world headquarters are located

---

[1] Every nine days, Otis moves the equivalent of the world population.
[2] ETO includes Africa and the Middle East.

> This case was written by Claudia Loebbecke, Research Assistant, under the supervision of Tawfik Jelassi, Associate Professor at INSEAD. It is intended to be used as a basis for class discussion rather than to illustrate either effective or ineffective handling of an administrative situation. Copyright © INSEAD-CEDEP 1992, Fontainebleau, France.

EXHIBIT 1 — The Legal Structure of Otis Elevator, Worldwide

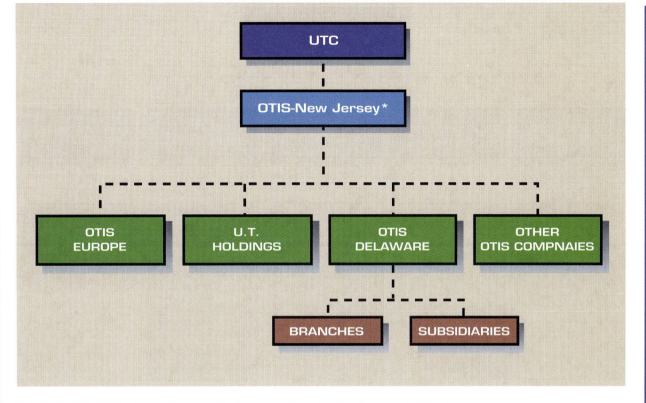

*Includes Otis HQ, Otis Engineering Center, and the U.S. part of North American Operations (NAO).

SOURCE: Company Document.

in Farmington, Connecticut, USA. For an overview of the management organization see Exhibit 2. The structure of Otis Europe, a holding company domiciled in France, is shown in Exhibit 3.

Otis worldwide revenues are almost twice that of its nearest competitor. Otis's rivals range from elevator divisions of multi-billion dollar conglomerates to small local firms with a handful of employees and no manufacturing capabilities of their own. Otis's worldwide competition comes mainly from six major companies: Schindler (Switzerland), Mitsubishi Electric Corp. and Hitachi Ltd. (Japan), Kone (Finland), Dover Elevator International (U.S.), and Thyssen (Germany).

THE ELEVATOR INDUSTRY

The two main business sectors of the elevator industry are "New Equipment" and "Service." Due to the direct correlation with the building cycle, elevator sales represent a cyclical business sector, while the elevator service market is characterized by strong stability. Of the two business sectors, service accounts for a significantly higher portion of profits. Elevator manufacturers therefore often accept a low margin on the sale of new equipment in order to obtain the service contract and sustain the company growth.

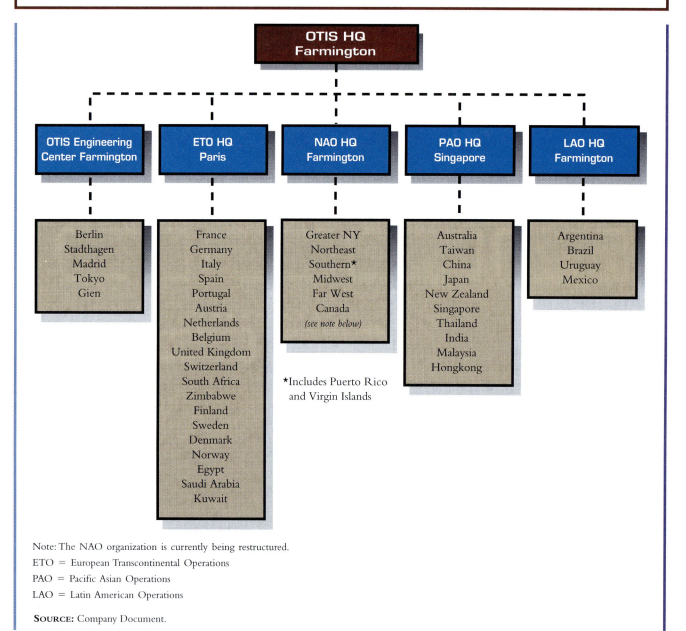

EXHIBIT 2 Otis Management Organization

Note: The NAO organization is currently being restructured.
ETO = European Transcontinental Operations
PAO = Pacific Asian Operations
LAO = Latin American Operations

SOURCE: Company Document.

The service market has attracted many small companies that did not produce elevators themselves. As long as elevators operated on the basis of electromechanical devices, these companies could compete successfully, since the interior design of almost all lifts on the market was very similar. With the introduction of microchips in the manufacture of elevators, some small companies had to reduce their service offers; they had neither the equipment nor the appropriately trained personnel to cope with these new developments in the elevator market.

> **EXHIBIT 3** Legal Structure of Otis Europe

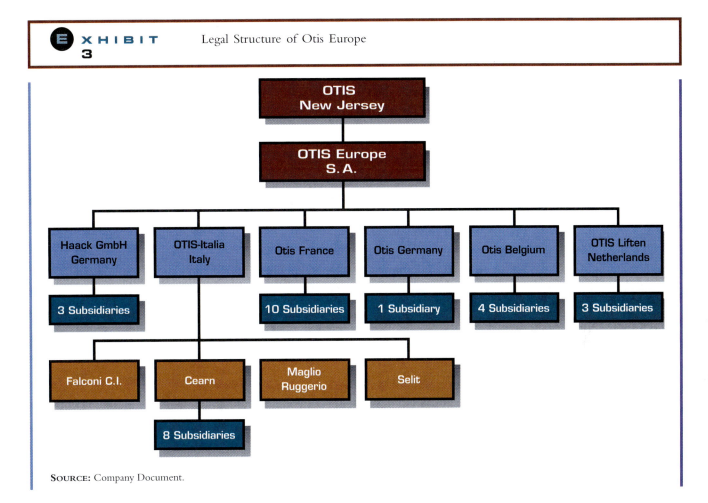

SOURCE: Company Document.

Thus the use of new technologies increasingly "regulates" the oligopolistic elevator market, providing additional benefits to the big players who are also producers of equipment: An elevator manufacturer typically receives service contracts for 60% to 80% of its newly installed equipment. Furthermore, for elevators with microprocessor-based control systems, the manufacturer is likely to keep the service contracts since small, local companies cannot provide appropriate maintenance. To support this trend, many elevator manufacturers offer discounts for long-term service contracts to attract and maintain customers.

OTIS FRANCE

While Otis has only one family of products—elevators/escalators—it nevertheless has two very different activities dealing with this product: New Equipment and Service. The New Equipment business is in turn made up of sales, manufacturing, and construction. There are three common types of elevators: gearless traction, geared traction, and hydraulic. Escalators and travolators can be viewed as complementary products.

The Service business is made up of some sales (spare parts), a small amount of manufacturing, and a large field labor force engaged in four types of services: contractual maintenance, repair, modernization, and replacement.

Contractual maintenance is about 70% of total service sales. Usually, the contractual maintenance customer is not the same as the new equipment customer (the construction contractor is seldom the final building owner). Therefore, the selling price of the maintenance contract is established once the building is completed and separately from the new equipment contract. Repair service consists of putting the elevator back in order, while modernization improves its operational condition. Repair margins are generally less than the margins for contractual maintenance, but higher than the modernization ones. However, modernization is a growth business in which—by definition—the market increases by age.

Otis France with about 6,400 employees serves approximately 40,000 customers. While about 1,400 people are employed in staff, management, sales, R&D, and administrative jobs, another 1,100 persons work in one of the two company factories in Gien (800) and Argenteuil (340), and almost 4,000 work in the field.[3] Due to the scope of its business, Otis France's organizational structure divides the country into three "zones" (East of France, West of France, and Paris with suburbs), 28 branches, and 180 commercial agencies. (The organizational structure of top management [the Executive Committee] is shown in Exhibit 4.) This organization also includes 10 subsidiaries (100% owned) grouped under the name of CFA and covering the whole country.

Otis France is the leader in elevator sales and service in the French market. With a turnover of more than $0.7 billion it has a market share of 39.6% of the elevator market in France. Its three main competitors in the French market are Schindler (18.3% of total turnover in the market), Kone (12.4%), and Soretex[4] (8.5%). (In 1988, Schindler acquired the elevator and escalator interests of Westinghouse Electric Company in the US.) About 60% of Otis turnover originates in service, while 40% results from new equipment sales or intercompany exports of equipment to Otis sister companies in Europe or agents in the third-world countries.

---

[3]The remaining people were employed in commercial positions in the branches.
[4]Soretex is a subsidiary of Thyssen (Germany).

Otis France Executive Committee (Top Management's Organizational Structure)

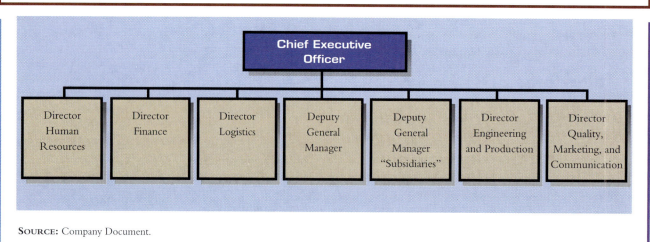

SOURCE: Company Document.

INFORMATION TECHNOLOGY AT OTIS FRANCE

In early 1986, Otis France used three main IT applications to support its elevator business: OTISLINE, the Customer Database, and REM (Remote Elevator Monitoring). OTISLINE was adapted from a successful implementation at Otis North America. REM was introduced to the French market after it had been developed and tested as a prototype in the United States.

OTISLINE

In late 1981, Otis North America (one of Otis's four regional divisions) began exploring the opportunities for enhancing their customer service operations through the use of information technology. This resulted in the development of OTISLINE, a centralized customer service center. Underlying OTISLINE was the concept of enhancing responsiveness to customer service requests. This necessitated the creation of a centralized dispatching unit with complete access to all customers and their associated product and maintenance data.

With these new capabilities Otis North America experienced dramatic improvements in their responsiveness to call backs. OTISLINE translated into not only a complete redesign of their customer information systems, but also into the creation of a new industry standard for service. Due to its success in North America, the OTISLINE concept was adopted and installed by other divisions within the company, including Otis France.

In France OTISLINE was also developed into a national communication center for the Otis maintenance activity. However, due to some local features (e.g., a different ZIP code and address structure and a telephone network that was much less accessible for technicians than in the United States) the installed OTISLINE was different from its U.S. counterpart.

OTISLINE in France, as in North America, operates 24 hours a day, seven days a week, receiving customer phone calls from building management and users and dispatching Otis service teams as necessary with the shortest possible delay. The French concept for this new use of IT led to offering OTISLINE as a service and charging the customer for it. This additional payment increased expectations on the customers' side, and thus in the beginning, led to hardly any increase in Otis benefits. Over time, Otis customers started to consider a service like OTISLINE more as a new industry standard than as a special offer. By dialing 05-24-24-07 (toll-free number) they communicate with Otis. 2,400 phone calls are received daily from customers and 800 from Otis technicians.

OTISLINE keeps a record on each lift; every event (e.g., an elevator inspection, repair, etc.) is stored in the computer database system. The Otis Maintenance Service as well as any other authorized employee within the company can access this database and use the relevant information for his/her activities.

Customer Database

With more than 40,000 customers stored, the customer database can be used by sales people, marketing, and communication. For each customer a variety of information is available. Address, phone number, name of people involved with elevator activity, annual turnover with Otis, pending negotiation, direct marketing campaigns, and results of customer satisfaction surveys can be launched from this database.

Remote Elevator Monitoring (REM)

Otis North America successfully introduced the prototype of a "Remote Elevator Monitoring" (REM) system which utilizes microchip technology to monitor an elevator and automatically notify Otis if it is malfunctioning. Through a master unit installed in the machine room, REM monitors lift performance. If performance deviates from predetermined standards, the REM Master Unit sends a message over a dedicated telephone line to Otis.

Functions with abnormal performance readings are corrected during regular maintenance. If a shutdown occurs, the REM system allows Otis to determine whether passengers are trapped (bidirectional automatic voice link between the cab and OTISLINE).

The major market for REM is France, where more than 7,000 units are implemented. In other European countries, only a few hundred REM systems are installed, while in the United States Otis North America has not sold any.

REM is characterized by the dual focus on external and internal business aspects. Introduced as an additional service to the customers (external focus), it is an excellent tool for the communication between the cab (trapped passengers) and the Otis Service division. From the internal perspective, it serves as a diagnostic tool which automatically feeds the shared company database. It leads to pre-emptive maintenance (striving for the goal of zero call backs) and thus to reduced maintenance/service costs and customer satisfaction improvement.

> With REM we should have no breakdowns anymore because we should be able to be on the job site before they occur.
>
> Pierre Amar
> Logistics Manager

THE BIRTH OF THE MASTER PLAN

In the summer of 1986, top management at Otis France contemplated the use of IT within the company. They were aware of the competitive advantage resulting from OTISLINE and REM, from both an external (customer) viewpoint and an internal (organizational) perspective. They thought that additional benefits could be gained from the development of new IT applications that improve efficiency and facilitate the flow of information across the company.

For internal processes, Otis was still using a system that was developed in the early 1960s, based on the technology that was available at that time. This system suffered mainly from a lack of providing business estimates and processing customer information. Every time during the last twenty years that a change was made in the organizational structure or in the business conduct, there was an attempt to adjust the computer system to the introduced changes.

> We realized that the system, the technology, and the organization were the three dimensions of the problem. So we felt that we'd try to understand where we go from now and we decided to set up the 'schema directeur' [the Master Plan] of our project.
>
> Pierre Amar

The idea of an IT system that could contribute to a redesigned retail system was introduced. However, top management was convinced that the development of further IT applications had to be based on an organizational redesign. They agreed that any new system could only serve as a tool for a predeveloped new strategy.

> The tool itself won't create the strategy, the motivation, the teamwork. The tool itself will create nothing. If it comes within a strategy, then it's outstanding; but it has to be prepared far in advance.
>
> Bruno Grob

THE "MASTER PLAN" PROJECT

The Concept

Otis France's goal was to design and implement a simplified version of the managerial and operational procedures surrounding the processing of a customer order. Central to the project was the interrelationship between the development of the procedures and the organizational structure, with decentralization of responsibility driving the design. The entire process, from the initial contact with the customer through the installation of the elevator, was reviewed and redesigned.

> Simplify processes and make them clearer, that was the main point. Once that was done, even imperfectly, we could design systems to respond to them. Obviously we had the computer in mind, but it was not the purpose of our exercise.
>
> Bruno Grob

The People Involved

The decision of top management to launch the Master Plan was the starting point for involving in the project a number of employees in different positions within the company. Pierre Amar noted that "the first step was not to leave that to the EDP people." Three committees (the Steering Committee, the Project Team, and the Users' Council) were officially formed to participate in a variety of tasks.

Otis started putting in place a Steering Committee. It consisted of the managing director (CEO) and all the directors in his first line. This committee was "in charge of talking to each other and trying to understand where they would like Otis to go in terms of systems to support the company strategies" (Pierre Amar).

The Steering Committee monitored the progress of the entire project, validated the results, and gave general guidelines. Bruno Grob, who started as Deputy General Manager in this committee, was later promoted to the position of CEO. From that point on, he became the key driving force of the project, even more than before.

The project itself was assigned to a newly set up dedicated team, what they called "La Direction de l'Organisation." Its composition was intended to cover a broad range of experience and knowledge about the company. It had five members from the Organization Department, including the Corporate Organization Manager.

The Users' Council, consisting of thirty individuals coming from the various areas of the company, examined and ratified the work and recommendations of the Project Team. It ensured the coherence and completeness of the project and carried out the management decisions. Furthermore, the User's Council submitted its own proposals to the Project Team and set up determined priorities among the Steering Committee's actions.

The Beginning of the Project

> Our approach was not to look at the problem from the system point of view, but to audit the existing situation, the organization itself.
>
> Pierre Amar

Otis started with investigating the characteristics of its business. The goals of that process were twofold. The first was to analyze the current business situation and to improve the understanding of what the company was actually doing in order to generate profits. The second goal was to increase awareness for the "Master Plan" project. The Users' Council became enthusiastic about the subject because its members were able to talk about what they knew. Thus the Project Team had successfully created broad commitment for the subsequent steps.

Pierre Amar described these steps as follows:

> We started explaining what we were doing: designing, manufacturing, selling, and maintaining elevators, managing people, etc. We tried to match the major business areas with the organizational units as they were at that time. This resulted in a matrix reflecting who did what. Afterwards we attached ratios to the matrix fields showing each person's resource allocation.
>
> We had two industrial locations: Did we need both of them or would one suffice? We were organized in branches which were providing two main services: modernization and maintenance

of elevators. Was that the right way to handle our business? People started looking differently at the way the company behaved.

During that process we discovered that one aspect was missing in our approach: the customers. We had never had the customer as a driving factor in what we were doing. In the branches we were driven by geography rather than by market segments, or even by the customer himself. We found that our whole business was contract-oriented: We were handling contracts rather than dealing with customers. That was the very big start.

Then we started thinking of what should be a) the processes and b) the system to support these processes. We described each process and analyzed who our customers were. Afterwards we investigated the communication: Who dealt with whom and what kind of information was exchanged?

We ended up with the target architecture of our processes rather than of our systems (which did not exist). We described the processes and determined the amount of the information we wanted to handle in the future.

The Development Methodology Applied

In defining their information systems requirements, Otis—with the help of an external consulting company—developed and applied a methodology which used the company's strategic goals to drive the system design process. This methodology divided the whole process into four main phases, which were implemented in a step-by-step manner. The four phases were: a) assessment of the current organizational structure and analysis of management areas, including a functional breakdown of its business as depicted in the strategic plan, b) assessment of the existing information systems, including the conceptual and data systems as well as resource feasibility studies, c) planning of the new organizational structure, and d) planning of the new information systems (including the systems' architecture and implementation). The outcome of these four phases was the "Master Plan" which detailed the functional and technical design of the new retail system. The development sequence of the Master Plan's phases and their associated time frames are shown in Exhibits 5 and 6.

The development phases determined three levels of investigation (conceptual, organizational, and physical) as well as two main tasks in the process (evaluation of the present situation and generation of solutions). The conceptual level, "What has to be done," provided the link with the strategic dimension and resulted in the redefinition of the business domains. The organizational level, "The way to do it," investigated alternative choices for the com-

Development Sequence of the Master Plan's Phases

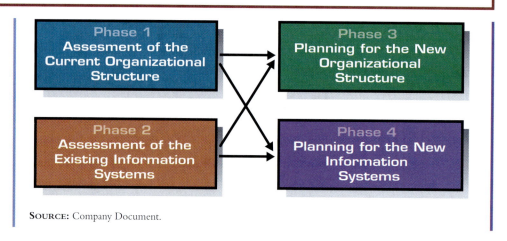

SOURCE: Company Document.

Exhibit 6   Time Frame for the Development Phases

	Feb. '86	March '86	April '86	May '86	June '86	July '86
Phase 1	21 X 24 Y					
Phase 2			7 X 24 Y			
Phase 3				5 X 14 Y		
Phase 4					6 X 18 Y	3 Y

X = Meeting of the Steering Committee
Y = Meeting of the User's Council

The meetings always mark the end of a phase.
Source: Company Document.

pany; its findings suggested a new organizational structure and a set of information systems. The physical level, "The means of doing it," determined the resources needed for the implementation of the project.

RESULTS OF THE MASTER PLAN

The results of the Master Plan can be categorized into two main areas: organizational changes and new IT applications. The interdependence between these two areas is obviously very important.

As far as information systems are concerned, the Master Plan includes a conceptual description of five new IT applications [SAGA, SALVE, STAR, SAFRAN-N,S,K, and SAFRAN-O] to be implemented between 1986 and 1992. These applications support negotiation, sales and contract management, invoicing and accounts receivable, purchasing management, and accounting. Their design is based on the concept that each type of sales activity (be it sales to a new customer or to an existing one, maintenance, repair, or modernization) follows the same basic procedure.

The New IT Applications

The five new IT applications include SALVE, a support system used by sales representatives in their negotiations with the customer from the initial contact to the booking stage. Once the order has been booked (order received by the factory), it is passed to SAGA, a contract management system, which creates and maintains the sales order. SAGA can be viewed as a special contract control system. The information gained from SALVE and SAGA serves as input for STAR, the purchasing and supplier management system. SAFRAN-N,S,K handles invoicing and other accounting functions regarding modernization as well as sales of new equipment for new or existing buildings. SAFRAN-O, planned to be implemented by May 1992, will handle the billing of maintenance services. Otis expects a high productivity increase from the introduction of SAFRAN-O, since the company has currently 60,000 maintenance contracts covering 130,000 elevators for which bills have to be prepared on a regular basis (quarterly). A short description of the functions and users of each of these systems is provided in Exhibits 7 to 11.

EXHIBIT 7   SALVE
(Systéme d'Aide à la Vente)
Negotiation Support System

Main Functions:
- Negotiation Support and Price Simulation
- Configuration of Products and Services Offered
- Price Calculations
- Preparation of Final Offers
- Real-Time Booking of Contracts
- Amendment to Existing Contracts
- Transfer of Orders to the Factories

Key Objectives:
- To Improve the Quality of Offers
  - Reliability (Feasibility, Zero Defects)
  - Speed (Reduced Delay)
  - Quality of Presentation
  - To Provide Sales Representatives with a User-Friendly and Flexible Negotiation Support Tool

Primary Users:
- Sales Representatives
- Secretaries/Assistants
- Field Superintendent
- Field Supervisor
- Sales Directors/Marketing
- Branch Managers

Source: Company Document.

The new IT architecture (see Exhibit 12) implies the development of systems for business functions (e.g., negotiation), compared to the previous systems, which were targeted toward specific activities such as repairs or sales. "SALVE, for instance," explains Jean-Claude Casari,[5] "is a system that offers capabilities for negotiation management up to the booking stage. It is the same system for new equipment or service sales. That was a big change compared to the old system where we managed operations by activity. For new sales, we had one type, and for repairs, we had another type of management. So we never had a global view of what we did per unit [elevator]." Pierre Amar goes on, "This choice was driven by our objective to get systems independent from organization. The previous architecture required a specialized sales organization for New Equipment and Modernization or Maintenance. The new one allows a high level of flexibility. A salesman can receive a mixed portfolio of whatever activity. Access to the related system functions is achieved through workstation customization."

For 1992, three additional accounting systems are planned to allow the full integration of the systems developed based on the Master Plan. These IT applications include SYGECO, a system handling accounts receivable, an accounting system managing accounts payable as well as an accounting and cost analysis system. Finally, a service management system, counterpart of SAGA for maintenance activity, will be developed.

---

[5]At Otis France until June 1991; now Strategic Planning Manager at Otis ETO headquarters.

SAGA
(Systéme d'Aide à la Gestion des Affaires)
Contract Management System

Main Functions:
- Support for Contract Management with Regard to
  - Relations with the Factories
  - Planning and Scheduling
  - Costs per Contract
  - Contract Financial Completion

Key Objectives:
- To Realize Contract Confirmations in Response to Customer Inquiries with Concern for
  - Planning
  - Efficient Contract Handling (Goal: Margin Completed versus Margin Booked)
  - Efficiency and Productivity (Number of Hours Used to Complete the Contract)

Primary Users:
- Field Superintendent
- Field Supervisor
- Control Department
- Audits

Source: Company Document.

STAR
(Système de Traitement des Achats en Région)
Purchasing and Supplier Management System

Main Functions:
- Management of Suppliers
- Purchase Orders Processing
- Invoice Validation and Processing
- Cash Management of the Local Branches

Key Objectives:
- Initiate (Regularly) Payments
- Manage all Contracts in Coordination with SAGA
- Ascertain Flexibility, Decentralization, and Control of Administrative Tasks

Primary Users:
- Purchasers in Local Districts
- Secretaries/Assistants

Source: Company Document.

SAFRAN N,S,K,*
(Système d'Aide à la Facturation en Région)
Invoice and Billing System for New Equipment in New and Existing Buildings as Well as Modernization

Main Functions:
- Invoicing Data
- Calculation and Printing of Invoices
- Credit Notes
- Bonds Management

Key Objectives:
- To Optimize Cost in Process Coverage
- To propose a Flexible Organization of Invoicing Procedures (Standardize Billing Rules)
- To Customize Invoices to Customer Needs

Primary Users:
- Accountants
- Employees in Charge of Invoicing
- Assistants/Secretaries
- Financial Director (Validation)

Source: Company Document.

*N = New Equipment in New Buildings
K = New Equipment in Existing Buildings
S = Modernization

SAFRAN O*
(Système d'Aide à la Facturation en Région)
Invoice and Billing System for Maintenance

Main Functions:
- Invoicing Data
- Automatic Quarterly Preparation of Maintenance Invoices
- Support Correction of Wrong Invoices
- Price Increases

Key Objectives:
- Increase Productivity
- Correct Invoice for the Maintenance

Primary Users:
- Accountants
- Employees in Charge of Invoicing
- Financial Director (Validation)
- Branch Manager Assistants

Source: Company Document.

*O = Maintenance

Activities and Readings in Information Systems

EXHIBIT 12 — Otis France Information Systems 1991

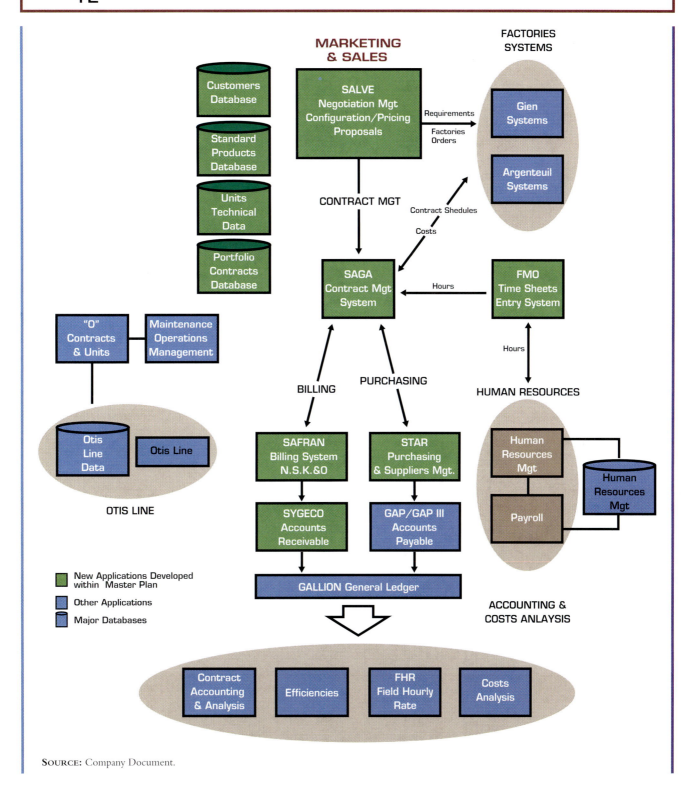

SOURCE: Company Document.

SALVE is the first system that was implemented; it served as a basis for the other applications that were developed later on. Giving the salesperson the authority and responsibility to set a price required implementing some control mechanisms.

The first consists of having built in the system a "plus/minus x percent" margin within which a price can be set. The second mechanism is basing the salesperson's premium on his/her sales performance (incentive).

From the salesforce's perspective, the major benefit of SALVE is the drastic reduction of lead time. The processing time from having a signed customer order to forwarding the material form to the factory was reduced from one month to 48 hours. In addition, the salesperson is in a stronger bargaining position with the customers since he/she has, through SALVE, a complete record of previous negotiations/contracts with each customer.

From a management perspective, SALVE offers two main advantages. First, orders get to the factory faster. Second, unlike in the past, when too many customized units were sold, there are now more sales of standard products because the salesperson could "bring" the customer to the product line.

At the beginning, the implementation of SALVE caused significant problems. There was major resistance to change by the salesforce, which had never been exposed to computers before. This necessitated a strong educational commitment and the need "not to change the tool and the process at the same time." In spite of the misfit caused by this situation, the company did not want to implement both changes simultaneously; "Otherwise," as Pierre Amar put it, "people [would have been] completely lost. We [Otis] found that adapting to a computer terminal is always a burden for people."

Before the introduction of SALVE, salespeople played the role of a "mail box," letting staff members in the corporate headquarters execute most tasks (e.g., determining prices for units, contract processing, etc.) for them. With SALVE they are able to, and they are also responsible for processing all such tasks themselves in the field. Of course, in the beginning, that appeared to them to mean a significant increase in their workload.

Management had expected that, once SALVE was in place, the salesforce would have more time to spend in the field meeting customers. However, experience proved the opposite: salespeople spent a lot of time in front of the computer screen. This turned out to be a major concern for customers as well, who did not want to pay somebody for operating a computer. (After one year SALVE became much more user friendly and salesmen reduced time spent on the keyboard.)

In spite of the Master Plan's goal of developing a common database throughout the company for the new IT applications, it was never intended to integrate the OTISLINE database with those of the internally oriented applications. Christian Madrus de Mingrelie, Organization Manager, explains the situation: "The two databases have to be meaningfully connected, but there will always be two databases."

Organizational Changes

The step-by-step implementation of the Master Plan's applications also resulted in a number of organizational changes in the company headquarters as well as in the field. Dominique André, Manager of the "West France" Zone, thinks that "the organizational changes were expected in advance, but not formally planned."

The main goal and the actual achievement of the Master Plan was "decentralization through centralization." The main areas of decentralization were data entry, invoicing, pricing, and booking. Consequently, the introduction of each new application was followed by changes in the human resources allocation. Although nobody was laid off, as the company proudly states, the number of headquarters employees has been reduced by about 20% since the launch of the project in 1986.

> For me as an outsider within the company,[6] the main idea of the Master Plan was decentralization. Once we had decided to give more responsibility to the people working in the region, we had to give them the tools to cope with that. And then, after they had more responsibility, we [in the headquarters] wanted to know what the salespeople did every day. Therefore, we needed to introduce control mechanisms.
>
> Tibor Gyoengyoesi
Marketing Studies Manager

Control as an inevitable consequence of increased autonomy and responsibility is also crucial from the financial department's point of view.

> You see that we give more autonomy to the salesman and thus dramatically improve our response time. On the other hand, we have also a dramatic control problem. Salesmen can cheat, purposefully violate the control rules. We realized that we had to be tougher regarding the control issue and created a new Audit Department.
>
> Charles Vo
Financial Manager

THE MASTER PLAN IN RETROSPECTIVE

The systems resulting from the Master Plan enable Otis to benefit from:

1. A major decentralization of responsibility resulting in reduced administrative overheads. Previously, all orders had to be verified at corporate headquarters in Paris (to assure that the requested elevator configuration is viable and the price is within the defined limits) prior to making an offer to the customer. With the new systems in place, because the computer system can perform all the necessary checks, the routing through Paris is no longer needed. Furthermore, the company benefits from the improved accuracy.
2. A drastic reduction of the order processing time (i.e., from the time a customer places an order until it is forwarded to the factory) from 1 month to 48 hours. This has significantly improved responsiveness and customer service.
3. Better management reports containing information on elevators sold or maintained, contracts finalized, or troublesome units. "For example," says Dominique André, "we now receive the bookings per branch every day; it used to be once a month with two weeks delay."
4. A complete flexibility enabling salesmen to prepare all types of affairs with an unlimited number of options and alternatives.

Dominique goes on listing decentralization, quality, and productivity as the major benefits of the Master Plan. He added: "Our situation is easy to understand: We are number one in the French market, both in New Equipment and Service, with more than 35% market share. All our competitors try to reduce our part of the elevator cake. It is a daily challenge to keep our maintenance contracts. For a strong market leader with a service that can be easily imitated the first strategic objective is to keep the number one position and market share. The Master Plan helped to reach this objective. As a next step we will try to improve it."[7]

Dominique goes on reflecting on the SALVE system, "Although, in the beginning, we had huge problems with the new applications, especially with SALVE, we would definitely do it again like that. Immediately after the introduction of SALVE, there was some resistance, but now [in 1991] even the sales representatives would not want to live without the system. They ask for more." "In any case," says Bruno Grob, "we feel comfortable with what we have done, since we know that our competitors now are trying to do the same thing as we did."

---

[6]Tibor Gyoengyoesi has been working for Otis France since, but was not directly involved in, the project.

[7]In this context, Dominique agreed that the results of the Master Plan were more a competitive necessity than a competitive advantage.

Regarding the other Otis subsidiaries in Europe, Bruno Grob adds:

> Yes, they all want to come to France and even though our Master Plan is not perfect, everyone wants to use it.

Nevertheless, the Master Plan is by no means viewed as perfect. Drawbacks and future threats are also recognized at different management levels. They include the lack of training, the time-consuming data input, and the reduced time that sales representatives have to be in the field.

Dominique elaborates on the latter point: "The biggest problem is the time that productive people have to spend in front of the computer. We want our sales representatives to be face to face with our customers, and SALVE is one obstacle to that."

Moreover, management is aware of the risk that a sales representative can leave the company and start his/her own business.

Management realizes the threat that competitors can easily imitate Otis products or service. There is the example of Servitel, a service offered by Schindler with similar capabilities as OTISLINE. Or, as reported in a business article, ". . . one competitor in the elevator industry copied the other's move to centralize service records. But the copycat company went a step further: it identified elevators that chronically failed, then approached the clients with proposals to rebuild those units. The innovator had [in 1987], at least temporarily, a whole new market to itself."[8]

In November 1991, four months after joining Otis, Christian Madrus de Mingrelie thinks that "user-friendliness, simplicity, and flexibility" are the three main areas needing further improvement. Bruno Grob took a different perspective when he commented on the future success of the systems and of the company as a whole by saying: "The major threat in the future comes from the Japanese companies. They have the ultimate in management, they all have the same goal, and that will finally outweigh the strengths of any information system."

SOME PERSPECTIVES FOR THE FUTURE

- **Zero callbacks as a new slogan for Otis**—A new USP (Unique Selling Point) or just an empty promise? Pierre Istace thinks that "zero callbacks are not yet expected by the customer. Would such a slogan raise expectations to a level that could not be guaranteed? Or would it be the best pre-emptive measure against the threat of Japanese companies entering the French market? Japanese companies, most likely, would base their marketing on such a slogan."

- **More flexible systems** to fulfill the needs of different units within the company—Such a development could also serve as a basis for a Pan-European system, which requires a high degree of flexibility. "We have to become more flexible," says Christian Madrus de Mingrelie. "We need subsystems for the different requirements of the regions where we have similar functional, but different physical, processes. Just look at the Paris area and the small local branches in the field. . . . And then we need to work on the interfaces between the different subsystems."

- **Shortened Cycle Time**—The optimal goal for the internal procedures is to shorten the "flow" path of a contract through the different business processes. "Two main steps are to be accomplished in order to pursue that goal," says Charles Vo. "Strict benchmarks will have to be introduced with the intention to save time in each process separately. Secondly, the integration of the different processes and systems within the headquarters and between the headquarters and the regions will have to be optimized."

---

[8]Burns, W. J. and McFarlan, F. W. "Information Technology puts power into control systems," in *Harvard Business Review,* September–October 1987, pp. 89–94.

European Integration—The goal is a common, standardized maintenance contract. One of the obstacles of this difficult project, which is "not yet very advanced," as Pierre Istace put it, is the variety of technical environments which are in place in different countries and the resulting problem of portability. "So far, a first agreement has been achieved on the programming language (NATURAL) and the database system (ADABASE) to be used," says Christian Madrus de Mingrelie. Other problems regarding standardizing the European maintenance contract stem from the diversity of legal frameworks (e.g., accounting procedures) and the different ways of doing business in various European countries.

THE END . . .

In the fall of 1991, about six months before the launch of the last system that resulted from the Master Plan, Bruno Grob, sitting in his office at the top floor of the new headquarters, was assessing the current corporate situation. He was not only pleased that the company was still market leader, but also that the investment in IT seemed to have paid off. He recognized that the use of IT had certainly played an important role in gaining and keeping Otis's position in the market. But had the investment in IT resulted in a sustainable competitive advantage? When pondering this critical question, he remembered a comment made previously by one of his subordinates:

> I think we have to look again, now that we have finished implementing the IT applications, how to simplify the organization. Of course, we have changed, but in my mind we have not changed enough. When you implement systems step by step, for instance in some applications we are still using the old system because we have not replaced it with a new application, we are obliged to design an organization that is not completely ideal. So the next step is to look again at the processes in the branches, to see again how to simplify, then to take advantage of our good on-line system. I have just (in 1990) hired some people to work on that. It's a never-ending process.
>
> Jean-Claude Casari

STEP 1: Read the Otis Elevator case. (This activity is especially suited for use in conjunction with Chapter 12 of *Information Systems*.)

STEP 2: Prepare the case for class discussion.

STEP 3: Answer each of the following questions, individually or in small groups, as directed by your instructor.

Diagnosis

1. What information needs did Otis's salespeople have? What information needs did Otis's customers have?
2. Why did Otis France develop an Information Technology master plan?
3. What strategy or strategies did Otis pursue?

Evaluation

4. How well did the OTISLINE, Customer Database, and REM systems meet Otis's strategic needs?
5. What deficiencies existed in Otis's information systems?

Design

6. What advantages did SALVE offer?
7. How did SALVE fit with Otis's strategy?
8. How did the other new IT applications (SAGA, STAR, and SAFRAN-N,S,K) fit with SALVE and with Otis's strategy?

Implementation

9. What problems did Otis's managers have to overcome to implement SALVE?
10. How effective was the implementation of SALVE?
11. What, if any, changes are still necessary?
12. Has the implementation of Otis's IT master plan provided a sustainable competitive advantage?

STEP 4: In small groups, with the entire class, or in written form, share your answers to the questions above. Then answer the following questions:

1. What strategy or strategies did Otis pursue?
2. What information needs did Otis have? How do these needs relate to Otis's strategy?
3. How well did Otis's information systems reflect its strategy and meet its information needs?
4. What factors influenced the implementation of Otis's information systems?
5. What changes are still necessary for Otis to accomplish its strategic objectives?

Activity 20: DMV

STEP 1: Read the DMV case. (This activity is especially suited for use in conjunction with Chapter 13 of *Information Systems*.)

"Why can't we go back to our old system? At least we know it works! Maybe it can get us out of this mess." Bill Maloney, the state's attorney general, was on the phone with Mark Bridger. Bridger, the director of the Department of Motor Vehicles (DMV), was doing his best to cope with a crisis that was becoming worse by the hour.

Two months earlier, the state began using a new data processing system designed to streamline operations at the DMV. Although the cutover—direct conversion—to the new system was without incident, problems began to mount soon after the system was placed in operation.

Now the system was unable to cope with the workload. More than a million drivers had been unable to register their cars. To make the situation even worse, many of those who registered their cars after the system went into operation were incorrectly listed in the database as operating unregistered vehicles. And renewal notices—issued automatically by the new computer system—had been sent to the wrong drivers. In fact, so many drivers had been forced to drive without a registration that the attorney general, Bill Maloney, had ordered the state police to cease citing drivers for this offense. No one, it seemed, had been spared: Even some of the vehicles operated by public works departments and local police forces throughout the state were registered to the wrong municipalities!

BACKGROUND

When the system was first conceived, a little over three years ago, the DMV expressed a need for a more up-to-date information-processing system than the ten-year-old system it was using. The DMV especially needed a system with a strong DBMS, to have more flexibility in accessing data and in making changes in the application software. Its current system used a conventional file-management approach.

In addition to performing all of the routine record-keeping functions such as maintaining automobile registration data, the DMV wanted the new system to automatically notify the state's five million drivers of license and registration renewals. It also wanted the system to be capable of allowing updates of the state's rating surcharge database to be made on a daily basis. This surcharge database keeps track of violation points against individual drivers and is used to penalize bad drivers by making them pay higher insurance rates. Under the old system, this database was updated periodically, but it was not unusual—due to inefficient update procedures—for the driver's record to be updated as much as three or four months after the conviction took place.

POLITICAL FACTORS

When the idea for a new computer system was originally suggested to the governor, he agreed that an effort such as this was long overdue. But he was not pleased to hear that it would take five years to develop and bring the project into full operation. It is alleged that

SOURCE: Selection from *Cases in Computer Information Systems* 'Yarmouth Inc.,' pp. 175–176 by B. Shore and J. Ralya, copyright © 1988 by Holt, Rinehart Winston, Inc., reprinted by permission of the publisher.

he then asked DMV director Bridger to find a consulting firm to develop the system in two years so that the completed system would be finished in time to be used during his reelection campaign as an example of his administration's accomplishments.

THE CONSULTANTS

Shortly after the governor's alleged request to expedite the development of the system, Bridger met with the information services division of Driscol and Russell, one of the country's leading public accounting firms. After studying the project's objectives, the manager of this division, Mike Price, suggested that the only way it could be completed in two years would be to use a fourth-generation language.

"We will still use a structured approach and build the system in modules," explained Price, "but the 4GL will save us a lot of time in programming, debugging, and testing the project."

Bridger was impressed with Price's confidence in his firm's ability to deliver the needed software and, above all, to deliver it on time. Within three months a $6.5 million contract was signed with Driscol and Russell.

The software development process went smoothly for the DMV. The senior systems analyst for Driscol and Russell spent six weeks at the DMV, during which time he learned about the current system and the characteristics of the new one. Once the systems analysis was complete and a preliminary plan approved, Driscol and Russell had few interactions with the DMV. According to the senior systems analyst at Driscol and Russell, the DMV preferred it this way, as the DMV was already overburdened with day-to-day problems.

THE SYSTEM FAILS

The system was delivered right on schedule, and during the first few weeks, as the workload on the new system increased, it seemed to perform well. Data entry was made from on-line terminals, and users found the system efficient. As might be expected at the start, those who used the system complained a little about the new procedures, but no serious problems emerged.

But as more and more new tasks were added to the system, the operators began to report an increase in response time. When the system was finally in full operation, the response time became intolerable. At best, response times were in the five-to-eight second range and frequently took as long as one to two minutes. The original contract specified that response times were to be no longer than three to five seconds.

An increase in response time, however, was just the tip of the iceberg. First, it was not possible to process all of the jobs on the new system. Even an increase to a 24-hour operation was insufficient to update the database. Within a few months, the backlog grew to such proportions that 1.4 million automobile registrations had not been processed. Meanwhile, when police stopped cars that did not have valid registrations, the drivers were arrested. As the protest from drivers began to mount, the attorney general's office stepped in and ordered the police to stop making arrests for invalid registrations.

Then an even more dramatic problem surfaced. It slowly became apparent that the database was contaminated with bad data, that the automobile registrations listed the wrong owners.

STATE DEPARTMENT OF DATA PROCESSING

With the system in total chaos, the DMV director and the attorney general decided to call in Gail Hendrix, the director of the state department of data processing. Hendrix had known about this project since its inception, when she had been appalled not only that her department had been frozen out of the development process but that the bid had apparently gone to a company without the usual competitive bidding process.

Hendrix was not surprised at the DMV's problems. During her first meeting with Bridger and Maloney, she shed some light on the sources of the problem. "I can't understand why Driscol and Russell used PROWRITE. Everyone knew it was a new 4GL, that it had lots of bugs to be worked out, and that no one had really tested it on a large project yet. Not only that, but PROWRITE was developed to run smaller MIS jobs. I don't think it was even meant to run transaction jobs where the system must handle several transactions per second."

Bridger asked, "How would you have developed the system?"

Hendrix replied, "I think COBOL should have been used for those modules that did the heavy processing. Then a 4GL, but not PROWRITE, could have been used for some of the other modules, especially the report-writing ones."

FINDING A SOLUTION

At the meeting with Hendrix and Bridger, Maloney insisted that they come up with a solution. "We've got our motor vehicle system in a shambles. To solve the problem tomorrow is even too late. What are we going to do?"

Bridger was in favor of holding a meeting with Driscol and Russell to determine what they could do to straighten out the situation. "Perhaps they could rewrite some of the transaction modules in COBOL, as Hendrix suggested."

Hendrix felt differently. "They've lost their credibility with me. I think we should write this software off as a complete loss and begin the development of a new system here in our own DP organization."

Maloney, however, was certainly not satisfied. "Look, why can't we bring our old system back into operation? At least we'll get the public and the politicians off our back."

"Bill, you asked me that on the phone last week, and I told you that it would take months to get the old software running again," replied Bridger. "And besides, we developed this new system to solve problems that our old software couldn't. I don't think yours is a reasonable solution."

STEP 2: Prepare the case for class discussion.

STEP 3: Answer each of the following questions, individually or in small groups, as directed by your instructor.

Diagnosis
1. What information needs did the DMV have?

Evaluation
2. How well did the old system meet these needs?

Design
3. What advantages did the new system offer?
4. What problems existed with the new system?

Implementation
5. Why did the system fail?
6. Can the DMV return to the old system?
7. How effectively did system development occur?
8. What should happen now?

STEP 4: In small groups, with the entire class, or in written form, share your answers to the questions above. Then answer the following questions:

1. What information needs did the DMV have?
2. How did it attempt to meet this need?
3. How effective was the resulting system?
4. How did the development of the system affect its performance?
5. What should the DMV do now?

Activity 21: A Case Study of Participative Systems Development

STEP 1: Read the following case. (This activity is especially suited for use in conjunction with Chapter 13 of *Information Systems*.)

BACKGROUND: THE REQUIREMENTS DATA BANK (RDB)

The Air Force Logistics Command's (AFLC) primary mission is to ensure that materiel resources are available to support Air Force weapons systems. This mission greatly depends on the AFLC Materiel Requirements Planning (MRP) process, which involves forecasting the acquisition and repair requirements of approximately 900,000 spares, repair parts, and equipment items worth nearly $28 billion (BDM 1986). This forecasting process involves predicting approximately $15–17 billion annually for acquiring and maintaining these items (Air Force 1982).

Beginning in the mid-1970s, the Air Force MRP process was criticized as inefficient. Specifically, in managing MRP tasks, the AFLC used 22 different data systems, and because these systems were developed in the 1950s and 1960s, they were antiquated. To meet logistics objectives, AFLC realized it had to improve the existing MRP process. To develop and implement these improvements, the Air Force undertook the Requirements Data Bank (RDB) (Air Force 1982)—a major MIS development project (which is still in progress).

A cadre of top functional people were identified and removed from day-to-day management activities to identify the requirements for the RDB. The result was a seven-year planning effort that culminated in the publication of a master functional description (MFD) for the RDB. The MFD was a general document that contained RDB goals and broke down development into several modules that could be developed relatively independently.

After thoroughly staffing the MFD, AFLC to management decided to develop a statement of work to solicit bids from professional services contractors to develop the RDB rather than attempt to develop it in-house. The statement called for each bidder to propose the best computer and functional architecture to meet MFD needs and for the selected contractor to submit specific functional descriptions for each MFD module. A later section of this paper discusses the practicality of this provision and the actual process of developing the specific module functional descriptions (FDs).

Bids were received from several contractors and a "fly-off" between the to two contractors was called for to verify that the contractors could deliver their proposed designs. aS a result, a contractor was selected to develop the RDB, AFLC funded the ten-year development, and development begain in January 1985 (BDM 1986).

The RDB has involved an enormous development effort. When completed, it will handle both the automated and manual areas involved in the AFLC MRP, developing nearly 3.7 million lines of code to replace the primarily batch-oriented 22 main data systems. It will involve over 5,600 users throughout the United States and will cost nearly $300 million to develop and operate over the next ten years (Air Force 1982).

SOURCE: Robert S. Tripp, "Managing the political and cultural aspects of large-scale MIS projects. A Case Study of Participative Systems Development." *Information Resources Management Journal* (Fall 1991): 2–13. Copyright 1991 by Idea Group Publishing.

THE RDB PROJECT MANAGEMENT ORGANIZATION

The main problem in managing the contractual development of such a large MIS involved bringing together three diverse cultures—users, in-house systems analysts, and contractor systems developers. Because users know little about MIS technology and in-house and contractor MIS professionals know little about functional processes, the project called for some means of coordinating these groups. To meet this challenge, AFLC established an RDB project management organization (PMO).

As indicated in the organizational chart shown in Figure 1, AFLC acknowledged the importance of information as a management resource by creating a headquarters organization to manage it—AFLC Director of Information Systems and Communications—and by placing this activity on the same level as the functional staff. The AFLC Chief Information Officer (CIO) holds the same rank and follows the same reporting channel to the AFLC Command Section as his functional counterparts.

As shown in Figure 1, the CIO has both line and staff functions reporting to him. To manage both functions, the CIO is "dual hatted"—he holds a headquarters staff position and controls a line organization simultaneously.

The CIO's staff functions include planning for future MIS directions and developments; obtaining the resources necessary to design, develop, operate, and maintain all AFLCMIS; establishing software and hardware architectural standards; developing database, application software, and hardware integration policies to coordinate major MIS developments; and producing contracts for MIS developments and hardware acquisitions. Because AFLC has several large, geographically dispersed operating sites, CIO staff responsibilities included providing MIS operating policy and guidance to each of the Chief Information Managers (CIMs), who report to the decentralized site commander and not to the CIO.

The CIO's line functions include managing and controlling the design, development, operations, and maintenance of all MIS to be used at each site. To accomplish these functions, the CIO has a separate organization that reports to him, as indicated in Figure 1. The line organization consists of several divisions that have a number of PMOs reporting to these divisions. The PMOs are responsible for major MIS developments. Another major part of the line organization is the unit responsible for current MIS operations at the AFLC's headquarters site.

The RDB is one of several MIS being developed for the Director of Materiel Management. This division is appropriately called the Materiel Management Systems Division. Five of these major divisions report to the CIO, which is responsible for developing the five major systems, with a total development cost of more than $800 million. Of these, the RDB is the largest and most important to AFLC.

The Project Manager and the User Representative

The RDB PMO, a variant of the "shared responsibilities" project team suggested by Synnott and Gruber (1981), was structured primarily to promote user participation in the project. The primary difference between the RDB PMO and "shared responsibilities" model is that the senior user representative reports directly to his functional line manager instead of to the project manager. The chief user representative is a senior functional manager with the same corporate rank as the RDB project manager. This arrangement is intended to foster strong user commitment and support during the development. The functional specialists, who work directly for the chief user representative, are assigned from the headquarters, but have the authority to "order" functional specialists in each area from AFLC operational sites to development sites when necessary.

Under this arrangement, the project manager is responsible for all aspects of the project, including costs and schedules, while the user representative is responsible for making sure

FIGURE 1 RDB Project Management Organization (PMO)

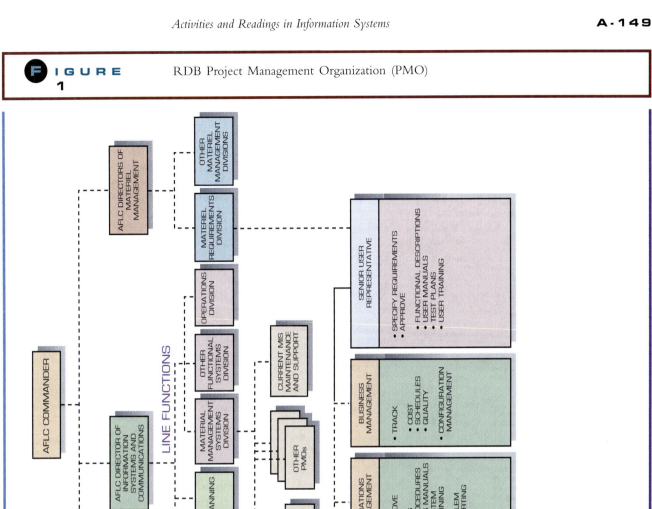

the system meets user needs. This organization demands that the project manager and user representative agree on costs, schedules, and capabilities. Under the Synnott and Gruber arrangement, the senior user would report directly to the project manager and have his effectiveness rating reviewed by the functional line manager. This approach aims to increase the user's cost and schedule commitment. The primary strength of the RDB approach is to make sure user views are considered in all aspects of project development. Control of the requirements baseline under the RDB approach must be given priority attention by the project manager. The senior user must also support stability of requirements specification.

As indicated in Figure 1, the RDB Project Manager reports to the Materiel Management Systems Division manager, while the senior user representative reports directly to a functional line manager with a rank and organizational level equal to the Materiel Management Systems Division manager. This arrangement allowed the RDB Project Manager to report to the same level of corporate management as the senior user representative, ensuring that user needs were balanced with cost and schedule considerations.

The selection of the project manager, senior user representative, and key members of their staffs in this organizational structure was very important, because the project manager and his team must be respected by the user representatives and vice versa. In the first four years of the RDB development, there were two project managers and two senior user representatives. In each "replacement," the project manager and senior user representative were screened for selection by both the AFLC's Chief Information Office (CIO) and senior functional manager to ensure that the project manager and senior user representative would work together to accomplish the RDB goals. In addition, both knew they would eventually move to functional positions that relied on the RDB, knowledge that increased their commitment to the project.

Most of the PMO and user representatives have remained with the project, and AFLC senior management plans to keep the attrition of team members to a very low level. On the other hand, the project manager and senior user representative positions will probably continue to be "stepping stones" for the growth of senior managers within AFLC. This set-up emphasizes the importance of having an RDB background credential for up-and-coming senior management prospects, thus encouraging the best functional people to serve in the development.

The Procurement Contracting Officer

As indicated in Figure 1, after program manager approval for actions, the Air Force procurement contracting officer (PCO) provided all directions to the development contractor. The PCO has the actual directive authority to enforce or change the provisions of the development contract. Like the senior user representative, the PCO does not work directly for the program manager but for a centralized procurement officer of the same rank as the project manager and the Materiel Management Systems Division manager. Because of a shortage of experienced PCOs within the contracting organization, the PCOs assigned to the RDB were usually junior people. As a result of this—but also because of the importance of the RDB to AFLC—major contracting decisions would frequently be deferred to the most senior contract management personnel. This arrangement placed an added burden on the project manager to communicate project needs to senior contract management people who were not involved in the day-to-day operations of the development to gain their support for needed contract changes.

From a project perspective, it would have been more efficient for the contracting representative to work directly for the project manager. In this way, the senior contracting officer could have reviewed and approved the contracting officer's effectiveness report. However, the reality here was that the contracting organization did not have enough experienced PCOs to support all PMOs in this manner. Since not all projects required a full-time PCO, AFLC's matrix approach ensured that PCOs were used efficiently and helped expedite routine contracting functions.

Structure of the RDB PMO

As shown in Figure 1, the RDB PMO consisted of three organizations that reported directly to the project manager. The Business Management Division of the PMO was responsible for monitoring development contractor costs, schedules, and quality of contractor-delivered products and for reporting significant deviations from planned performance in these areas. The Operations Management Division was responsible for approving contractor-proposed operations procedures, operations manuals, and training programs for Air Force operations personnel who would operate contractor-delivered software at the AFLC sites. This division was also responsible for coordinating AFLC site-preparation activities to accept hardware at each site selected by the development contractor for RDB operations. The Information Engineering Division was responsible for approving detailed software designs and associated documents produced by the development contractor.

In addition, the PMO structure included an independent verification and validation (IVV) contractor, who reviewed the development contractor's documentation and software products to ensure that high-quality products were delivered. The IVV contractor reviewed acceptance test plans and conducted independent tests of software for the PMO. The project manager was responsible for providing technical direction to the IVV and development contractors.

The organizational approach used to develop the RDB placed a substantial communications and coordination burden on the project manager and other members of the PMO team to obtain the cooperation of people beyond their direct control; as a result, they needed strong communication and persuasion skills. Senior management took this burden into account when selecting the project manager and other PMO senior members. Locating the user representatives and the PMO at the development contractor's facility facilitated communications between these groups. Moreover, to facilitate coordination, the RDB PCO also spent two or three days each week with the PMO.

PROJECT RESPONSIBILITIES DURING EACH PHASE OF DEVELOPMENT

Specific RDB project responsibilities during each phase in the development cycle closely resembled those suggested by Synnott and Gruber for MIS project organizations (1981). To make steady progress on the RDB development, all the organizations involved in the development had to understand their roles and responsibilities clearly. Figure 2 outlines the responsibilities of the development contractor, users, and in-house systems analysts in the various phases of the RDB development. The figure explains how the major responsibilities shifted in the group depending on the particular phase of the life cycle of the development.

The Requirements Definition Phase

In the Synnott and Gruber model, the user is directly responsible for developing the functional requirements and for writing the functional description. The RDB contract, however, assigned this responsibility to the development contractor, assuming that the selected—rather than in-house—people would best understand the AFLC MRP process. However, it soon became apparent that in-house senior people were better suited to articulating a clear vision of the RDB. As a result, the PMO and users jointly developed a concept of operations that functionally described the "new world" the RDB was expected to achieve and how it would change current operations. Once the concept of operations was specified, the user representatives wrote descriptions that revised their functional processes accordingly.

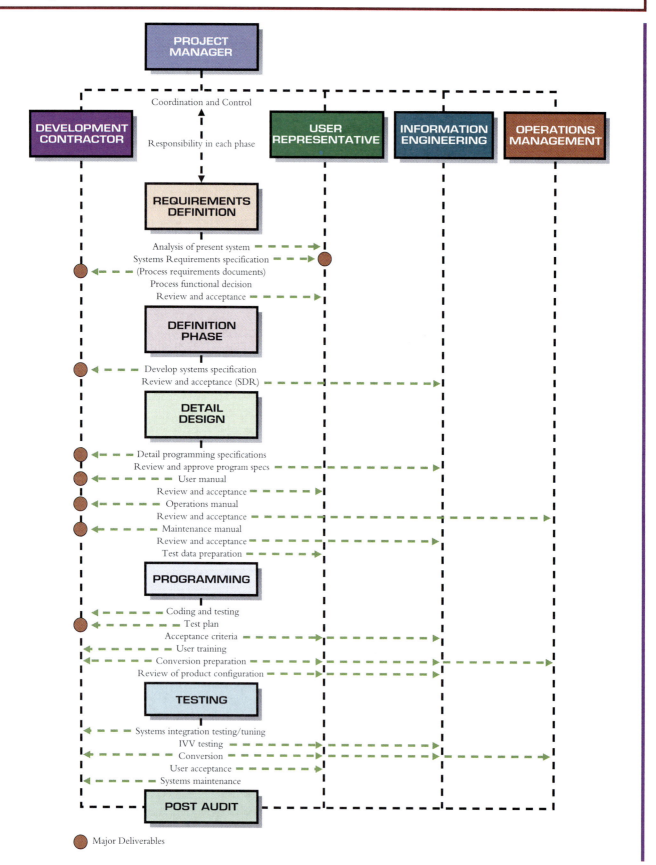

FIGURE 2 RDB Responsibilities by Stage in Project Life Cycle

These descriptions, called process requirements documents, were delivered to the contractor, who then refined these documents and issued process functional descriptions (PFDs) that defined the details for all requirements of the RDB's sixteen segments. These PFDs had to be consistent with the concept of operations and the process requirements documents. The portfolio of sixteen completed PFDs were large and complex. They included over 6,500 pages, describing more than 2,200 processes.

The PFDs, which took over two years to develop, spelled out the functional requirements and offered details of all the process activities. The extra steps involved in this process paid off—the development contractor understood the requirement more fully, often helping to write the PFDs.

Traditional wisdom suggests that only the user can specify requirements. While this may be the case, the cost and political pressure associated with a large MIS development contract probably "forced" AFLC to specify the requirements sooner than would have been done without that pressure.

As indicated in Figure 2, the user organization has primary review and approval authority for the contractor-delivered PFDs. Formal mechanisms were established to provide direction to the contractor to correct deficiencies in the various documents and software products, as will be explained below.

The Definition Phase

The definition phase emphasizes how—rather than what—things are built in each RDB segment. The primary document in this phase was the systems specification. The primary responsibility for AFLC review and approval shifted from the users to the PMO systems analysts, who were housed in the Information Engineering Division.

The Detailed Design Phase

As the design for each segment progressed into detailed design, the contractor was required to submit several documents for review and approval before the next phase of development could proceed. The primary document during this phase was the program specifications, although the contractor also had to deliver drafts of the user's manual. Figure 2 indicates which PMO organization had primary responsibility for review and approval of each document.

The Programming Phase

During this phase, the development contractor coded the segments. The AFLC maintained a basically "hands off" role, except to answer questions.

The Testing Phase

During the test phase, AFLC activity was intense to ensure that the product met its requirements. Because the PMO had established good working relations with the development contractor, AFLC and IVV contract personnel were allowed to observe the development contractor integration testing activities. This practice helped build confidence that the system was meeting its objectives. Also, if problems were spotted by AFLC personnel, the contractor test department could document the problems before official AFLC acceptance testing started. This process helped shorten the process for making software changes when they were needed. The IVV contractor played a key role in this phase, as did the user. The user led the testing activity and was assisted by the IVV contractor. If problems were uncovered, which they invariably were, the user prioritized the problems that required software modifications. Usually, the highest-priority changes were made as soon as possible, while lower-priority changes were scheduled for later releases of the software.

The Post Audit

Six months after official acceptance of a segment, the user population was sent questionnaires to determine the extent of user satisfaction with the system and to determine if the segments met the requirement. If serious problems were found, software modifications would be developed for release to users.

ESTABLISHING AND MAINTAINING CONTROL: IMPORTANCE OF CONFIGURATION MANAGEMENT

Establishing control over any MIS development requires configuration management procedures—procedures that specify how the team members go about approving or modifying the contractor documents or software products during the MIS development cycle.

As discussed above, AFLC team members reviewed each of the contract documents and software products. Figure 2 shows who had the primary responsibility for accepting specific products during each phase of the development. Initial deliveries of documents and software products always required some correction or modification. To control the configuration of these documents, the appropriate members of the AFLC PMO wrote Design Problem Reports (DPRs) or Software Problem Reports (SPRs). DPRs were written against functional descriptions, systems specifications, users' manuals, operation manuals, maintenance manuals, data base specifications, and any other written document before these documents were accepted. SPRs were written against software deliveries, primarily in the test phase of development, before acceptance. Baseline Change Requests (BCRs) and Data Base Change Requests (DBCRs) were written after acceptance of products to change their configuration.

Because sixteen major segments were developed in RDB, the processes in Figure 2 had to be traversed at least sixteen times. (Actually, some of the segments were broken into several modules, so the process was repeated many more times). Thus, at any given time, several documents or software products were in process, involving different phases of development for the sixteen segments. To maintain control, AFLC provided written instructions to the contractor, using the appropriate configuration management documents described above.

Automated configuration management reports were developed to indicate the status of each document and software product, including information on how many problem reports were outstanding on each product. Using these reports, the project manager could determine where to focus management attention. Thus, a strong configuration management organization was needed just to track documents and software products and to correctly assign the products for corrective comments or acceptance.

The Business Management Division of the PMO handled configuration management, and because of its importance, configuration management was given special emphasis by the project manager.

Figure 3 illustrates the procedures used to propose and process BCRs. The procedures for processing other change requests and problem reports were similar. Users, PMO members, or the development contractor could initiate a change request. Upon receiving a change request, configuration management people within the Business Management Division of the PMO assigned the request a number for tracking purposes and prepared a letter for the project manager to forward the request to the development contractor for evaluation. The PCO endorsed the letter to the contractor to "authenticate" the request for evaluation. The development contractor then routes the change request to all potentially affected departments. After affected departments evaluate the proposed change, the contractor consolidates all responses and prepares a configuration change directive with the appropriate cost and schedule impacts of the change clearly specified. The contractor submits the change directive to configuration management, which logs the response and submits the change directive for user, PMO, and PCO coordination. If the change directive is submitted by the contractor

FIGURE 3 Configuration Management

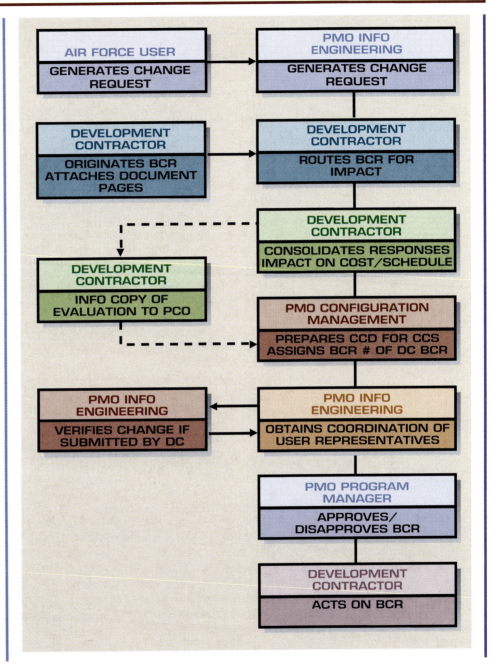

with no request from the AFLC team members, it receives a number and is routed to PMO and users for evaluation and approval. Finally, after the senior user representative has coordinated the change directive, it is approved or disapproved by the project manager. After the project manager's action, configuration management updates the BCR log and prepares a letter for the PCO to notify the contractor based on the outcome of the project manager's decision. The contractor then takes the appropriate action.

Although the procedures outlined above may seem bureaucratic, they are necessary to establish and maintain control in large-scale MIS developments. To be effective, users must support the process, the project manager must insist on following the procedures to the letter, and this discipline must be followed or control will be lost.

SOME LESSONS LEARNED

Initially, the roles and responsibilities of each group in the RDB development were not clearly defined (GAO 1986). The user representatives understood their role, but their perception of development goals differed from that of the development contractors. The users were accustomed to dealing informally with in-house developers, who traditionally pay little attention to the cost of information relative to its value. Users would request work through formal channels and the in-house developers would determine how many hours it would take to perform the work. If a conflict arose over resources, users and developers would sit down and prioritize the work to be done. In this environment, AFLC users had never been told that any job was impossible or beyond the project's scope. In short, the users had never worked in a formal, constrained environment where procedures were used to direct and modify MIS development efforts.

The development also faced a new situation. As mentioned earlier, the contractor was selected after prototypes of portions of two contractors' proposed designs were compared. (Several other contractors submitted proposals, but only two were selected to build design prototypes). During the prototype demonstrations, relations between AFLC personnel and the contractors were at arm's length. To prevent any possible favoritism to a single contractor, contractors received only information they specifically requested. Thus, normal customer relations were not established early in the program. As a result, the contractor developed the attitude—reinforced in the prototype competition—that there would be little feedback from users in the RDB development. This meant that contractors grew to feel their job was done when the product was delivered to the user. This attitude impaired necessary communications between users and development contractors. In a complex undertaking like the RDB, initial attempts to describe the system in any formal document are very likely to contain errors or inadequate descriptions that need modifications. In the early days of the RDB, the contractor was unprepared to engage in this dialogue in a controlled and disciplined manner.

PMO Coordination Failures

The initial RDB PMO was not prepared to coordinate these two groups or integrate their differing views of what was to be developed in the RDB. Disciplined configuration management procedures for directing and controlling the contractors' efforts were omitted, as were formal reviews for checking contractor progress at the critical design and development milestones. Too much informal dialogue between users and the contractor resulted in the contractor receiving conflicting and incomplete guidance. In addition, the PMO did not "preach" cost control or convince users that delays in decisions or incomplete disclosure of requirements lead to cost overruns and schedule slippages. Also, the PMO had former in-house systems people evaluating the proposed designs of the contractor. Some of these people resented having someone else work on a development they thought they should be doing. As a result, the contractor did not receive some information he needed to know.

Failing to control and manage these diverse cultures resulted in a large project with cost and schedule overruns projected barely six months after contract award. (The results of this failure have been documented [GAO 1986].) The root cause was a lack of understanding of roles and missions among the groups involved. As a result, a new PMO and senior contract staff were appointed to straighten out the situation.

Implementing Formal Procedures

Project management learned from initial problems and installed new leadership to correct them. The major task facing the new management team was to establish control over the project and clearly define the roles and responsibilities of each organization involved in the development. The new team explained the responsibilities of each group during the phases of development outlined above, emphasizing the importance of specifying requirements and minimizing changes, and implemented firm configuration management. The AFLC and contractor members of the design team were told flatly that contractor guidance must be in writing and must be approved by the project manager using appropriate configuration management procedures.

Users at first reacted negatively to these changes, expecting they would be criticized if several BCRs were written about their particular segment. When the project manager insisted upon implementation, he promised that no user representatives would be singled out for criticism based on number of BCRs. This promise induced the senior user representative to support the formal procedures.

Another problem about BCRs emerged. As indicated in the last section, each BCR had the schedule and cost to implement the change clearly identified on the bottom line. As a result, all PMO members became "independent cost estimators" and criticized the contractor estimates. Some of the criticisms were justified and were pursued through official channels. Most, however, resulted from failure to understand the full cost of changes. The project manager had to explain to PMO members that the contractor costs included not only direct costs for programming the changes but also charges for documentation changes and pro-rata charges for contractor overhead.

The RDB was the AFLC's first experience in contracting out MIS developments; as a result, users and in-house analysts had never seen the full cost associated with information system developments. (In-house resource requirements had shown only direct labor hours with changes.) To quell this uneasiness, functional people suggested that cost information be removed from the BCRs. The project manager vetoed this suggestion and insisted that the cost of each proposed change remain as the bottom line on the BCRs. He was supported by the senior user representative. Eventually, this problem disappeared, and users began to consider the value of the information versus the cost of the proposed change.

Figure 4 shows the cost of BCRs approved after the implementation of the procedures. After procedures to control informal talk were instituted, the number and cost of approved BCRs dropped dramatically, due in large part to the users' disapproving BCRs based on cost/benefit analyses before they reached the project manager for decision. While the costs of approved BCRs may appear to be large, they represent far less than 10 percent of the development costs during the periods shown. Figure 5 shows the cost of BCRs that users disapproved as a result of cost/benefit considerations during this period. As shown, users' cost considerations have introduced a good deal of restraint into the program. This form of self-control is the best form of discipline and is supported by all parties now.

CONCLUSIONS

Defining and controlling system requirements heavily depends on user attitudes and commitment to developing the system within the project's cost and schedule constraints. These user attitudes and this commitment can be directly affected and strengthened in turn by actions the project manager and corporate staff can take. This paper outlined some of those actions and pointed out that they are largely political and cultural in nature and, thus, should be managed accordingly.

Carefully selecting the lead user representative and organizationally placing user representatives in the MIS project team are key determinants of how successful the identification and

FIGURE 4 Costs of Approved Modification BCRs

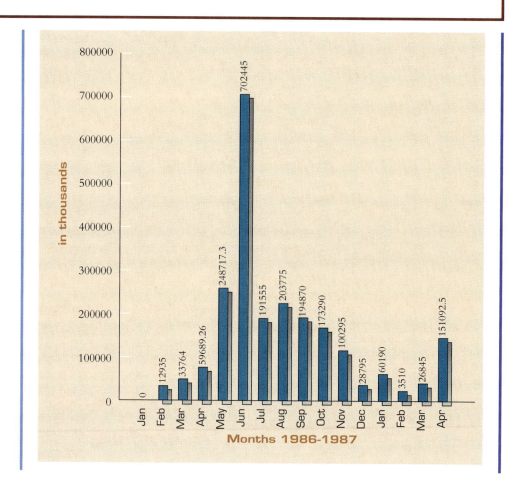

communication of requirements with the developer will be. Creating the proper organization and manning it with the right staff are political acts.

Once the requirements have been defined, user involvement in maintaining the requirements baseline is absolutely necessary. To make sure "requirements creep" is held to a minimum, the senior user must play a fundamental role in making sure the baseline is maintained. Specifically, he must be involved in the approval process during various steps in the design process and must participate in strict configuration management processes to review and approve all suggested changes before they are considered by the developer for cost and schedule effects. Making sure the requirement is maintained and not changed frequently is a cultural phenomenon that needs to be taught and nurtured.

References

Ahituv, Niv and Newmann, Seev (1984, June). A Flexible Approach to Information System Development. *MIS Quarterly,* 69–78.

Appleton, D. S. (1986, January 15). Very Large Projects. *Datamation,* 63–70.

BDM Corporation (1986). *The Air Force Requirements Data Bank Master Functional Description (MFD),* Revision B.

FIGURE 5   Costs of Disapproved BCRs

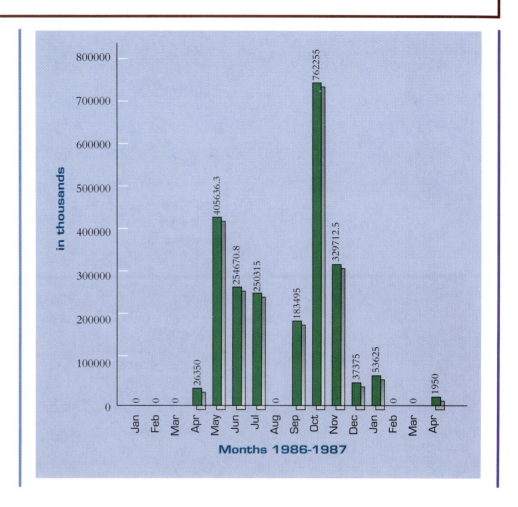

Doll, W. J. (1985, March). Avenues for Top Management Involvement in Successful MIS Development. *MIS Quarterly,* 17.

Hirscheim, R. A. (1985, December). User Experience With the Assessment of Participative Systems Design. *MIS Quarterly,* 295–304.

Juergens, Hugh F. (1977, June). Attributes of Information System Development. *MIS Quarterly,* 31–41.

King, William R. (1982). Alternative Designs in Information System Development. *MIS Quarterly,* 31–42.

Markus, M. L. (1983). Power, Politics, and MIS Implementation. *Communications of the ACM,* 26 (6), 430–444.

McFarlan, F. W. (1981). Portfolio Approach to Information Systems. *Harvard Business Review,* 59, 142–159.

Snow, Terry (1984). Use of Software Engineering Practices at a Small MIS Shop. *IEEE Transactions on Software Engineering,* SE-10 (4), 408–413.

Synnott, W. R. and Gruber, W. H. (1981). *Information Resource Management: Opportunities and Strategies for the 1980s.* New York: John Wiley and Sons.

Tait, P. and Vessey, L. (1988, March). The Effect of User Involvement on Systems Success: A Contingency Approach. *MIS Quarterly,* 91–108.

U.S. Department of the Air Force (HQ AFLC/LO[RDB]) (1982). *The Air Force Requirements Data Bank (RDB) Economic Analysis.* Wright-Patter AFB, OH.

U.S. General Accounting Office (GAO) (1986). Continued Oversight Crucial for Air Force's Requirements Data Bank. Report Number GAO/IMTEC-87-6. Washington, DC.

White, K. B. and Leifer, R. (1986, September). Information Systems Development Success: Perspectives from Project Team Participants. *MIS Quarterly,* 214–223.

Wong, Carolyn (1984). *A Successful Software Development. IEEE Transactions on Software Engineering,* SE-10 (6), 714–727.

STEP 2: Prepare the case for class discussion.

STEP 3: Answer each of the following questions, individually or in small groups, as directed by your instructor.

Diagnosis
1. What information needs did the Air Force have in the area of tracking materiel resources?
2. Why did the Air Force develop the RDB?

Evaluation
3. How well did existing systems meet the identified needs?

Design
4. What advantages did the proposed system offer?

Implementation
5. What steps in the SDLC did the Air Force follow?
6. What key decisions did they make in implementing such a large-scale MIS project?
7. What roles did the project manager, user representative, and procurement contracting officer play?
8. How were project responsibilities allocated during each phase of development?
9. How effective was project development?
10. What changes would you recommend if the Air Force implemented a similar MIS project?
11. What steps would comprise a quality development process for the Air Force?

STEP 4: In small groups, with the entire class, or in written form, share your answers to the questions above. Then answer the following questions:

1. What information needs did the Air Force have?
2. How did it attempt to meet these needs?
3. How effective were the resulting systems?
4. Did a quality systems development process exist?
5. What changes should be made in the development process?

Activity 22: It Won't Work in Kanji: The Case of Expert Systems Standardization at Global

STEP 1: Read the following case. (This activity is especially suited for use in conjunction with Chapter 14 of *Information Systems*.)

As Mr. Tanaka read Mr. Brown's memo, he could foresee many problems for Global Sekiyu's (GS's) Applications Development Group and for the company as a whole. The Applications Development Group, to which Tanaka belonged, was responsible for creating and maintaining computer programs to support GS's operations. The Group enjoyed a high level of success and status within GS and generally operated independently of GS's parent, Global Oil. Even so, GS often used software developed by Global, and vice versa. This strategy was possible because many software vendors produced products in both English and Kanji, the dominant Japanese language for business. Where this had not been the case, GS had developed programs on its own to meet its users' needs.

Brown's memo signaled a possible end to this happy state of affairs. Previously, Global Corporate had never exerted control over the application development of its subsidiaries. Now, Brown's memo asked GS to use a product called ADS for GS's Grease Project. As Brown and Tanaka both knew, ADS was not ideal from the Japanese perspective—it did not support Kanji on personal computers (PCs) and its vendor had no Japanese offices. However, the Grease Project was part of a larger effort that would involve Global Corporate and all its subsidiaries. For this reason, Global had insisted that all members of the "team" use a standard product. Global had selected ADS after an extensive evaluation procedure despite ADS's lack of Kanji support on the PC, despite the absence of other ADS customers and ADS vendor support in Japan, and despite the fact that GS had already begun its work on the Grease Project using a product called GURU, which supported Kanji. Tanaka had just completed an experiment to evaluate the difficulty of converting software from GURU to ADS and found that this took almost as much time as it had originally taken to develop the software from scratch!

Brown's memo had not taken Tanaka entirely by surprise. The Grease Project is an Expert Systems (ES) application (see Exhibit 1). Ever since the ES Subcommittee produced its enabling-strategy white-paper over a year and a half ago, Tanaka had foreseen the possibility that Global might issue ES standards that would be difficult for GS to endorse. As the ES Senior Supervisor, reporting directly to the Application Development Manager at GS, Tanaka had followed developments at Global, evaluated Global's policies as they related to GS, and given as much feedback to the Subcommittee as was diplomatically possible.

GLOBAL CORPORATION

Global Oil began in 1871 as Bearing Oil Company. Today, Global Oil Corporation is a large, integrated oil company that refines and sells petroleum products in over 100 countries. Global has centralized the management of its marketing, refining, and related operations at its headquarters in Virginia. The centralized Marketing and Refining Division (MRD) is divided into U.S. and international departments and is responsible for the foreign affiliates. Among the worldwide subsidiaries, Global Sekiyu is one of the strongest.

GS, founded in 1898, is a marketing and sales company. Although it owns no refineries, it does have partial shares in two, Keio Kabushiki Kaisha and Tohoku Petroleum Industries, Ltd. GS employs approximately 1,300 people in Japan, over 100 of whom are in the Information Systems (IS) department at the head office. Nearly half of the IS department are contractors from computer consulting companies.

Technical Note—Expert Systems

Introduction

An Expert System (ES) is a computer program that mimics the way a human expert in a given field uses his or her expertise to solve complex and ambiguous problems. To do this, the ES must first "capture" the knowledge and judgement that the expert has acquired through years of experience. Second, it must be able to generalize and reason from this experience to solve problems that are similar yet somewhat different from those that the expert has seen. Finally, it must be able to communicate its answer or decision in a way that laymen can understand and believe as if they were dealing with a human expert.

How Expert Systems Are Used

Human experts, in most fields, are in short supply. Typically, a person recognized as an expert has acquired his or her expertise through twenty or thirty years of experience beyond formal schooling. As their expertise peaks, such people tend to seek new challenges or perhaps to retire. As a result, at any time, the supply of experts in most companies is wanting.

The primary use of ES technology is to duplicate, rather than replace, an expert. An ES application, in effect, allows the expert to be in two places at once. For example, General Electric's DELTA helps maintenance personnel to find and repair problems with its diesel electric locomotives. Although all GE's repair people have been trained and are skilled, it takes many years for them to develop the experience that DELTA can provide. With DELTA, they have an expert immediately at hand to assist with problems that they cannot solve on their own. Similarly, medical ES applications assist physicians in making diagnoses and suggesting treatments, particularly at rural hospitals where specialists may be unavailable and time is critical. Legal ES applications advise lawyers in the formulation of trial strategies; financial ES applications assist traders and advisors in managing portfolios; manufacturing ES applications assist operations managers and designers in process control.

Occasionally, as with GS's Help Desk system, ES applications are used to replace an expert. The motivation for this is usually to reduce costs, although it often also improves service by increasing the availability of the expert. ES applications have also been built to capture the knowledge of an irreplaceable expert who is due to retire. Finally, ES applications have been built for the sole purpose of training novices.

How Expert Systems Are Built

Most ES applications start with an ES "shell." The shell is a computer program that knows how to reason, how to recognize patterns, and how to make judgements when given facts, rules-of-thumb, and representative situations; however, it lacks specific expertise, the facts, rules-of-thumb, etc., that are known to the human expert. It is normally equipped with a "knowledge engineer," along with a human expert, to train it in its intended expertise. Depending on the sophistication of the shell, it may also have the ability to learn from its own mistakes as it works side by side with the expert on the same problem. Finally, the ES shell has an "explanation module" which describes how the ES arrived at its decision. Therefore, the expert can determine where the ES thinking may have gone astray, and can train it to respond properly in the future. The explanation module is also important when the finished ES application is used to train novices and when it must convince a reticent human that its decision is reasonable.

The direct reporting relationship between GS and Global Oil is from Mr. Ozawa, President of GS, to Mr. Schiffman, Executive Vice-President of the MRD international division (see Exhibit 2). Although this relationship has the ultimate reporting responsibility, individuals within GS confer and report to their counterparts at Global Oil. Mr. Ozawa is the first Japanese to be the president of GS.

INFORMATION SYSTEMS

The IS department at GS communicates frequently with MRD via phone, video conferencing, and electronic mail. The electronic mail system spans all of Global's affiliates, allowing any Global employee to communicate with any other employee at any time despite time-zone differences. However, communication among divisions is primarily at the manager level or higher. GS guidelines state that company-related telecommunications must be approved by the IS director.

GS employees are rarely assigned to corporate headquarters for extended periods. Likewise, corporate employees are rarely transferred to GS. When employees are exchanged for project assignments, it is usually at the manager level or higher.

The Development and Technology Services (D&TS) is a division of the IS department. Its function is to develop and research new products and applications for use within GS. The Manager of D&TS, Mr. Kobayashi, has an MBA from a U.S. business school and has worked

Marketing and Refining Division—International

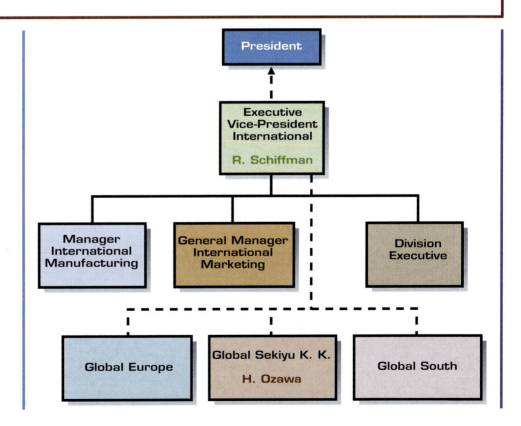

for several different departments within GS, as well as for other subsidiaries. He reports directly to the IS director (see Exhibit 3) and is responsible for everything that goes on in the division. Reporting to him is the Applications Development Manager, Mr. Matsui. Like Kobayashi, Matsui received an MBA from a U.S. business school, and has worked at many other divisions within GS. He supervises all development and research of new applications. Among the people he supervises is Tanaka, who also received an MBA from a U.S. business school and has worked in other divisions of GS. When Global decided to begin developing ES applications, Tanaka was selected to become GS's expert. He developed both ES applications currently in use at GS. The first application was for a computer help-desk, which allows users to find answers to their computer problems quickly and easily. The second, and larger, application is the Grease Project. When the project is completed, the Grease Expert System will allow engineers and salespeople to analyze customer problems and needs. Ultimately, it will be combined with a customer response center so that customers can call GS and get an immediate answer from the technician without having to wait for an engineer.

EXPERT SYSTEMS ENABLING STRATEGY

In early 1989, the steering committee for applications development at Global Corporate spun off an ES Subcommittee and charged it with the task of developing a strategy for enabling ES use within Global. The Subcommittee was composed primarily of managers from the Systems and Computer Services Group of the MRD. In June of 1989, the Subcommittee issued its report finding that

- ES technology had emerged as a valuable technique for providing cost-effective solutions to certain categories of business problems.
- The tools available for developing ES applications were evolving rapidly.
- Although Global's use of ES technology had been limited, various projects within Global and its subsidiaries confirmed the maturity and value of the technology. Five projects were cited.
- Competitors appeared to be increasingly active in ES; Global was behind and needed to accelerate its activity. The report cited statistics on staffing, etc., for 14 competitors.
- Many companies outside the oil industry had reported significant benefits of ES development. Nine well-known cases of strategic uses were summarized in the report.

The committee recommended a strategy of disbursing ES knowledge throughout the company while concurrently improving centralized support. To implement this strategy, specific changes were needed in the infrastructure supporting ES development. Among the recommendations was one to develop a guideline to "define a method for selecting the most appropriate (ES) tool for an identified application."

One section of the report was devoted to ES tool selection. It recommended that divisions with little or no experience in ES use one of several PC-based products to address small- to medium-sized problems. In addition, it recommended that an "interdivisional project be established to evaluate and recommend tools which can be used both on the mainframe and on the personal computer."

Tanaka had concurred wholeheartedly with the findings and recommendations of the report. At the time the white-paper was issued, Tanaka had just taken on the task of developing GS's first ES application. As part of this task, he had evaluated a variety of ES tools and settled on GURU, one of the products recommended in the white-paper, because of its support for Kanji and its support of image files (graphics). The development of this first system was highly successful and convinced Tanaka and others at GS that there was a greater role for ES in GS's future.

Exhibit 3: Information Systems at Global Sekiyu

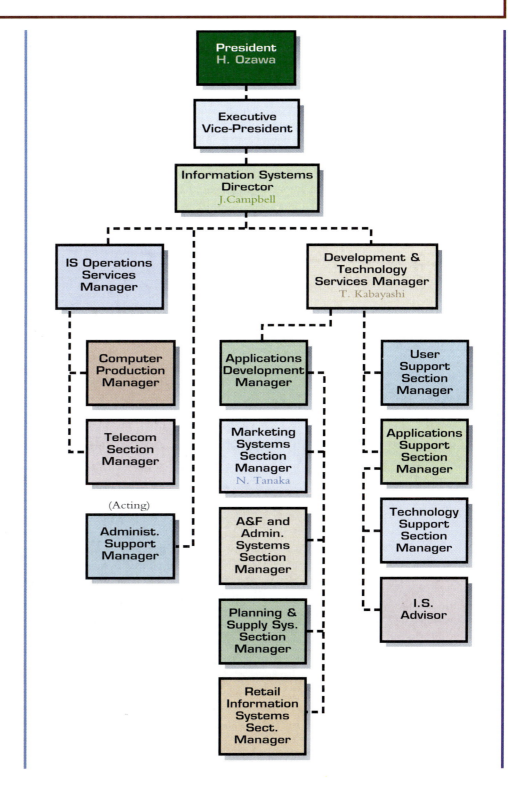

SELECTION OF ADS AS A STANDARD

On July 10, 1989, less than a month after the strategy report was published, the recommended ES evaluation project was initiated with a kick-off meeting at the MRD offices in Omaha, Nebraska. Prior to the meeting, Steven McKenzie, Tanaka's counterpart at Global Corporate, issued a memo identifying a preliminary list of factors that would be considered essential, important, and desirable in the selected ES product. Vendor support in Japan was listed as important but not essential, and support of Kanji was listed only as desirable. The committee charged with selecting the ES standard was composed of nine members from Global, six of whom were from MRD, including just one representative of International Applications Development.

After some deliberation, the committee limited its evaluation to programs that ran both on the IBM PC and on IBM mainframes. The purpose of this limitation was to minimize effort in transferring software from one platform to another, to increase the ability to share information among applications, and to reduce the number of products being used for ES development. This would maximize the availability of support and minimize the amount of training necessary. As a result, only four products were examined. Among these products, ADS was the only one deemed satisfactory in the PC environment. In April, 1990, the committee completed its report recommending ADS as a "standard-gap" product (one that should be considered the standard for the next one to three years).

Upon receipt of the Selection Report, Tanaka immediately undertook a review of ADS from GS's perspective. His report, issued less than three weeks later, confirmed that the Grease Project could be undertaken using ADS; nevertheless, based in part on the assumption that the Grease Project was a standalone application, he recommended that it be developed in GURU. As a caveat, Tanaka noted, "We will need to ask (MRD) whether ADS will be used as a tool for the Lube Knowledge Base and also whether GS should use the same tool for future integration with a master program. Even (if) that is the case, I will propose that GS postpone the investment decision (in ADS). . . ."

ISSUES FROM THE JAPANESE PERSPECTIVE

GS agreed with Global's policy to standardize the ES shell. It would eliminate duplication of effort by one or more subsidiaries as different ES applications were developed, and it would facilitate exchange of knowledge and expertise. However, GS had had no input into the selection of the standard; Tanaka was informed of the progress made by the U.S. task force. In turn, he had notified Global Corporate by memo that ADS would be difficult for GS to accept because of the following: 1. lack of Kanji support on the PC; 2. lack of vendor support; 3. lack of image support; and 4. absence of commercial sales in Japan.

The people who were to use ES applications at GS, while able to speak and read some English, were not proficient enough to use a program in English. In addition, the Grease Project in development was intended partly for the benefit of GS's customers, most of whom do not speak or read English.

The Japanese culture is highly visual. Most Japanese managers find that a picture is far clearer and easier to understand than its description in words. Therefore, graphics capability was crucial for any application at GS. ADS lacked support for graphics.

The lack of vendor support in Japan was also an obstacle. Who could Tanaka or other users call if there were problems? The vendor of ADS, Aion, is located in California. Because Tokyo is 11 hours ahead of the West Coast, support directly from Aion was impractical.

The fact that the product had never been sold in Japan also made GS uneasy. Also, with the absence of significant sales, Aion had little incentive to develop a Kanji interface or to create a support staff in Japan.

EXHIBIT 4 Worldwide Lube Expert Systems

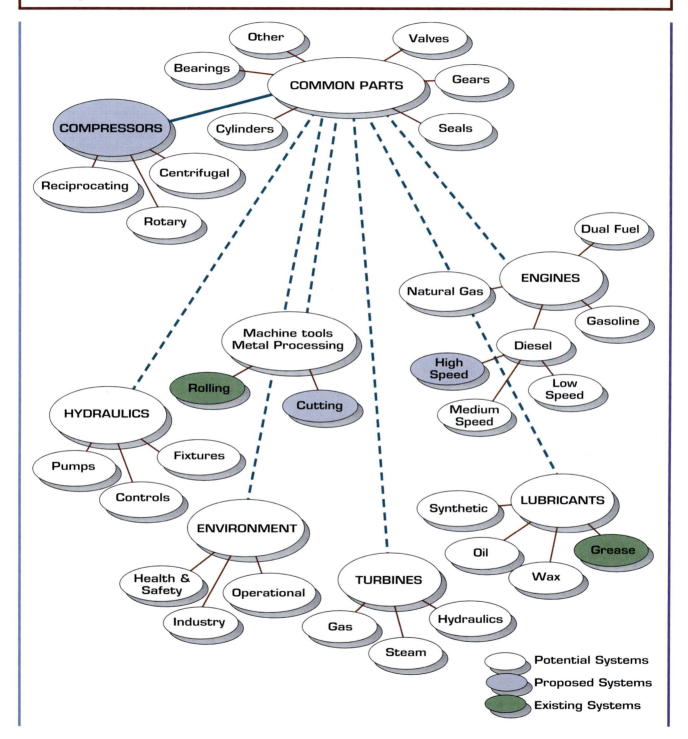

GS had few obvious alternatives, and none seemed very promising. It could switch its ES development to ADS, complying with the Global standard; it could use a program such as GURU that would be more useful for its own applications; or it could develop parallel systems in GURU and ADS satisfying both Corporate and local needs but incurring substantial "unnecessary" development costs and possible inconsistencies among the finished products. Mr. Campbell, the IS director, believes that given a valid reason and a solid case, GS can deviate from the corporate standards. However, everyone understands that this is a relatively short-term solution, and that whatever product(s) are chosen must be able to fit with long term corporate goals. Given that Japanese versions of software are often different from the original versions, with different features and capabilities, GS often has no choice than to go with a different product.

Tanaka had originally planned to develop the Grease Expert System in GURU so that it could be used by GS's engineers, technicians, and sales staff. This would satisfy GS's needs and would be extremely useful to its employees and customers. However, it would not help other Global affiliates, as very few people are fluent in reading Kanji.

The development of parallel systems is complex and costly. It is estimated that to convert one small portion of GURU to ADS would take over one man month and require a programmer or programmers fluent in ADS, GURU, English, and Japanese. Against these costs, GS must weigh the benefits of compatibility with Global Corporate and ease of use for its employees.

ISSUES FROM GLOBAL'S PERSPECTIVES

Global envisions the eventual development of a comprehensive, integrated, worldwide Lube Knowledge Base. As currently conceived, the Lube system would include components for compressors, hydraulics, environment, turbines, engines, lubricants (including GS's Grease system), and other common parts as well as machine tools metal processing (see Exhibit 4). The benefits of such a system include

- the ability to capture knowledge which would otherwise be lost through retirement, transfers and promotions;
- increasing the availability of knowledge and expertise to all field marketers;
- facilitation of knowledge sharing among affiliates; and
- reduction in duplication of common resource files and information.

By mid-1990, Brown began to realize that development of a Lube Expert System would be a long-term objective that would demand coordination on a worldwide bases. By late 1990, in conjunction with other managers throughout Global, he began to design an architecture that would encourage this development and enable it to flourish. The architecture laid out the various components of the system and began design of common systems such as the user interface and security system. It also laid out some ground rules for developers of other parts of the system. In particular, it required that development be done with the ADS ES shell.

STEP 2: Prepare the case for class discussion.

STEP 3: Answer each of the following questions, individually or in small groups, as directed by your instructor.

Diagnosis
1. What information needs did Global Sekiyu have?
2. How did these needs resemble and differ from the needs in other parts of Global Oil?

Evaluation

3. How well did the company's information systems meet those needs?
4. Why did Global Corporate want to introduce a standard application development in all subsidiaries?
5. What problems did such an introduction create for Global Sekiyu?

Design

6. What alternatives are available to Global Sekiyu?

Implementation

7. How did Global Sekiyu respond to Corporate's selection of the ADS standard?
8. What should Mr. Tanaka do now?
9. What challenges remain in defining IT policy?

STEP 4: In small groups, with the entire class, or in written form, share your answers to the questions above. Then answer the following questions:

1. What information needs did Global Sekiyu have?
2. How did Global Corporate attempt to meet this need?
3. What problems did the ADS standard pose for Global Sekiyu?
4. What should Global Sekiyu do now? ●

The Information Systems Infrastructure at AT&T

STEP 1: Read the AT&T Dream Team case. (This activity is especially suited for use in conjunction with Chapter 14 of *Information Systems*.)

THE AT&T DREAM TEAM

In July 1993, 60 of AT&T's top technology managers gathered nervously in a Berkeley Heights, N.J. conference room to meet their new chief information officer, Ron Ponder. "Morale was surging, anticipation was rising," recalls Rudolph Alexander, the company's VP of strategic information planning and the meeting's organizer. "It was like waiting on the arrival of the Messiah."

Ponder—lured away from Sprint, where he had also headed information systems (IS)—surprised his new colleagues with a talk that was decidedly nontechnical. "He said he was there to do two things," says Alexander. "Get customers and serve customers." Ponder, also a former CIO at Federal Express, made it clear he expected everyone else in the room to concentrate on customers, too.

In the nearly 28 months since that meeting, Ponder and AT&T, the third-largest company in the world, have embarked on what is probably the biggest, most ambitious information technology (IT) project under way anywhere.

To complete the project within his five-year deadline, Ponder is assembling a crack team of 26 CIOs, from within AT&T and from the outside. Of these, 23 have been assigned to AT&T business units, some of which are bigger than many corporations. They report directly to both Ponder and their business-unit managers, and all have technology projects of their own in the works.

In all, more than 50,000 AT&T employees—roughly one-sixth of the company's entire work force—report to Ponder and his all-star team of CIOs. At stake is nothing less than AT&T's ability to compete in the deregulated telecom marketplace.

The Problem Defined

Today, AT&T runs a hodgepodge of incompatible computer and communications systems. It allows each of its 23 business units to maintain customer records in forms that can't be shared with other units. Some business units can't even swap electronic mail with other business units without problems. "We've been like the shoemaker's children," says CEO Robert Allen. "We've been so focused on IT for the customer that we haven't spent enough time looking at our own operation. It's important to our cost structure to be able to make a connection between various business units." Ponder's project includes building a single, unified IT architecture around industry standards that will enable business units of the $75 billion telecom powerhouse to share selected data about customers.

At the heart of Ponder's vision is enabling AT&T to develop what he calls a "single view of the customer," from the time a company salesperson knocks on a customer's door throughout the life of their relationship. Or from the time teenagers get their first phones and computers, and even AT&T Universal Credit Cards. "I'm going to laser in, understand as much as I can about their buying habits, living habits, and lifestyles," says Ponder. "It's easy to invent

SOURCE: "The AT&T Dream Team" Mary Thyfault, *Information Week,* (March 6, 1995: pp 26–29, 34, 39. Copyright © 1995 by CMP Publications, Inc.

the products if I can find the customer. Right now, we have the services but can't find the customers."

Company watchers, while admiring Ponder's talent and experience, warn that completing the IT project will be difficult. Sharing data is a challenge for a company that has its fingers in every slice of the communications-computing pie, including microchips, telephone systems, computers, and, of course, long-distance lines.

Ponder's vision of sharing data across the company runs counter to AT&T tradition. And the pressure is on to get it done. Even Ponder admits the clock is ticking. "We need to be well into this in the next three years because the marketplace won't wait on us, the customer won't wait on us," he worries. "Our enemy is time." In fact, according to Howard Anderson, managing director of the Yankee Group Inc., a consultancy in Boston, Ponder "faces the toughest and biggest job of any IT professional at any company in the world."

The Journey So Far

To appreciate how far Ponder and his team must travel, it helps to know where they started. When Ponder joined AT&T in June 1993, he found what he describes as a "disaggregated IT structure, operating in relatively low-level ways." Specifically, each business unit had its own IS structure, with William Osl, VP of new business development, overseeing information resources for AT&T's internal operations. "Overall, there was very little alignment of resources with the primary goals of the businesses and very little synergy between businesses," says Ponder. The Yankee Group's Anderson describes it more harshly: "They had very competent IT professionals that were being beat up by their divisions. And they've got every networking and operating system ever invented."

AT&T's technology structure made it difficult to get a single view of an AT&T customer, even within a business unit. Take AT&T's phone systems business—known as Global Business Communications Systems—where Bob Napier, the new CIO, found six IT organizations supporting different segments of the business. "If you wanted to get, say, a profitability statement by a customer prior to sitting for final negotiation on a deal," he says, "you'd have to go through some rather lengthy overnight batch jobs."

Customers weren't happy either. When Rino Bergonzi, now head of corporate IT services, was CIO at United Parcel Service, he used to get "very upset with AT&T," he says. "AT&T was an impossible company to deal with. Every time they visited me, they used to show up with 20 people. There was not one that knew my business." To change that, Ponder and his All-Stars will have to make great technical strides. For starters, Ponder has made a crucial breakthrough by convincing senior AT&T executives on the importance of merging the company's network and technology functions with the back-office billing and customer-care operations.

"This represents a whole new vision about the importance of information technology at AT&T," says Dan Elron, an analyst with Coopers & Lybrand in New York. "Traditionally in the telephone world, there was a definite wall between the two."

To further break down those walls, Ponder and his team have spent the last six months in heated debate over a crucial document known as the "foundation architecture." It will dictate technologies, standards, and products to all the company's CIOs. "When we get this fixed, we can move on the data in a very practical way," says Ponder. Already, the document calls for AT&T to use its own internal services and products where they make sense and where they are competitive. With that, the Yankee Group's Anderson estimates that AT&T may provide as much as 10% of sales for its Global Information Solutions (GIS) unit.

Back to Basics

The AT&T All-Stars are selecting a series of common industry standards on which to base their companywide systems. They've already decided to use TCP/IP to link 22 internal networks into one corporatewide frame-relay backbone that will eventually be migrated to asynchronous transfer mode (ATM) lines. Bergonzi estimates that standardized networks will save about $75 million and, more important, shave precious time spent cobbling together the business units' networks.

While Ponder refuses to provide additional details about the foundation architecture, a source close to the company says AT&T's networks will use Cisco and Wellfleet routers and Cabletron hubs. In the messaging arena, the source adds, AT&T will rely on the X.400 E-mail and X.500 directory standards. For enterprisewide computers, it will run client-server networks based on Unix VI.4. On desktop computers, AT&T will use DOS and Windows with a smattering of Unix VI.4.

Ponder also plans to regain control of billing from the local exchanges. While each business unit will be allowed to continue running its own systems, the difference is that those systems will all adhere to the common standards. "We want control of billing for time-to-market," he says. "Billing is key to databases, and databases allow you to become a market-facing organization."

The billing take-back and a move to client-server architecture centered around customers—as opposed to products—are enabling the consumer communications unit to add billing features 83% faster and improve order processing by 85% compared with previous measures, according to the company.

AT&T also hopes to use the companywide architecture to support common global applications for sales support, order entry, finance, and human resources. "People from Hong Kong to Pittsburgh can collaborate electronically rather than put their files in Federal Express," says Ponder. The architecture also enables AT&T to negotiate billions of dollars in volume discounts. "We saved millions of dollars already with just one vendor," Ponder adds.

People, of course, will make it all happen, and Ponder has done his best to recruit and promote the best business-technology managers he could find. Before he did, however, Ponder studied AT&T's business units. "Everybody kept looking for Ron in IS," says Alexander. "But he was spending his time with key business leaders and some of their customers, trying to understand all the needs of the businesses."

After Ponder got to know those needs, he recruited seven key CIOs. Jim Zucco, one of MCI's visionaries and key architects, left that company to be CIO and VP for AT&T's Business Communications Services (BCS). Jones of consumer long-distance was recruited from Tektronix. Bergonzi left UPS to become VP and division executive for Corporate Information Technology Services and run AT&T's internal operations. William Lewis joined from United Technologies' Pratt & Whitney division to run IT for Network Systems. Robert Napier came from Lockheed and is now CIO at Global Business Communications Systems. Gerald Corvino was recruited from mainframe maker Amdahl Corp. to be CIO at Microelectronics. Ronald Fowinkle left Sequent Computer Systems Inc. and is now the CIO at AT&T GIS.

Homegrown Talent

Ponder also recruited from within. His group of AT&T executives includes Judy Page, CIO and investment officer in the Network Services division, Robert Forte, CIO of Paradyne, and Norm Pancoast, CIO of Bell Labs. He also inherited Ingvar Peterson, CIO at newly acquired McCaw Cellular Communications Inc. in Kirkland, Washington.

"It's some pretty high-powered, impressive talent," says Jack Kelley, managing partner of the communications industry group, northeast region, for Andersen Consulting of Chicago. Adds Alexander, "Each one of these people is a contender to run one of our businesses in the future." Case in point: Zucco was promoted in January to chief of operations and general manager of BCS and was replaced by Les Lichter, formerly service engineering and development VP of BCS.

Each CIO sits at the senior management table of their business unit, with dual reporting responsibility. They report to the subsidiary president and to Ponder, who wants to keep the CIOs focused on meeting business needs, but at the same time create an infrastructure that enables AT&T to share customer information corporatewide. That dual reporting responsibility can be stressful, especially when Ponder and a business unit president call meetings at the same time. Microelectronics' CIO Corvino jokingly wishes for cloning technology "so that I can be in two places at once."

To finish arranging his team, Ponder came up with a way to segment the business-unit CIOs into four communities of interest—services, products, global, and support division—that meet monthly. "It brings a lot more focus and discipline to what we do," says Alexander. Additionally, all 26 CIOs meet quarterly, and a group of about 200 people from the company's IT community meets every six months. The interaction extends beyond the formal meetings. "I can pick up the phone and know I've got somebody I can talk to who understands the things I'm trying to do and is working the same issues," says Microelectronics' Corvino. Also, each AT&T business unit has its own consolidation and renewal initiatives. At AT&T GIS, for example, CIO Fowinkle is building teams to implement global ordering systems that are receiving high marks from users.

Network Systems, meanwhile, is creating the world's third-largest data warehouse—a terabyte in size—by year's end. Network Systems—the long-distance factory that manufactures goods for AT&T's business and consumer long-distance groups—isn't building from scratch: instead, it's cloning GIS's data warehouse. In the last year, Lewis has focused on an intensive training program for software developers while shifting his development budget from 80% legacy support to half the budget going to new projects. The legacy developers "pulled off a miracle to keep those running," he says.

Network Systems also is consolidating 150 systems to 30 or 40, deploying an online documentation system, and installing CAD/CAM (computer-aided design/manufacturing) systems that will enable real estate folks to see square footage and engineers to spot where equipment is stored.

Tracking Solutions

Corporate IT services is developing network-management tools that dynamically track a transaction through the network from the time it leaves a PC. "If something goes wrong with that individual transaction, we will know, whether it be a network, network node, or mainframe," says Bergonzi. "We can solve it immediately instead of having people constantly calling each other around the world."

McCaw is upgrading the network to meet regulatory demands that require it to offer customers a choice of any long-distance carrier to carry their cellular service. It is, they concede, a crucial project. In fact, until it's finally completed, regulators have legally separated McCaw's cellular company and AT&T.

In the consumer long-distance market, Jones will finish taking over the billing processes—and the wealth of billing data—from the local phone companies. In business long-distance, Lichter is upgrading the network so customers can share videoconferencing, spreadsheets, and Lotus Notes applications more easily and less expensively.

Several factors threaten to trip up Ponder and his All-Stars. For one, Ponder admits that other approaches to developing a corporatewide data warehouse haven't worked. "Many companies, including AT&T, have failed at this," he says. The most common mistake: "They get dozens of people together, and they do an enterprisewide data model, top down. Everybody would say, 'Yes sir, yes sir, you got it.' But you go back a year later and nothing's happened. The only thing you know when you start is it's going to fail—you just don't know how long it's going to take." Yankee Group's Anderson agrees: "If you build it right interoperability is free. If you build it wrong, you build black holes."

Laying the Groundwork

Even AT&T's brass knew Ponder's greatest challenge would be overcoming barriers within a company that has a very deeply embedded technology base. In the six months prior to Ponder's arrival, Alexander, acting as an emissary for then CFO Alex Mandl, began visiting senior executives within AT&T to sell them on the idea of bringing in a CIO. "We wanted to make sure Ponder landed on an undefended beach to the sounds of bands and music and would not have to fight his way in," says Alexander. "We wanted to make sure he was thought of as having value from Day One."

Naturally, AT&T's technologists were "probably the most resistant" to the CIO idea, explains Alexander. "I spent a half day in shirtsleeves tangling with that crew, and when I came out I had them convinced." The key: helping them understand the value of information—something quite different from technology. Once Alexander did that, he says, "there was an outcry. 'When is the CIO coming?'"

Another challenge: Ponder's counterparts at rival carriers aren't sitting still. Long-distance competitors such as MCI have already closely aligned their systems and operations. Quips one analyst, "The joke at MCI used to be 'Watch the television commercials in the morning, and program the service in the afternoon.'"

While MCI officials declined to comment, John Kresovsky, VP of IT services at Sprint, says his company is moving to distributed systems. But the comparison isn't exactly fair: Unlike AT&T, which competes in 23 businesses, MCI and Sprint are limiting themselves to just one—telephone services.

At times Ponder has felt overwhelmed by the enormity of his job, say associates. Alexander recalls him saying, "This is an impossible task. There is no one brain that can absorb all that has to be absorbed here. I need to think of this in bits and bytes and find a way to connect those." But it also helps that Ponder has support from the top.

Mandl, now executive VP and CEO of the Communications Services Group, says he's counting on Ponder to bring AT&T's information resources capabilities up several levels. "Building a robust information platform within AT&T is a very critical part of our strategy," he says. "It's the enabler for getting a bunch of other things done."

The complexity of it all threatens even the best. "It can get you confused, add to your costs, and slow your response," says Alexander. But he believes Ponder is leading the All-Stars' team meticulously. "He's walked very deliberately in the direction he needs to move," says Alexander. "He gains a lot of foresight and thought before he takes a step. When he puts that foot down, it's solid. He doesn't wiggle it; it doesn't move."

STEP 2: Prepare the case for class discussion.

STEP 3: Answer each of the following questions, individually or in small groups, as directed by your instructor.

Diagnosis
1. Describe AT&T's information infrastructure before the arrival of Ron Ponder.
2. What information needs did AT&T have?
3. How will AT&T's information needs change in the coming years?

Evaluation
4. How well did the company's information architecture support its needs?
5. How do the current information technology infrastructure and corporate culture at AT&T support or oppose a change in the architecture?

Design
6. How has Ponder proposed to streamline AT&T's technology structure and architecture?
7. What is the likely impact of the imposition of standards on the individual business units? What is its likely impact on the organization as a whole?
8. How has Ponder proposed to regain control of billing?

Implementation
9. What are the key elements of Ponder's restructuring plan?
10. Why did Ponder spend his time initially with key business leaders rather than with his CIOs?
11. What is the reporting structure for the CIOs? How does this reporting structure support Ponder's view of AT&T's information systems architecture? What problems does this reporting structure present?
12. How does the organizational structure support continued development of the architecture?
13. What challenges remain in defining IT policy at AT&T?

STEP 4: In small groups, with the entire class, or in written form, share your answers to the questions above. Then answer the following questions:

1. What information needs does AT&T have now and expect to have in the near future?
2. How did it attempt to meet these needs?
3. How effectively did the company manage the recent changes?
4. How effective are the changes likely to be?
5. What should AT&T do now? ●

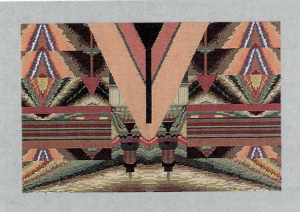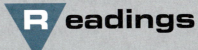

"Hot New PC Services," by David Kirkpatrick

(This reading is especially suited for use in conjunction with Chapter 2 of *Information Systems*.)

You're at the PC in your den, planning a weekend trip to San Francisco. First you call up airline schedules, pick the lowest fare, and type in a credit card number. Your ticket will arrive in tomorrow's mail. Next you check an up-to-the-minute hotel guide with ratings, select one, and make a reservation. What about an elegant restaurant to impress that important customer? Press a key to search the Zagat restaurant survey for San Francisco. If you have any doubts about your choice, type a public query asking if anyone has a better idea. Tomorrow or the next day you'll find responses from people you've never met. Send your customer a note inviting him to dine at that chic Italian place you picked. Take a peek at the weekend weather forecast for the Bay Area. Now get up and start packing.

All this and more can be done right now by subscribers to Prodigy, the interactive on-line service created by IBM and Sears Roebuck. But it's only the beginning. You'd better get your tongue around the term "interactive multimedia," because it's shorthand for a revolution. Sound, still photos, even video—anything that can be turned into bits of digital code—will zip in *and out* of your home and office, perhaps within three or four years. Information and entertainment will come to you when you want it, not when some TV network or pay-cable channel says you do. You will have far more control over what and when you watch. You'll be able to exchange video, pictures, and text with anybody.

This two-way communication with the world will have a profound impact on culture, markets, government, and daily life. Says Robert Stanzione, vice president for product development at AT&T Network Systems: "We are at the edge of a new age, where visual communication will be just as ubiquitous as voice communication is today." In this "new age," innovations in compressing and transmitting digital data will cause a vast upheaval in the way people receive and exchange information.

No one business will be able to create this brave new world single-handedly. Companies in a dizzying range of industries—including telecommunications, computing, print and broadcast media, entertainment, and consumer electronics—are jockeying and negotiating with one another for position in the interactive digital future. Says CEO Bill Gates of Microsoft, who is determined to play a central role in this evolving world: "We look at lists of those companies to see which ones we should be doing things with. A lot of guys are going to win and lose big." The most sought-after partners at the moment: cable television companies. Their coaxial links may be better suited than telephone wires for getting the new technology into the home.

A growing number of early voyagers are already testing the interactive future by logging on to today's relatively primitive services like Prodigy and CompuServe. Using PCs with modems attached to phone lines, these pioneers are defining a new kind of electronic connectedness. Consumer-oriented interactive services are now used in 3.3 million of the 92 million U.S. households, and the number is growing more than 30 percent a year, according to Arlen Communications, a Bethesda, Maryland, research company. These services will take in $473 million in 1992, predicts Link Resources, a New York City consulting firm, which projects a compound annual revenue growth rate of 28 percent for them. Some 9.6 million households have the requisite PCs with modems, Link figures; an additional 17.4 million have PCs but so far are modemless.

SOURCE: David Kirkpatrick, "Hot New PC Services" *Fortune* November 2, 1992, pp. 108–109, 112 and 114. © 1992 Time Inc. All rights reserved.

Today's services are limited mostly by their inability to display anything besides text and crude graphics. The services are also often annoyingly slow and difficult to operate. But subscribers are flocking to them anyway, simply for the rich variety of material they provide (see table). Most important, these services are *interactive,* meaning users within each service can talk to each other, through their keyboards, of course. They can communicate privately through electronic mail or publicly via bulletin boards and real-time gabfests. A huge percentage of the information available is created not by anonymous writers but by the actual users. This is not a passive medium. You are not a reader or a viewer, but an author and a contributor.

Users post more than 80,000 public messages on Prodigy's hundreds of bulletin boards each day, on topics ranging from heavy metal rock to vegetarian cooking to investment theory. At any given time over 500,000 messages are on tap for viewing. Says Esther Dyson, who publishes the technology newsletter *Release 1.0:* "If you go to a party and don't meet people you like, what's the point? When you go to the on-line party, you almost inevitably meet new people who share your interests."

Prodigy is merely the largest and most consumer-oriented of a burgeoning array of PC-based interactive services. It has jumped to 1.75 million users in 850,000 homes in the two years since it went national. Other top services include CompuServe, which offers the most data; America Online; General Electric's GEnie; and the Sierra Network, and independent all-game national network. Local and special-interest bulletin boards abound, including such offerings as GayCom and Christian Net.

Logging on to Prodigy for an hour or so a couple of times a week changed the life of Gayle Kinsey, 38, a part-time computer consultant, paralegal, and single mother in Corrales, New Mexico. When she wanted to start a newsletter to help promote her consulting business, she found about 15 others on the service who were eager to join the project. "We worked the whole concept through on Prodigy, even took a vote," she says. When she had an idea for a new kind of children's bed, she posted a query on Prodigy's Money Talk bulletin board and heard from several potential investors and a metallurgist in Pennsylvania who will build a prototype.

Of all Kinsey's adventures with Prodigy, probably none is more telling than what happened when she got angry with it. She didn't like the narrow focus of many of the bulletin boards, which are restricted to particular subjects; oddly, all health matters used to be discussed on the parenting board. So she posted critical notes on a number of the boards suggesting that users suspend their memberships in protest until Prodigy added more categories.

Several hundred other members responded. They began sharing the phone numbers of prodigy officials and discussing insurrectionary strategy. Here was a unique interactive phenomenon: using the service to change the service. The effort paid off in early September. Prodigy announced that in response to many member "requests" it was tripling its bulletin boards to 420. Kinsey pronounces herself very pleased.

Ross Glatzer, Prodigy's CEO, says he is awed by his customers' intensity. In midsummer he brought together 19 members from around the country, many of whom had become persistent on-line critics. Glatzer recalls: "One member said to me, 'I want you to understand that it may be your company, but it's *our* service.' How many companies would kill to have their customers embrace the product with such fervor?"

Besides Sears, Prodigy merchants that offer catalogues and individual items on-line include Hammacher Schlemmer, Lands' End, J.C. Penney, and Spiegel. Enthusiast Patricia Johnson of North Falmouth, Massachusetts, particularly appreciates the convenience: "I hate to shop. So sometimes when I don't want to waste time going to the store, I just call up Prodigy at 10 P.M. and buy basic items like sheets. They are delivered to my door two days later. That's a huge time saving for me." Johnson also cut through the crowds in June when air fares suddenly dropped and even many travel agents had a hard time grabbing tickets. She bought five cut-rate round trips to the West Coast for family members by logging on to Prodigy early in the morning.

Interactive Services You Can Use Now

All the services listed, except the Sierra Network, include late news, sports, weather, entertainment news and reviews, investing information, some games, shopping, on-line discount brokerage, electronic mail, and bulletin boards for discussions with other subscribers.

American Online 180,000 users	$7.95 a month for two hours, then 10 cents a minute; 800-827-6364.	Specializes in live discussion and bulletin boards on all sorts of subjects. Relatively easy to use. A fast-growing startup that went public this year.
CompuServe 1,070,000 users	$49.95 initial charge plus $7.95 monthly for basic services. Other material available at $12.80 an hour and up; 800-848-8199.	More data than other services but difficult for nontechies. Special strength: on-line computer hardware and software support. Owned by H&R Block.
GEnie 350,000 users	$4.95 a month for basic nonbusiness-day service, otherwise $6 an hour and up; 800-638-9636	Lots of games, and bulletin boards on subjects including jokes, real estate, religion and ethics. Extensive computing information. Owned by General Electric.
Prodigy 1,750,000 users	$49.95 initial subscription, then $14.95 a month plus some charges for optional services; 800-776-3449.	The easiest to use but sometimes very slow. Owned jointly by Sears and IBM.
The Sierra Network 12,000 users	$12.95 a month for 30 hours evenings and weekends, $2 to $7 an hour otherwise; 800-743-7721.	All games and chat. Went national last year. Owned by Sierra On-Line, a publicly held computer games company.

One snag: Prodigy continues to lose money—$30 million to $50 million this year, according to Gary Arlen, president of Arlen Communications. He calculates that Sears and IBM have sunk well over $800 million into the service so far but projects a possible breakeven next year. (CompuServe, by contrast, has been profitable since 1979.)

Interactive services have broad implications for politics in particular. Ross Perot has proposed using them for electronic town meetings to resolve national issues. Already members debate political questions in a variety of forums on many of the services. Specially organized Prodigy events offer genuine interaction with politicians. During both nominating conventions this summer, Prodigy members who were also delegates (12 from each party) volunteered to answer specific questions from members. Want to know how your Congressman voted on family leave? On Prodigy, just type in your zip code for the voting record of your Representative and your Senators, and while you're at it check how much political action committees contributed to their latest campaigns.

The candidates have recognized the power of the on-line electorate. Both President Bush and Governor Clinton posted campaign statements on Prodigy in September and personally approved answers to questions from members. The spirited debate that ensued went on for weeks. Jerry Brown logged on to CompuServe in June, discussing his campaign, debating issues, and answering questions.

The new technologies also have intriguing potential in education. A study last spring at Northern Kentucky University suggests that in some situations on-line classes may be better than conventional ones. Students in six college courses in education, sociology, geology, and business law were divided into conventional sections and on-line sections that met only occasionally with teachers. The on-line section, used Macintosh computers and an educational interactive system called Olé, developed by Cincinnati Bell. In general, the on-line students got better grades and rate the course more highly than the control group did. Total costs per student are 30 percent lower with Olé than with traditional methods, the university says—a boon in the age of spiraling tuitions.

So how soon will you be able to add video, sound, and pictures to all this neat stuff? Bill Gates thinks such advanced systems may extend to a million homes within four years. In early October a consortium organized by Microelectronics & Computer Technology Corp. (MCC), a cooperative research group in Austin, Texas, announced that it hopes to deploy a multimedia interactive network by early 1995. The new venture, called First Cities, includes Apple Computer, Bellcore (the research arm of the Baby Bells), Corning, Eastman Kodak, North American Philips, Kaleida labs (an Apple joint venture with IBM), Tandem computer, and several telephone and cable companies. Says First Cities executive director Bruce Sidran: "Our vision is to provide multimedia information when, where, and how you want it—in your home, your car, an airplane, or while you're walking down the street."

Lucie Fjeldstad, IBM's general manager of multimedia, says Big Blue already has the technology to manage a nationwide system that would allow users anywhere to hold video conferences, collaborate on projects with people scattered in different cities, take a course from any university, and select from a cornucopia of entertainment options. Her notion of one way shopping interactively might work is striking: "Say you tell the system you need a new jacket. You can find one you like and have the machine call up a hologram that looks like you so you can try it on and order it if you like it."

Today's services are limited to text and graphics because phone lines, the only existing two-way connections between homes and offices and the outside world, have limited bandwidth—the capacity for carrying information. Technicians are making progress on several ways to expand it. First, telephone wires can be made to carry more data. A technology called ISDN, for Integrated Services Digital Network, expands the maximum bandwidth of conventional phone lines as much as sevenfold. It's widely used in Europe. In parts of Maine, Massachusetts, New York, and Vermont, ISDN is already available for roughly twice the cost of a conventional phone line; telephone companies plan a national rollout over the next two or three years.

Second, as the pipes are widening, the stuff that flows through them is getting smaller. Telecommunications standards-setting bodies are debating a number of methods for compressing digital data. Compression involves eliminating redundant or unnecessary parts of a signal—for example, the pauses in a conversation. By next year phone and cable companies in some test locations will be able to compress a video signal so that it takes up one-eighth the space on a wire it does today.

While telephone companies struggle to squeeze more stuff into their skinny little wires, the cable television industry is working to bypass the telephone system entirely. Cable's higher-capacity coaxial lines now run past more than 90 percent of American homes and connect to 65 percent of them. Any compression method that works on a phone line would open up even more usable space on cable. Today most big cable companies are installing fiber-optic strands as their systems' backbones, using coaxial cable only for the final link to consumers' homes.

A network combining fiber optics and coaxial cable could carry a gigabit of information per second—a billion digital bits, the equivalent of 30,000 single-spaced typewritten pages. That's roughly 500 times the capacity of a phone line. Until recently most experts believed that national interactive networks equipped for video would have to wait until millions of homes were strung individually with fiber-optic telephone lines, at the daunting cost of roughly $2,000 per home. (A cable connection costs an average of $500.) but since sufficient bandwidth already makes its way into homes via cable systems, the time frame has shortened drastically. The digital device you'll use to control all this interactive stuff will probably be some combination of a TV and a cable box rather than a supersmart telephone.

IBM and AT&T each claim to be best positioned to manage the vast digital networks that would feed material down the cable. Says IBM's Fjeldstad: "We believe we have the lead to establish this service over time." But at AT&T, Robert Stanzione isn't convinced: "It is our intention to be the leader in visual communication products and services. When it comes to networking, I know of no other company that has as much experience as AT&T." Other giants vying to manage future high-capacity networks include Alcatel Alsthom, Digital Equipment, Ericsson, Fujitsu, Hitachi, Matsushita, Northern Telecom, and Siemens.

Whoever ends up controlling the networks, cooperation between telephone and cable companies may be the best way to make interactive multimedia happen. Federal Communications Commission Chairman Alfred Sikes aims to break down the regulatory barriers that have kept companies in each industry from either cooperating or poaching on the other's turf. Says he: "I think competitive markets will deliver more quickly, just as increasingly competitive long-distance telephone markets have delivered better networks and services."

Following a favorable FCC decision, New York Telephone announced in early October that it would work with Liberty Cable Television to install a test system for interactive video in three Manhattan apartment buildings. It said it would replace the buildings' old-fashioned phone lines with coaxial cable—essentially adopting cable technology.

Phone companies have a crucial skill that the cable companies lack—experience in managing two-way communications. Says Eric Martin, a specialist at Gemini Consulting of Morristown, New Jersey: "Remember that the U.S. phone companies have built the most complex switched networks in the world and have a fantastic reputation for reliability and quality. And what's the bad rap on cable? That their service and transmission quality is relatively low."

Tele-Communications Inc., the largest cable system operator, is already a partner with US West, a major phone company. Their jointly owned system in Britain provides both telephone and television service on the same cable. In Denver the two companies have hooked up with AT&T to test "video on demand" over cable TV lines. Users can order from a catalogue of more than 1,000 movies and special events, watch them whenever they want, and stop each offering at will for up to ten minutes.

Cable companies will use their new capacity at first to offer a vastly expanded menu of movies and entertainment shows. Time Warner's experimental Quantum system in Queens already allows viewers to select from among 15 movies and special events at any one time; soon customers equipped with keyboards will be able to send each other messages. Within a few years Quantum will probably provide interactive classified ads, yellow pages, videogames, and retail catalogues with photographs, says Geoffrey Holmes, a Time Warner senior vice-president. IBM and others are especially interested in establishing a partnership with Time Warner. It is the nation's second-largest cable company, with 6.8 million subscribers, and it also produces and owns huge libraries of potential multimedia material—such as movies, music, and magazines (including *Fortune*). Holmes says recent FCC rulings mean he can quickly add long-distance phone service and, within five years, high-quality videophones.

Mitchell Kapor, founder of the computer software firm Lotus Development, left Lotus in 1986 and now heads the Electronic Frontier Foundation, which promotes a free and open flow of communication on information highways. It has won many influential ears, including those of FCC Chairman Sikes. Kapor worries that if cable companies control future multimedia networks, they will restrict access to them. "In print there are hundreds of thousands of publications with all shades of opinion," he says. "My dream is that we could get that same range of expression and ideas in this new interactive medium. But I fear that we'll just get more least-common-denominator, entertainment-oriented, advertiser-controlled stuff."

He points out that while the phone system is accessible to everyone, the cable system has been structured and regulated as a one-way flow controlled by the operators. "So either we need to change the policy regime under which cable is done, or we need to have phone companies do this," he says. Only if cable systems support independent origination of content, he believes, will nonprofit alternative information and entertainment sources flourish.

Replies Bob Thomson, a spokesman for Tele-Communications Inc.: "Nobody's going to make the huge investments necessary if that sort of model is imposed on them. We go out and buy our products wholesale and then retail them to our customers, and shape those offerings to best suit our marketplace. Some portions of our network may be totally open to all comers, just as public-access cable channels are today. If there's a market for that kind of service, it will have to be met."

The new industry that emerges could be a major force in the U.S. economy. Says Microsoft's Gates: "This is the information age, and we're talking about the deployment of a new generation of information technology to the homes of America. It's going to change things, big time. It will create a lot of wealth, and a lot of easier ways of doing things." Gates foresees more efficiency in virtually every market as companies develop ways to search quickly and easily through vast databases of available goods and services—including investments.

In pursuit of that vision, Gates has privately funded his own company, called Interactive Home Systems, in Redmond, Washington. Its 35 employees are trying to find and commercialize means of scanning through those huge databases of the future. Another project involves making digital representations of artworks for a high-quality on-line museum. Says Gates: "In the same way that Microsoft bet on the microprocessor, IHS is making bets on very, very broad-bandwidth and high-resolution screens connected to very intelligent interactive devices. It's the only company I know that's completely worthless unless this stuff all really happens."

The U.S. could gain a tremendous competitive advantage globally if it moves rapidly into on-line multimedia. No other country except Canada has a comparably sophisticated communications infrastructure that includes pervasive cable television. Says Brendan Clouston, chief operating officer of Tele-Communications Inc.: "One of the next great positives for America in the world community is that we are the leader in moving toward this kind of information network." See you on-line.

Discussion Questions

1. How do interactive information services affect the daily conduct of business and leisure activities?
2. How do interactive services help meet individuals' needs for information?
3. What role will the telephone and cable industries play in interactive services of the future? ▼

"Mrs. Fields' Secret Ingredient," by Tom Richman

(This reading is especially suited for use in conjunction with Chapter 3 of *Information Systems*.)

Part of the late Buckminister Fuller's genius was his capacity to transform a technology from the merely new to the truly useful by creating a new form to take advantage of its characteristics. Fuller's geodesic designs, for instance, endowed plastic with practical value as a building material. His structures, if not always eye-appealing, still achieved elegance—as mathematicians use the word to connote simplicity—of function. Once, reacting to someone's suggestion that a new technology be applied to an old process in a particularly awkward way, Fuller said dismissively, "That would be like putting an outboard motor on a skyscraper."

Introducing microcomputers with spreadsheet and word-processing software to a company originally designed around paper technology amounts to the same thing. If the form of the company doesn't change, the computer, like the outboard, is just a doodad. Faster long division and speedier typing don't move a company into the information age.

But Randy Fields has created something entirely new—*a* shape if not *the* shape, of business organizations to come. It gives top management a dimension of personal control over dispersed operations that small companies otherwise find impossible to achieve. It projects a founder's vision into parts of a company that have long ago outgrown his or her ability to reach in person.

In the structure that Fields is building, computers don't just speed up old administrative management processes. They alter the process. Management, in the Fields organizational paradigm, becomes less administration and more inspiration. The management hierarchy of the company *feels* almost flat.

What's the successful computer-age business going to look like in the not-very-distant future? something like Randy Fields's concept—which is, in a word, neat.

What makes it neat, right out of the oven, is where he's doing it. Randy Fields, age 40, is married to Debbi Fields, who turns 31 this month, and together they run Mrs. Fields Cookies, of Park City, Utah. They project that by year end, their business will comprise nearly 500 company-owned stores in 37 states selling what Debbi calls a "feel-good feeling." That sounds a little hokey. A lot of her cookie talk does. "Good enough never is," she likes to remind the people around her.

But there's nothing hokey about the 18.5 percent that Mrs. Fields Inc. earned on cookie sales of $87 million last year, up from $72.6 million a year earlier.

Won't the cookie craze pass? people often ask Debbi. "I think that's very doubtful . . . I mean," she says, "if [they are] fresh, warm, and wonderful and make you feel good, are you going to stop buying cookies?"

Maybe not, but the trick for her and her husband is to see that people keep buying them from Mrs. Fields, not David's Cookies, Blue Chip Cookies, The Original Great Chocolate Chip Cookie or the dozens of regional and local competitors. Keeping the cookies consistently fresh, warm, and wonderful at nearly 500 retail cookie stores spread over the United States and five other countries can't be simple or easy. Worse, keeping smiles on the faces of the nearly 4,500, mostly young, store employees—not to mention keeping them productive and honest—is a bigger chore than most companies would dare to take on alone.

Most don't; they franchise, which is one way to bring responsibility and accountability down to the store level in a far-flung, multi-store organization. For this, the franchiser trades off revenues and profits that would otherwise be his and a large measure of flexibility. Because

---

Reprinted with permission. *Inc.* magazine, October 1987, copyright 1987 by Goldhirsh Group, Inc., Wharf, Boston, MA 02110. Tom Richman, "Mrs. Fields' Secret Ingredient."

its terms are defined by contract, the relationship between franchisor and franchisee is more static than dynamic, difficult to alter as the market and the business change.

Mrs. Fields Cookies, despite its size, has not franchised—persuasive evidence in itself that the Fieldses have built something unusual. Randy Fields believes that no other U.S. food retailer with so many outlets has dared to retain this degree of direct, day-to-day control of its stores. And Mrs. Fields Cookies does it with a headquarters staff of just 115 people. That's approximately one staffer to every five stores—piddling compared with other companies with far fewer stores to manage. When the company bought La Petite Boulangerie from PepsiCo earlier this year, for instance, the soft-drink giant had 53 headquarters staff people to administer the French bakery/sandwich shop chain's 119 stores. Randy needed just four weeks to cut the number to 3 people.

On paper, Mrs. Fields Cookies *looks* almost conventional. In action, however, because of the way information flows between levels, it *feels* almost flat.

On paper, between Richard Lui running the Pier 39 Mrs. Fields in San Francisco and Debbi herself in Park City, there are several apparently traditional layers of hierarchy: an area sales manager, a district sales manager, a regional director of operations, a vice-president of operations. In practice, though, Debbi is as handy to Lui—and to every other store manager—as the telephone and personal computer in the back room of his store.

On a typical morning at Pier 39, Lui unlocks the store, calls up the Day Planner program on his Tandy computer, plugs in today's sales projection (based on year-earlier sales adjusted for growth), and answers a couple of questions the programs puts to him. What day of the week is it? What type of day: normal day, sale day, school day, holiday, other?

Say, for instance, it's Tuesday, a school day. The computer goes back to the Pier 39 store's hour-by-hour, product-by-product performance on the last three school-day Tuesdays. Based on what you did then, the Day Planner tells him, here's what you'll have to do today, hour by hour, product by product, to meet your sales projection. It tells him how many customers he'll need each hour and how much he'll have to sell them. It tells him how many batches of cookie dough he'll have to mix and when to mix them to meet the demand and to minimize leftovers. He could make these estimates himself if he wanted to take the time. The computer makes them for him.

Each hour, as the day progresses, Lui keeps the computer informed of his progress. Currently he enters the numbers manually, but new cash registers that automatically feed hourly data to the computer, eliminating the manual update, are already in some stores. The computer in turn revises the hourly projections and makes suggestions. The customer count is OK, it might observe, but your average check is down. Are your crew members doing enough suggestive selling? If, on the other hand, the computer indicates that the customer count is down, that may suggest the manager will want to do some sampling—chum for customers up and down the pier with a tray of free cookie pieces or try something else, whatever he likes, to lure people into the store. Sometimes, if sales are just slightly down, the machine's revised projections will actually exceed the original on the assumption that greater selling effort will more than compensate for the small deficit. On the other hand, the program isn't blind to reality. It recognizes a bad day and diminishes its hourly sales projections and baking estimates accordingly.

Hourly sales goals?

Well, when Debbi was running *her* store, *she* set hourly sales goals. Her managers should, too, she thinks. Rather than enforce the practice through dicta, Randy has embedded the notion in the software that each store manager relies on. Do managers find the machine's suggestions intrusive? Not Lui. "It's a tool for me," he says.

Several times a week, Lui talks with Debbi. Well, he doesn't exactly talk *with* her, but he hears from her. He makes a daily phone call to Park City to check his computerized Phone-Mail messages, and as often as not there's something from Mrs. Fields herself. If she's upset about some problem, Lui hears her sounding upset. If it's something she's breathlessly exu-

FIGURE 1 The Information Flow

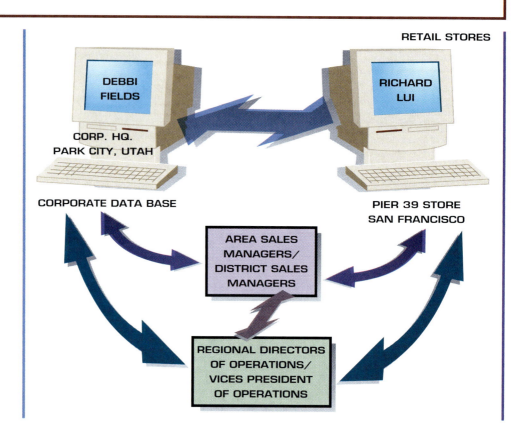

berant about, which is more often the case, he gets an earful of that, too. Whether the news is good or bad, how much better to hear it from the boss herself than to get a memo in the mail next week.

By the same token, if Lui has something to say to Debbi, he uses the computer. It's right there, handy. He calls up the Form-Mail program, types his message, and the next morning it's on Debbi's desk. She promises an answer, from her or her staff, within 48 hours. On the morning I spent with her, among the dozen or so messages she got was one from the crew at a Berkeley, Calif., store making their case for higher wages there and another from the manager of a store in Brookline, Mass., which has been struggling recently. We've finally gotten ourselves squared away, was the gist of the note, so please come visit. (Last year Debbi logged around 350,000 commercial air miles visiting stores.)

Here are some other things Lui's computer can do for him.

- Help him schedule crew. He plugs his daily sales projection for two weeks hence into a scheduling program that incorporates as its standards the times Debbi herself takes to perform the mixing, dropping, and baking chores. The program gives him back its best guess of how many people with which skill levels he'll need during which hours. A process that done manually consumed almost an hour now takes just a fraction of that time.
- Help him interview crew applicants. He calls up his interview program, seats the applicant at the keyboard, and has him or her answer a series of questions. Based on the answers given by past hirees, the machine suggests to Lui which candidates will succeed or fail. It's

still his choice. And any applicant, before a hire, will still get an audition—something to see how he or she performs in public. Maybe Lui will send the hopeful out on a sampling mission.

- Help with personnel administration. Say he hires the applicant. He informs the machine, which generates a personnel folder and a payroll entry in Park City, and a few months later comes back to remind Lui that he hasn't submitted the initial evaluation (also by computer), which is now slightly past due. It administers the written part of the skills test and updates the records with the results. The entire Mrs. Fields personnel manual will soon be on the computer so that 500 store managers won't forget to delete old pages and insert revised ones every time a change is made.
- Help with maintenance. A mixer isn't working, so the manager punches up the repair program on the computer. It asks him some questions, such as: is the plug in the wall? If the questions don't prompt a fix, the computer sends a repair request to Park City telling the staff there which machine is broken, its maintenance history, and which vendor to call. It sends a copy of the work order back to the store. When the work gets done, the store signs off by computer, and the vendor's bill gets paid.

That's a lot of technology applied to something as basic as a cookie store, but Randy had two objectives in mind.

He wanted to keep his wife in frequent, personal, two-way contact with hundreds of managers whose stores she couldn't possibly visit often enough. "The people who work in the stores," says Debbi, "are my customers. Staying in touch with them is the most important thing I can do."

It's no accident, even if Lui isn't consciously aware of why he does what he does, that he runs his store just about the same way that Debbi ran her first one 10 years ago. Even when she isn't there, she's there—in the standards built into his scheduling program, in the hourly goals, in the sampling and suggestive selling, on the phone. The technology has "leveraged," to use Randy's term, Debbi's ability to project her influence into more stores than she could ever reach effectively without it.

Second, Randy wanted to keep store managers managing, not sweating the paperwork. "In retailing," he says, "the goal is to keep people close to people. Whatever gets in the way of that—administration, telephones, ordering, and so on—is the enemy." If an administrative chore can be automated, it should be.

Store managers benefit from a continuing exchange of information. Of course, Park City learns what every store is doing daily—from sales to staffing to training to hires to repairs—and how it uses that information we'll get to in a minute. From the store managers' perspective, however, the important thing is that the information they provide keeps coming back to them, reorganized to make it useful. The hour-by-hour sales projections and projected customer counts that managers use to pace their days reflect their own experiences. Soon, for instance, the computer will take their weekly inventory reports and sales projections and generate supply orders that managers will only have to confirm or correct—more administrative time saved. With their little computers in the back room, store managers give, but they also receive.

What technology can do for operations it can also do for administration.

"We're all driven by Randy's philosophy that he wants the organization to be as flat as possible," says Paul Quinn, the company's director of management information systems (MIS).

"There are a few things," says controller Lynn Quilter, "that Randy dislikes about growth.... He hates the thought of drowning in people so that he can't walk in and know exactly what each person does.... The second thing that drives him nuts is paper."

"The objective," says Randy, "is to leverage people—to get them to act when we have 1,000 stores the same way they acted when we had 30."

He has this theory that large organizations, organizations with lots of people, are, per se, inferior to small ones. Good people join a growing business because it offers them an opportunity to be creative. As the company grows, these people find they're tied up managing the latest hires. Creativity suffers. Entropy sets in. Randy uses technology to keep entropy at bay.

He began by automating rote clerical chores and by minimizing date-entry effort. Machines can sort and file faster than people, and sorting and filing is deadly dull work, anyway. Lately he's pushed the organization toward automated exception reporting for the same reason. Machines can compare actual results with expected results and flag the anomalies, which are all management really cares about anyway. And within a few years, Randy expects to go much further in this battle against bureaucracy by developing artificial-intelligence aids to the running of the business.

Understand that it's not equipment advances—state-of-the-art hardware—that's pushing Mrs. Fields Cookies toward management frontiers. The machines the company uses are strictly off the shelf: an IBM minicomputer connected to inexpensive personal computers. It is, instead, Randy's ability to create an elegant, functional software architecture. He has, of course, had an advantage that the leader of an older, more established company would not have. Because Mrs. Fields is still a young enough company, he doesn't have to shape his automated management system to a preexisting structure. Every new idea doesn't confront the opposition of some bureaucratic fiefdom's survival instinct. Rather, the people part and the technology part of the Fields organization are developing simultaneously, each shaped by the same philosophy.

You see this congruence at corporate headquarters and in the company's operational management organization.

Between Debbi as chief executive officer and the individual store managers is what seems on paper to be a conventional reporting structure with several layers of management. But there's an additional box on the organization chart. It's not another management layer. It transcends layers, changing the way information flows between them and even changing the functions of the layers.

The box consists of a group of seven so-called store controllers, working in Park City from the daily store reports and weekly inventory reports. They ride herd on the numbers. If a store's sales are dramatically off, the store controller covering that geographical region will be the first to know it. If there's a discrepancy between the inventory report, the daily report of batches of cookies baked, and the sales report, the controller will be the first to find it. (It is possible for a smart thief to steal judiciously for about a week from a Mrs. Fields store.) "We're a check on operations," says store controller Wendy Phelps, but she's far more than just a check. She's the other half of a manager's head.

Since she's on top of the numbers, the area, district, and regional managers don't have to be—not to the same degree, at any rate. "We want managers to be with people, not with problems," says Debbi. It's hard, Randy says, to find managers who are good with both people and numbers. People people, he thinks, should be in the field, with numbers people backing them up—but not second-guessing them. Here's where the company takes a meaningful twist.

Problems aren't reported up the organization just so solutions can flow back down. Instead, store controllers work at levels as low as they can. They go to the store manager if he's the one to fix a discrepancy, a missing report, for instance. Forget chain of command. "I'm very efficiency minded," says Randy.

So the technology gives the company an almost real-time look at the minutiae of its operations, and the organizational structure—putting function ahead of conventional protocol—keeps it from choking on this abundance of data.

Some managers would have problems with a system that operates without their daily intervention. They wouldn't be comfortable, and they wouldn't stay at Mrs. Fields. Those who do stay can manage people instead of paper.

If administrative bureaucracies can grow out of control, so can technology bureaucracies. A couple of principles, ruthlessly adhered to, keep both simple at Mrs. Fields.

The first is that if a machine can do it, a machine *should* do it. "People," says Randy, "should do only that which people can do. It's demeaning for people to do what machines can do. . . . Can machines manage people? No. Machines have no feelie-touchies, none of that chemistry that flows between two people."

The other rule, the one that keeps the technological monster itself in check, is that the company will have but one data base. Everything—cookie sales, payroll records, suppliers' invoices, inventory reports, utility charges—goes into the same data base. And whatever anybody needs to know has to come out of it.

Don't enforce this rule, and, says Randy, "the next thing you know you have 48 different programs that can't talk to each other." Technology grown rampant.

Having a single data base means, first, that nobody has to waste time filing triplicate forms or answering the same questions twice. "We capture the data just once," says controller Quilter.

Second, it means that the system itself can do most of the rote work that people used to do. Take orders for chocolate, for instance. The computer gets the weekly inventory report. It already knows the sales projection. So let the computer order the chocolate chips. Give the store manager a copy of the order on his screen so he can correct any errors, but why take his time to generate the order when he's got better things to do—like teaching someone to sell. Or, take it further. The machine generates the order. The supplier delivers the chips to the store and bills the corporate office. A clerk in the office now has to compare the order, the invoice, and what the store says it got. Do they all match? Yes. She tells the computer to write a check. The more stores you have, the more clerks it takes. Why not let the computer do the matching? In fact, if everything fits, why get people involved at all? Let people handle the exceptions. Now, the clerk, says MIS director Quinn, instead of a processor becomes a mini-controller, someone who uses his brain.

The ordering process doesn't happen that way yet at Mrs. Fields, although it probably will soon as Randy continues to press for more exception reporting. You can see where he's going with this concept.

"Eventually," he says, "even the anomalies become normal." The exceptions themselves, and a person's response to them, assume a pattern. Why not, says Randy, have the computer watch the person for a while? "Then the machine can say, 'I have found an anomaly. I've been watching you, and I think this is what you would do. Shall I do it for you, yes or no. I yes, I'll do it, follow up, and so on. If no, what do you want me to do?'" It would work for the low-level function—administering accounts payable, for instance. And it would work at higher levels as well. "If," Randy says, "I can ask the computer now where are we making the most money and where are we making the least and then make a decision about where not to build new stores, why shouldn't that sort of thing be on automatic pilot too? 'Based on performance,' it will say, 'we shouldn't be building any more stores in East Jibip. Want me to tell [real-estate manager] Mike [Murphy]?' We're six months away from being able to do that."

The ability to look at the company, which is what the data base really is, at a level of abstraction appropriate to the looker is the third advantage of a single data base—even if it never moves into artificial-intelligence functions. It means that Debbi Fields and Richard Lui are both looking at the same world, but in ways that are meaningful to each of them.

The hurdle to be overcome before you can use technology to its best advantage—and that isn't equivalent to just hanging an outboard motor on a skyscraper, as Buckminster Fuller said—isn't technical in the hardware sense. Randy buys only what he calls plain vanilla hardware. And it isn't financial. For all its relative sophistication in computer systems, Mrs. Fields spends just 0.49 % of sales on data processing, much of which is returned in higher productivity.

Much more important, Randy says, is having a consistent vision of what you want to *accomplish* with the technology. Which functions do you want to control? What do you want your organization chart to look like? In what ways do you want to leverage the CEO's vision? "Imagination. We imagine what it is we want," says Randy. "We aren't constrained by the limits of what technology can do. We just say, 'What does your day look like? What would you *like* it to look like?'" He adds, "If you don't have your paradigm in mind, you have no way of knowing whether each little step is taking you closer to or further from your goal."

For instance, he inaugurated the daily store report with the opening of store number two in 1978. The important thing was the creation of the report—which is the fundamental data-gathering activity in the company—not its transmission mode. That can change, and has. First transmission was by Fax, then by telephone touch tone, and only recently by computer modem.

Having a consistent vision means, Randy says, that he could have described as far back as 1978, when he first began to create it, the system that exists today. But he doesn't mean the machines or how they're wired together. "MIS in this company," he says, "has always had to serve two masters. First, control. Rapid growth without control equals disaster. We needed to keep improving control over our stores. And second, information that leads to control also leads to better decision making. To the extent that the information is then provided to the store and field-management level, the decisions that are made there are better, and they are more easily made.

"That has been our consistent vision."

Discussion Questions

1. What information needs do the top executives of Mrs. Fields Cookies have?
2. What needs do the store managers have?
3. What systems exist to meet these needs?
4. How effective are these systems? ▼

"Prometheus Barely Unbound," by Tom Peters

(This reading is especially suited for use in conjunction with Chapter 4 of *Information Systems*.)

From Rutland, Vermont, to Timbuktu, business practice is being set upon its ear. Business and many general press publications chronicle the brave new world of commerce: There are tales of junk bonds and takeovers and LBOs, the so-called "market for corporate control." There were three consecutive days in mid-August 1989 when—ho-hum—Kodak, Digital Equipment, and Campbell Soup announced yet another round of thousands of staff reductions. No crisis triggered these decisions. Just business as usual. Or, as is increasingly the case, unusual.

More business as usual/unusual: A visit with the chief information officer (a new title/idea) at KG Stores, a 118-store menswear chain based in Denver. Using information technology, KG has reduced its order and replenishment cycle with Levi Strauss from about nine weeks in 1987 to three or four days.

Publications such as *Fortune, Industry Week, Business Week,* and *Business Month* often compile lists of competitive needs for managing the '90s. Such lists are helpful, but incomplete—they ignore the context which makes all this necessary. Competitive practices required to survive in the '90s—pursuit of "six sigma quality" (99.9997 percent perfect, a Motorola goal touted even in its ads), shrinking innovation and order cycles by orders of magnitude, the use of team-based organizations everywhere and the subcontracting of anything to anyone from anywhere—are downstream links in a chain of immutable forces sweeping the world's economy. Nothing less than "millennia change" is afoot, says Boston consultant and *Future Perfect* author, Stan Davis. Exhibit I (see chart) is primarily an effort to untangle the larger context.

PRIMARY FORCES AT WORK

The left side of the chart appears grossly oversimplified. But after much though, I am convinced that just *two* intertwined, primary forces are animating the massive economic transformation: globalization and information technology.

Globalization

Everybody talks about it. But what does it mean? For Americans—whether they run a multi-billion-dollar, old-line manufacturing outfit or the corner mom-and-pop shop—it means that any remnants of isolationism must go.

Consider the four top blocks under "Primary Forces at Work." Globalization concerns the recovered dominant economies—Japan and West Germany in particular. In simple terms, these big and great economies are every bit the match of the United States economy: witness Japan's high positive trade balance and the even higher positive trade balance from non-protectionist West Germany. Yet new sources of high-quality commodities and non-commodities are emerging from the Newly Industrialized Countries (NICs) like Korea, Taiwan, Singapore, and Hong Kong (assuming it's capitalist after the 1997 Chinese takeover). These "four dragons," along with other Asian growth nations such as Thailand, the Philippines, and Malaysia, now actually account for more trade with the United States than does Japan.

There's more. Italy continues to be the fastest-growing economy in the European Economic Community. And if you want to see electricity in the air, try Spain; real estate mar-

SOURCE: Tom Peters, "Prometheus Barely Unbound," reprinted with permission of Academy of Management Executive, 1990, Vol. 4, pp. 70–84.

EXHIBIT 1 Primary Forces at Work

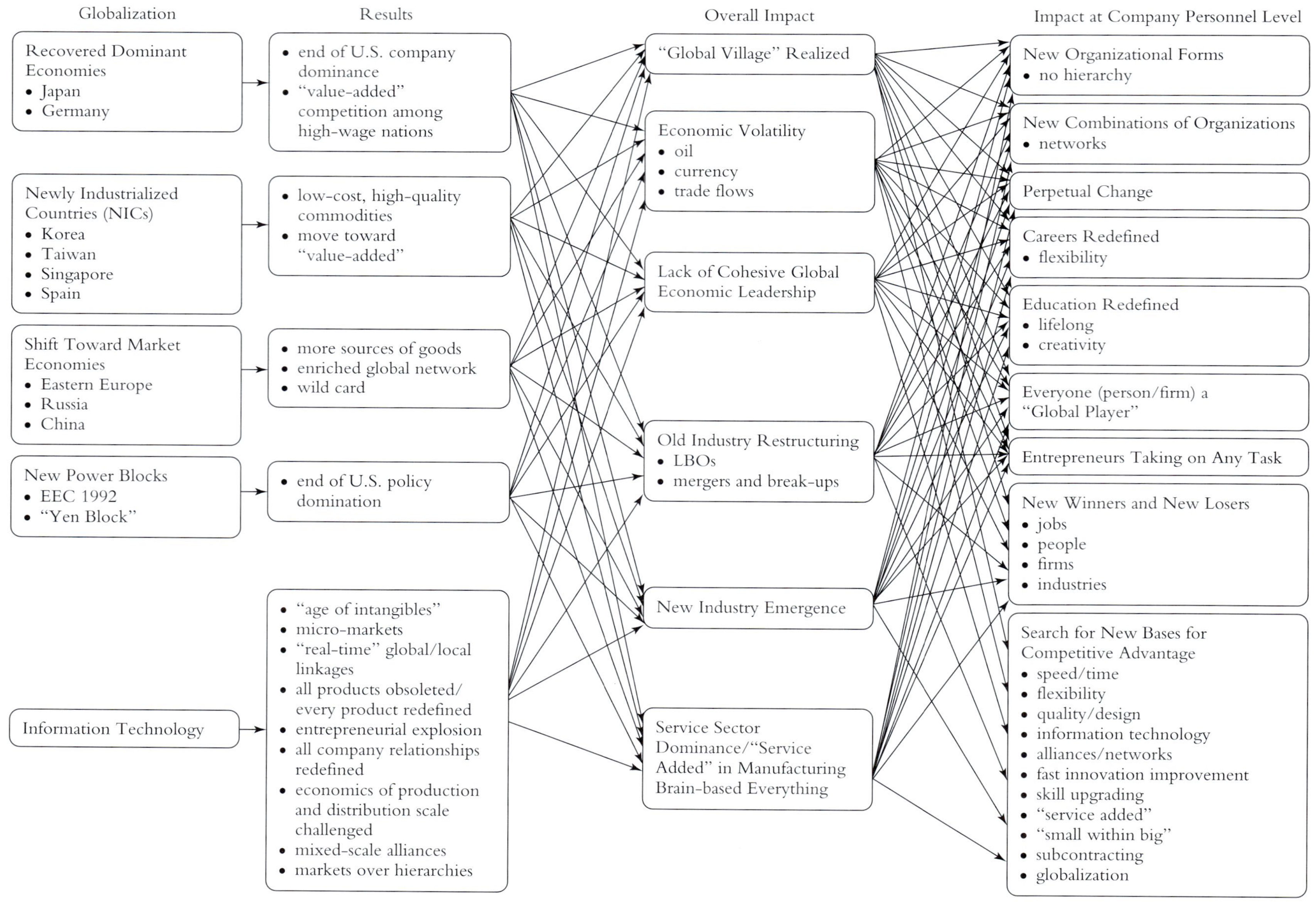

Globalization

Recovered Dominant Economies
- Japan
- Germany

Newly Industrialized Countries (NICs)
- Korea
- Taiwan
- Singapore
- Spain

Shift Toward Market Economies
- Eastern Europe
- Russia
- China

New Power Blocks
- EEC 1992
- "Yen Block"

Information Technology

Results

- end of U.S. company dominance
- "value-added" competition among high-wage nations

- low-cost, high-quality commodities
- move toward "value-added"

- more sources of goods
- enriched global network
- wild card

- end of U.S. policy domination

- "age of intangibles"
- micro-markets
- "real-time" global/local linkages
- all products obsoleted/every product redefined
- entrepreneurial explosion
- all company relationships redefined
- economics of production and distribution scale challenged
- mixed-scale alliances
- markets over hierarchies

Overall Impact

"Global Village" Realized

Economic Volatility
- oil
- currency
- trade flows

Lack of Cohesive Global Economic Leadership

Old Industry Restructuring
- LBOs
- mergers and break-ups

New Industry Emergence

Service Sector Dominance/"Service Added" in Manufacturing Brain-based Everything

Impact at Company Personnel Level

New Organizational Forms
- no hierarchy

New Combinations of Organizations
- networks

Perpetual Change

Careers Redefined
- flexibility

Education Redefined
- lifelong
- creativity

Everyone (person/firm) a "Global Player"

Entrepreneurs Taking on Any Task

New Winners and New Losers
- jobs
- people
- firms
- industries

Search for New Bases for Competitive Advantage
- speed/time
- flexibility
- quality/design
- information technology
- alliances/networks
- fast innovation improvement
- skill upgrading
- "service added"
- "small within big"
- subcontracting
- globalization

kets for plant sites are shooting toward the heavens as the Japanese and others race to enhance their "insider status" before 1992.

The growing market orientation of the planned economies throws a real spanner into the works. I don't expect the Soviet Lotta automobile to sweep North America off its feet the way VW Beetles, Honda Civics, and Hyundai Excels did. Nonetheless, the surge toward a market orientation in the Soviet Union, Eastern Europe and China—despite the latter's on-and-off gyrations—may profoundly affect the global economy by the late '90s.

Three balanced "power blocs" set the pace as the world economy charges headlong into the 21st century: North America (strengthened by the U.S.–Canada Free Trade Agreement), the European Single Market (today, more so post-1992 and still more as Eastern Europe becomes a partner) and the yen bloc, the more or less Japanese-led Asian powerhouse nations. It will never again be safe—or wise—to think of commerce in a local fashion. The rubble of the Berlin Wall is merely the most dramatic evidence of the movement to destroy borders that has begun in developed and developing nations.

Information Technology

While globalization has occurred somewhat autonomously, it has received a big boost from the new power of information technology. That doesn't just mean the transistor, microprocessor, computer, microwave relay, satellite dish, or fiber optic cable. It means all those things, increasingly woven together and abetted by thousands of networked systems and software packages tossed in for good measure.

The management and coordination of information have always driven economic change. The rise of the merchant class, which created the market economy, effectively broke feudalism's hold and ended the Dark Ages. What does information have to do with the Dark Ages? A Middle Ages crossroad, where a literal market stood, is nothing more than a dense knot of information (multiple buyers and multiple sellers). Another example: The Industrial Revolution was important for its smokestack technology and accompanying standardized production. But it blossomed in the United States, which had a rich transportation network in the world's biggest and most vigorous free-trade zone (the 48 contiguous states); in turn, the railroads' power to connect the nation was multiplied by the telegraph, which allowed timely market coordination. Then the telephone emerged (though routine long-distance calling is only 20 years old), and markets were once more compressed. Next came the computer, the definitive information processor, and along with it the arrival of fiber optic cable, microwave relays and satellites, creating the ultimate "information highways."

Information is power. Information technology allows us to instantly disperse power globally. It's not just economic power. Former Citicorp Chairman Walter Wriston and economist George Gilder are among those who argue that global computer-telecommunications networks destroy old political power blocs. This is no fantasy. Fax machines and television cameras played a leading role in Eastern Europe at the end of 1989.

Information technology (IT) affects a J.C. Penney store boss who sees a great sweater at Neiman Marcus. She buys it, photographs it, and faxes the reproduction to JCP buyers around the glob. In a day or two, a buyer finds a factory in Kuala Lumpur or Bangkok that can copy it. In a week or two, thousands of replicas are winging toward Penney stores. IT also means that CRSS, the giant Houston-based architectural firm, can exchange corrected drawings with client 3M on CAD machines almost instantly. IT permits an IBM engineer, stuck on a problem, to ask 70,000 expert colleagues around the globe for overnight help. IT causes GE to spend hundreds of millions of dollars to create a private global phone network to permit instant, seven-digit dialing from anywhere to anywhere. And IT makes the finance ministers of America and Germany and Japan almost powerless in the face of global financial trading networks. (In a symbolic watershed, the London Stock Exchange in 1989 replaced its trading floor with a computer-telecommunications network.)

RESULTS

What are the results of these primary forces (please look at the chart again)?

Globalization

Bid farewell to United States companies as peerless stars in the world economies; while Boeing and GE surely still play a big role, the "greats" today also include the world's 10 largest banks (9 are Japanese), Hitachi, Sony, Honda, Toyota, Nissan, and from West Germany, BASF, Bayer, BMW, and Bertelsmann.

Examine the recovered dominant economies of Japan and West Germany: Each giant and the entire manufacturing (and service) economies of the dominant nations shed commodities to swiftly climb the "value-added chain," as business strategist call it. There is little room for "commodity production" in the great economies if they wish to sustain high wages and continued growth. The battleground has shifted from "more, more, more for bigger, bigger, bigger markets" (the traditional American trump card) to "better, better, better for ever more finely diced markets." Note the growing role of the Japanese in upscale automobiles, where Honda (Acura), Nissan (Infiniti), and Toyota (Lexus) are altering the North American market. Superb quality, faster innovation (for individual firms and networks of firms), and "smarter" distribution (electronic data interchange networks) are hallmarks of these value-added economies.

There is a puff or two of air left in dominant and fully developed nations' commodity sails. Yet the big news is the burgeoning flow of increasingly fine goods pouring in from the newly industrialized countries. (Singapore's emphasis on education, value-added products and services and telecommunications networks is testimony to this.) Nonetheless, NICs and others like them have become, for reasons of relatively lower wages as well as mastery of advanced production techniques, the heartland for commodity production. However, "commodity" has a new meaning. In the past, "commodity" meant cheap—both inexpensive and far from the leading edge. Today commodity still means inexpensive, but the new technologies are equalizers. The *new* commodities (microwave ovens, television sets, and semiconductors from Korea, PCs from Taiwan, garments from Hong Kong) are of the highest quality and not far from state of the art technologically. Perhaps the most significant problem facing the exporters and partners is that commodity and low quality still go hand-in-glove in these nations.

(Among other things, this change turns up the competitive heat under the developed countries. Even superb quality is not enough to qualify as "high value added." High value added now hinges upon rapid distribution networks, service-added features, lightning-fast innovation—more on that later.)

The shift toward market economies by the Russians, Eastern Europeans, and Chinese is a wild card on the global game board. At the very least, it means more product choices for a world already choking on choices. (The *Economist* calls it "manic specialization.") If any of these undernourished areas can lick the infrastructure issue (computers, telecommunications networks—and basics such as highways, which are deficient in Russia and China), the global commercial network of nations will truly become the long-awaited little village.

Information Technology

Intangibles now dominate tangibles, a fact that is difficult for many to deal with. Matter doesn't matter so much anymore. "Lumps are out, brains are in," according to one colleague. It's the age of "no-mater," says consultant Stan Davis. Dun & Bradstreet sold the Official Airline Guide, a well-packaged compilation of publicly available information, for $750 million in 1987—twice what Donald Trump paid for the Eastern Shuttle. The ultimate intangible—well-packaged information—is more valuable than the aircraft, the pilots, the mechanics, the flight attendants, and the administrators of huge airlines!

A company's true worth increasingly bears little relationship to the lumps it owns. When Philip Morris shelled out $12.9 billion for Kraft, the accountants determined that the company had just $1.3 billion in "hard" assets (plants, equipment, cheese)—leaving a whopping $11.6 billion in "intangibles." Or consider Kimberly-Clark, which used IT to create a huge database for a Huggies diaper launch. With the names of 75 percent of the year's 3.5 million new American mothers in hand, the firm aimed direct mail barrages at the women. Each mother becomes a discrete market, catered to in a unique fashion. Kimberly-Clark officials insist that the database is as valuable as the trees that go into the product.

Then there is the "smart bathtub" from American Standard, priced at over $35,000—it includes a VCR, presettable bath temperatures, and a host of other features. And "smart" shopping carts which give shippers detailed information about specials, the location of goods and display interactive games or local news while shoppers wait in line. In short, "information-added" technology redefines and reconstructs every product, new or mature.

When it comes to IT, the changing nature of the links *within* and *among* organizations is as profound as the "smartening" of discrete products. Instant access to every corner of the globe is a 1990 reality. We're blasé as we read in David Lodge's novel on the industrial economy, *Nice Work,* about a London bond trader who always goes to bed with her remote, automatic price-quotation calculator stuffed under her pillow; instant information availability has redefined the entire financial services sector. Manufacturing is affected at least as much. Instant computerized order entry and instant interaction over product design issues are things of the present. Take Motorola's pager operation: Manufacture of a custom pager starts 17 *minutes* after the order is transmitted by a remote salesperson.

Or consider this discussion of Hitachi taken from the November–December 1989 *Harvard Business Review*. The story is not really about Hitachi; instead it's about the big firm's subcontractors and the subcontractors' subcontractors. In earlier times the task in question would have required weeks:

> There is a Japanese maker of high-precision dies that serves the burgeoning consumer electronics industry. . . . During the past five years, this small company has organized itself around an electronic network linking it to such giant electronics companies as Hitachi and to a highly specialized family of suppliers. Designers at Hitachi sketch a new part and sent it by fax to the diemaker. Die engineers review the sketch and, using computer-aided design (CAD) systems, generate the specifications for a new die in a matter of hours. The company then decides whether to make the die itself or subcontract it to one of the suppliers—all of whose skills, current capacity and work-in-progress have been logged. As often as not, it chooses a supplier and sends the specifications by fax, along with supplementary information about materials and stresses. The supplier, using advanced numerical control tools, makes the die, also in a matter of hours. It is not uncommon for Hitachi to get the die for some parts back in one day: the sketch arrives in the morning, the die is finished in the afternoon.

Another impact of monumental significance is the surge of entrepreneurs in the information age. With everything literally being reinvented and long production lines for mass widget-making dissolving, new players are entering all fields at an unprecedented pace. A prime example: the tens of thousands of software entrepreneurs who have recently sprung up. (What an industry: Microsoft's founder Bill Gates recently joined *Fortune's* list of billionaires.) But new entrepreneurial opportunities also arise in old-line industries, such as steel and packaged goods and financial services. Time-honored tenets of vertical integration just don't cut it anymore; businesses today go to whomever, wherever, of whatever size that can do this little bit of that little job best. Giant firms with 11- or 12-figure sales will probably still exist tomorrow. But beneath the surface, plant watering chores, cafeteria management, legal services, accounting, and even specialized R&D will be "outsourced" from a loose collection of small, efficient, and effective outfits gathered in a tight, electronically linked network. This shift is in its infancy; as global electronic highways proliferate in the next 10 to 15 years, we will see a much greater entrepreneurial surge.

Adversarial, arms-length dealing that have marked American companies' relations—with vendors, middlepersons, and customers—won't (*can't,* for survival's sake) exist in the new world. Recall the KG-Levi Strauss relationship: To cut an order cycle from nine weeks to four days, the two firms had to create intense technological links—*and they have to trust each other.* This increasingly commonplace "competing-in-time" (another new phrase) example is occurring again and again throughout the textile and garment industry: A 66-week cycle, which begins with design and ends with the production on the consumer's shelf, is shrinking to 11 weeks. For this to happen, the garment maker has to be closely tied to the fabric maker (as has happened with Levi Strauss and Milliken); the fabric maker needs tight links to its chemical suppliers (a Du Pont with a Milliken); and all must plug into even the fashion designer's curious world.

We can no longer think productively or profitably about "the company" alone. All models of "the firm" must include seamless global connections with vendors, vendors' vendors, middlepersons, customers, and customers' customers.

Embedded in all of the above is radical change to the economics of production and distribution scale. The biggest are losing out to the "bestest." And the new "bestest" will probably be alternative outfits that consist of *networks* of small, medium, and large firms gathered to do today's (and not necessarily tomorrow's) task as best they can. It is common to see a proud company like Digital Equipment make the following product announcements: Its top-of-the-line workstation (where Digital lags) contains a brain (a pioneering microprocessor) developed by relatively small MIPS computer of Sunnyvale, California. Efficient Tandy Corporation will manufacture Digital's personal computers. Ultimate sales end up on Digital's revenue line, but Digital itself adds unique value by providing the network, sales, and service skill, long-established customer relations, and an intellectual framework that ties the products together.

Markets will increasingly win out over hierarchies. We've favored hierarchies as a way to organize complex commercial affairs for the last several hundred years. In the late '50s, John Kenneth Galbraith labeled America's biggest corporations "perfect machines." Efficiency of coordination via massive, specialized staffs led to effectiveness on the bottom line. No more. Thanks to information technology (and numerous supply sources for everything), those specialists will most often be full-scale *outside* partners. Inside the firm, information readily available in sophisticated forms (via the use of expert systems, groupware, and networked PCs), dramatically reduces the need for management layers. After all, a hierarchy is only an information-processing machine. Formerly a firm needed a cast of thousands to collect receipts in hundreds of shoe boxes and a horde of senior financial analysts to count the shoe boxes. Not today.

OVERALL IMPACT

Look at the chart: Now the real mess begins! Each of the boxes and bullets under "Results" is a jumble of cause and effect leading to what I have labeled "Overall Impact." Sorting out the links is hopeless—and not particularly valuable. Each force impacts, and is impacted by, any number of other forces in a multiplicative way.

Begin with the "global village" that Marshall McLuhan predicted in the late 1950s. It's here, though we ain't seen nothing yet. Financial markets are globally connected 24 hours a day. No trader can afford to be out of touch at any time. Perhaps a more interesting window on tomorrow comes from assessing our and others' multinational companies. My daughter's IBM typewriter was made in West Germany, doubtless with components from a dozen nations. On the other hand, her Honda Accord, which sits in a sorority parking lot in Ithaca, NY, was made in Ohio. The issue of trade (and trade deficits) is no more about Japan's NEC competing with the United States' Cray in supercomputers than it is about Apple Japan and Apple Europe and Apple Singapore competing with Apple USA. Everyone is everyone else's subcontractor. Companies automatically scan the globe for the best solution to the make/buy decision. In *The Age of Unreason,* British professor Charles Handy even reports that London firms are sending their daily typing to Taipei, courtesy fax and global telecommunications networks!

The lack of cohesive economic leadership, also spurred by the homogenized effects of information technology networks, impacts our world and has destabilizing results. The Great Depression of 1930 is often attributed to Britain's loss of global economic leadership and America's hesitation to pick up the mantle. Subsequently, our cohesive global leadership contributed to the astonishing worldwide economic growth following World War II. Now we have the beginning of a leadership standoff among Japan and the yen bloc, the European Single Market and the United States. Though information technology networks have a homogenizing effect (feedback loops have been reduced from years in Columbus' time to nanoseconds today), the absence of firm leadership will most likely be destabilizing.

Can the absurd land values in Japan continue? Or the equally extraordinary valuation of the Tokyo and Taipei stock markets? Will oil cost $15 a barrel or $35? Will inflation run at 4 or 14 percent? This perpetual volatility on a previously unknown scale is especially significant. The reason: *All* modern business-planning techniques assume predictability. Capital budgeting methods using discounted cash flow analyses so popular the West depend on the ability to more or less accurately predict product supply and demand, competitors, technologies, interest rates, inflation, and raw material prices over a 10- to 25-year period. This was possible for a couple of decades following World War II, when such techniques took root. Such predictive accuracy is long gone.

The interaction of volatility, globalization, and information technology is leading to wholesale, speedy restructuring of *all* old industries, even in Japan. The changes (e.g., downsizing, shifting portfolios) in two successful Japanese industries—shipbuilding and steel—have been at least as dramatic as, and even quicker than, the highly touted United States Basic-industry restructuring. Historically, Japan has had no true multinationals, just exporters—the automakers first among them. Not today. Hardly a month passes without notice of a new Japanese automobile manufacturing operation to be opened on North American or Japanese automobile manufacturing operation to be opened on North American or European soil. The same is true in semiconductors and consumer electronics. Now the cycle is repeating itself in other countries: As wages soar, newly industrialized countries such as Korea and Taiwan are rapidly shipping their mundane textile and electronic assembly jobs offshore and pursuing higher value-added tasks at home.

Stir in the mergers and de-mergers sweeping the United States. Again cause and effect is impossible to sort out: While merger mania has been abetted by (some would say, caused by) such new financial instruments as junk bonds, it's equally fair to say that the instruments are a response to a deeper need for restructuring.

In fact, de-mergers (spinoffs, breakups, management-led LBOs) may turn out to be a bigger story than the mergers. Most often, after a merger, a massive sell-off of business bits to managers follows. Though some are frightened of this trend, LBO performance looks good overall. The failures lasso headlines; but the mounting empirical evidence suggests that most LBOs will readily weather a sizable recession. One recent study of the United States and British LBOs, for instance, observes that first- and second-year debt repayment exceeds plan by 400 and 500 percent respectively! Such success stems from the new owners' quick rationalization of hopelessly inefficient operations. Real value has been unlocked.

So old industries are restructuring wildly and new industries, especially information-related ones, are emerging just as fast. Already, information technology may contribute as much as 20 percent directly to the GNP; add indirect effects, like smart products and processes and networks, and that number easily could be doubled—and the IT age is still in diapers.

The direct role that silicon, microprocessors, computers, software codes, and fiber optic networks play is apparent. The less apparent role has just as great an impact. The young biotechnology revolution is as much a computer revolution as it is a biological sciences revolution; the ability of the computer to sort through and deal with billions of possible compound combinations is as important as the new theoretical scientific foundations. Information is changing and rearranging material sciences, too. Look at the massive array of new, customized compounds being developed by the chemical companies, and the overall shift among big firms from commodity to specialty production. Case in point: A decade ago, 70 percent of giant Monsanto's revenues flowed from commodity-grade chemicals; now that number is 2 percent.

Then there's the biggest shift of all—toward service-sector dominance. Consider these words from recently retired Motorola Chairman Bob Galvin: "The nation that masters the management of information for the service industries—along with owning the key parts of the service sector in the world's major developed markets—is destined for global economic leadership of historic proportion."

The service sector already directly employs 75 percent of Americans, a slightly lesser share of Europeans and about 60 percent of the Japanese. Moreover, service employees account for the lion's share of the payroll in what we still choose to call manufacturing companies. Take Hewlett-Packard: About 75 percent of its employees perform service tasks—accounting, MIS, research, marketing, sales, distribution, engineering, and design. The idea of a distinction between "manufacturing" firms and "service" firms is becoming useless or, worse, counterproductive. The most effective service firms today are those with the most sophisticated "factories": American Airlines' reservation system, the information systems and networks of a Federal Express or an American Express. The most effective manufacturers today, in turn, are those with the most extensive service operations—remember that huge General Electric investment in an independent, global telecommunications network.

Service is already the most sophisticated sector of the economy. Value-added and technology spending per employee stands above manufacturing. Via applications-pull, the service sector is dragging the manufacturing sector into the future.

Now look anew at the chart and reflect on all the "Overall Impact" elements: realization of the global village, economic volatility, lack of cohesive global economic leadership, old industry restructuring, new industry emergence, service-sector dominance, service-added strategies. It's an unmistakable snapshot of a world turning upside down. Yet, I cannot emphasize enough that we have barely begun to experience the impact of these multiplicative, intertwined forces. We are still largely "unwired," even with the explosive growth of global telecommunications networks. Globalization might appear to be well advanced, but the changes going on in the NICs and in Eastern Europe, and the radical transformation of Western European and Japanese companies, are also barely out the gate.

IMPACT AT COMPANY/PERSONAL LEVEL

This is the "meat and potatoes" of the seminars I normally conduct, and the heart of such revolutionary new management books as Charles Handy's *The Age of Unreason,* Stan Davis' *Future Perfect* and Harvard Professor Rosabeth Moss Kanter's *When Giants Learn to Dance.* The suggestions that spew forth from a Handy, Davis, Kanter or me are not "nifty-to-do" ideas. They are survival musts, driven by the interaction of all the destabilizing, youthful forces just reviewed.

New Organizational Forms

New ways of organizing are upending the applecart of about two millennia of management practice. Hierarchies—the only organizational format since the Chinese invented it 2,000 years ago (and the United States perfected it following World War II)—are being quickly dismantled. Multibillion-dollar, dozen-layer-deep organizations are being trampled in the global marketplace by multibillion-dollar, three-and four-layer organizations—witness Sears' trouncing by Wal-Mart in the '80s. Firms like Wal-Mart, The Limited, Nucor Corp., Federal Express, Compaq Computer, Quad/Graphics, and Cypress Semiconductor simply don't look like firms of old.

And firms of old are shedding *their* skins. In 1981, Jack Welch took over General Electric, the firm known in the '70s as *the* model for industrial excellence. Welch's predecessor, Reg Jones, was an "industrial statesman," spending as much time in Washington D.C. as in the corporate headquarters. When Welch took over, he dismantled corporate staffs including the fabled central strategic planing operation; and he tossed out many ill-fitting pieces in the business portfolio, such as Utah International, a natural resource company bought by Jones in the '70s to soothe earnings hiccups. He bought into the service sector with a vengeance—financial services, the media. GE of 1989 bears little resemblance to GE of 1981 in shape, attitude, or portfolio.

Other old-line firms are catching on. GM, Ford, and Chrysler are de-integrating and calling on subcontractors to make anything and everything. Thanks to the new information-technology linkups, the subcontracting relationship differs wildly from the past. After installing just-in-time inventory management schemes aided by electronic data interchange, companies like GM, for one, are now insisting that all supplier transactions soon be paperless!

New Combinations of Organizations

Little firms are signing up big firms to do this or that. Big firms are signing up little firms to do this or that. These relationships are creating additional new relationships. For example, the Ford Taurus development project brought outsiders into the design loop at the very beginning. The revolutionary aim was speed and more innovation from those who knew their business best. Makes sense? Of course. But it also wiped out a hundred years of conventional wisdom about product development.

Perpetual Change

"We eat change for breakfast," says Harry Quadracci, chairman of innovative Quad/Graphics, a half-billion-dollar revenue printing firm. "Our workers see change as survival," he adds. Dick Liebhaber, executive VP of $6 billion MCI, chimes in: "We don't shoot people who make mistakes; we shoot people who don't take risks."

Behaving in a "button-down fashion," "keeping one's nose clean" and acting as a "steward" were once the hallmarks of the climb up the corporate career ladder. Forget it. Firms that change—fast, constantly, and from bottom to top—have a chance at survival. Those that resist disorder and change don't.

I recall my doctoral studies at Stanford, examining the internal structures of organizations. The largest body of literature involved resistance to change at the company, small group, and individual level. Change *is* threatening. Yet those who welcome it will be the only contenders for survival, whether small or large, in an old industry or new one. How do we square characteristic resistance to change and the bedrock requirement to "eat change for breakfast?" Answer: It won't be easy. The attitudes and philosophies of the Quadraccis and

Liebhabers must become the norm. Perpetual change means perpetual retraining and worker reassignment, perpetual new alliances among companies of varying sizes, perpetual reorganization. The surviving organization will resemble a floating crap game of projects embedded amid networks of multiple companies.

Careers Redefined

The change process will redefine *every* career. Rosabeth Kanter claims that the only survivors will be those who "perpetually seek to add value." Her favorite word is "project." Everyone, janitor to vice president, must be "seeking out projects to add value."

So who's left to sweep the floor? A visit to a 3M facility in Austin, Texas, suggests that floor sweeping, food handling and security guarding are fast becoming almost as sophisticated as engineering. Computer-based floor sweepers and new security systems call for a sophisticated worker in virtually every job. A new, highly automated facility belonging to the huge drug distributor, Bergen Brunswig, is illustrative: Most manual work is done by machine. Work teams that dot the facility are not so much in the business of "doing" (by old standards), but in the business of improving the system. They are brain-involved, improvement-project creators, not muscle-driven lump shifters. There is no room on the staff for anyone who sees himself or herself as a pair of hands, punching a time clock.

Education Redefined

The nature of worker education must change. Employees have seldom loved "training"—as in second-rate instructors stuffing outdated material down throats. Yet Quad/Graphics is a university disguised as a company. Workers spend a day a week in the classroom—a "day a week, forever" as a leader in the firm's educational program puts it. "Training" is out. "Life-long learning" is in. Every thriving firm, from bank to burger maker, will look like a university—period.

Besides training in the new technologies and techniques, like statistical process control and problem cause-and-effect analysis, there's a need for massive doses of "inter-firm relationship training," according to Stan Davis. It's a must if seamless links with "foreign" firms (suppliers, producers, middlepersons, customers from everywhere) are the norm.

Society's educational needs will differ too. Fads may stress a return to the three Rs (and that apple surely needs polishing), but the opposite is actually the more pressing requirement. Every viable worker will be required to think and create. Consider these words from Stan Davis:

> Mass production means meticulous attention to repetitive detail . . . Socialization in the industrial world was to make [children] capable of sustaining boredom in adult life. An example . . . is the way children who are naturally creative were punished in schools a few generations back. A not uncommon punishment was to write something like "I will not say _ again" one hundred times on the blackboard. The purpose . . . was to adapt them to carrying out repetitive detail in the industrial labor force. Perhaps today a more creativity-producing punishment for the same act would be to list a hundred different ways of saying the same "_" thing.

Every Person a "Global Player"

Recall Handy's description of London firms sending typing to Taipei. To survive, London typists must realize they are competing with Taipei typists. They must learn to "add value" (e.g., know more software programs, more languages than their Taiwanese counterparts) or else they'd better learn to love pounding the pavement. This is especially tough for xenophobic Americans, who grew up believing in the god-given invincibility of the United States economy. Every American work force survivor, receptionist to computer scientist, must become obsessed with Europe and Asia—and how to add more value than their counterpart at the big firm 6,000 miles away or the start-up next door.

Entrepreneurs Taking on any Task

As change accelerates, we will see more entrepreneurs like the software start-up, the biotech lab, the new financial services boutique, the specialty food maker, the personal-shopper outfit, the custom magazine producer (there were 491 new, customized magazines launched in the United States alone in 1988). But new *forms* of entrepreneurs will spring up, too. For example, middle managers at big firms will become "project creators," to use Kanter's term; smart ones will move quickly to create an independent skill base.

Let's fantasize for a moment about how the endangered middle manager might survive in the new "lean-and-mean" environment. Pretend you are a mid-level accounting boss in a $100 million division of a bigger firm. In the past, your job description was narrow: keep the books accurately. Bird dog (i.e. harass) those who don't get their numbers in on time. Stay in your office, ready to instantly answer queries from higher-ups.

Suppose your division has three factories, two distribution centers, a couple of sizable engineering groups, a marketing operation, and four sales branches. Your survival strategy today should begin with a wandering jag. Meet with your dozen groups' leaders: How can you and your gang help? You'll likely spark the enthusiasm of a couple of middle managers. Schedule a briefing session with each unit leader to talk about "the revolution in project accounting." Give your spiel quickly then discuss cooperative efforts. Volunteer one of your staff or yourself to work on an experimental project—e.g., a major modification to a costing system to accompany the next product launch. Aim to have a half-dozen pilot projects in various stages at any time; each of your people should be working on at least one, and 10 percent should be on full-time pilot assignment at any time.

Think like a consultant: Eventually, you should propose to sell your service to other divisions. This not only makes you and your team more valuable, it also prepares you for the next bold step: peddling your group's expert services for a profit *outside* the corporation. If later you are a victim of "pyramid flattening," you will have proven, marketable skills. You might even propose to cut the umbilical cord, go independent, incorporate, and then sell half your services back to the company. Of course, the story is no fantasy; it's practiced in outfit after outfit today.

So, "entrepreneur" means anybody from anywhere who can figure out some way to do *something* better. And the faster one can figure that out, and the quicker one is willing to become or consider becoming an independent purveyor of unique skills, the better the chances for continued participation in the work force.

New Winners and New Losers

New winners and new losers pop up every day. New losers include over 40 percent of the 1979 Fortune 500 that have disappeared from that list in the last decade. Losing means gone out of business, being swallowed up by another firm and reconfigured or dismantled, being supplanted by an up-start—Apple in computers, Nucor in steel. MCI CEO Bill McGowan may have described the new context best. The former "rags-to-riches-to-rags cycle," he says, was about three generations. Now it's down to five years. Never has an employee's, company's, industry's toehold been so precarious.

The same trauma even besets regions. The sluggishness of the Rust Belt versus the vitality of the Altanta-Tampa-Austin-Los Angeles-Portland "golden crescent," as I call it, is now old news. But the disparities will become more pronounced with time. In his superb book, *Job Creation in America*, economist David Birch comments that, "Most of the new firms taking the place of the older ones offer different kinds of locations and work forces, present different needs for capital, transportation, government services, education, recreation, and energy." A firm no longer gravitates to North Carolina for low wages, but for the prowess of Duke. Regions with skilled workers, great universities, a sound K–12 school system, a clean environment, and a ready flow of entrepreneurial capital will grab the lion's share of tomorrow's brain-based jobs and firms.

Search for New Bases for Competitive Advantage

Finally, all of the above comes down to the frantic pursuit of new bases for competitive advantage. Chief among them:

1. *Speed/time.* Time compression is becoming the principal basis for competitive advantage, according to one rapidly developing school of thought. Businesses are squeezing production cycles, slashing product development cycles, shrinking delivery time. Companies that can bring the "newest and most improved" to the market fastest, ensure instant delivery anywhere and everywhere, and then quickly upgrade the product stand a chance of surviving. Those that don't learn to play this very complicated game don't stand a chance. For example, KG Stores' chief information officer insists that soon his company will not accept orders from vendors that are not hooked up electronically. In another case, a mid-sized plumbing supply distributor in the deep South threatened mighty plumbing products manufacturer Kohler of Wisconsin: Speed up (a lot) or else. Kohler had to comply.

2. *Flexibility.* Quickly getting into and out of things is a necessity today, since "leap-frogging" takes place regularly in virtually any industry you can name. Quality improves dramatically overnight. New performance standards eclipse old ones in a flash. Rapidly forming new alliances is a parallel requirement. Thus the paradox: Flexibility means raw speed, but there is also an unprecedented need for patient investment in developing relationships and alliances, at home and in overseas markets.

3. *Quality/design.* Superb quality alone won't be enough for future survival. But superb quality is an absolute requisite for any developed (or developing) nation/firm in virtually every market. Quality moved atop the United States corporate priority list in the early 1980s. Now we are talking about other "top priorities," such as speed and service added. That's sensible. However, the average American firm has not "licked the quality issue." There is much more to be done in training and education, in employee involvement and adoption of self-managing teams to provide autonomy to those closest to the action. "World-class quality" may be a "given," as all my friends tell me, but it's a given at damn few of the firms I work with.

    Quality's handmaiden is design—aesthetics, user friendliness, functionality. Putting design "in the loop" from the start of the product development process, as a Ford now does and as a Herman Miller always has done, is one of the many new horizons that will distinguish tomorrow's winners from the losers.

4. *The astute—and pioneering—use of information technology.* Getting everyone to experiment brashly with information technology in every part of the organization, *and* in every "outside" business relationship, is a survival essential. "Fast followership" is not enough: Pioneering, scary or not, is required.

5. *Forming alliances and becoming a network partner.* Creating new temporary or permanent alliances and embedding the organization in tightly linked networks with suppliers, middlepersons, and customers are also absolute survival requirements. "Network management" skills will quickly become the most cherished in the firm.

6. *Fast innovation/perpetual improvement.* Dramatically compressing development cycles, tough as that job is, constitutes only a part of the emerging innovation equation. Most sizable firms still quake at the smallest failures, can't deal with obstreperous new-product champions, refuse to grant true autonomy and requisite spending authority to "low-level" units and overinvest in yesterday's winners. They are, in short, lousy innovators with a pronounced anti-innovation bias: It is tomorrow's kiss of death.

    The perpetual improvement of everything (another flavor of innovation) is also an absolute necessity that represents a stunning departure from the past. Fast-paced quality improvement can go on forever—and must. Fast-paced productivity improvement can go on forever—and must. Fast-paced organizational and business process improvement can go on forever—and must. Everyone, literally, must picture himself or herself in the "perpetual improvement business, full time," to quote one exec.

7. *Perpetual skill upgrading.* The skill package that the corporation and its network brings to the marketplace, and the pace at which that package increases compared to the skill package of its competitors and their networks, will determine competitiveness like no other factor. "World-class work force" must become a more common phrase than "world-class quality." Why? Because the former drives the latter.

8. *Service added.* Adding service—another form of intelligence—to every product and its distribution and marketing is yet another *survival* necessity. For example, Levi Strauss is betting the company on its ability to be responsive to customers, more than on its fashion design skills.

9. *Small within big.* Scale is changing. "New big" is neither beautiful nor ugly, just profoundly different from "old big." Big in the traditional sense—7,000 people under one auto factory's roof—is an almost guaranteed loser today. But big *networks* of various-sized firms is an oddball form that will likely survive and prosper.

    Other winners: Smallish, self-contained units within very big firms and big networks composed of specialist pieces of firms of various sizes. In fact, the successful "new big" outfit is probably best conceived as a "network/alliance manager," rather than a vertically integrated behemoth. Even goliath Boeing says its chief skill is "systems integration."

10. *Subcontracting.* In *The Age of Unreason* Charles Handy describes an exercise conducted by executives at a multibillion-pound British company; they aimed to determine what *couldn't* be subcontracted. They decided that everything could be farmed out "except for the chief executive officer and his car phone." That's a bit extreme, but only a bit. In the conservative publication *Business Month,* a wag recently predicted that "by the year 2010 there may be no CEOs" in the new, flat, network forms of organization.

    Consider what is perhaps today's ultimate example, the FI Group, one of Britain's largest software systems houses. FI employs about 1,100, most of who are part-time freelancers who need toil no more than 20 hours per week. More than two-thirds of the firm's work is done at home: All told, employees live in 800 sites and serve 400 clients at any time. Life at FI is captured in the November 1988 issue of *Business:* "Chris Eyles, project manager, sat down in her office in Esher, Surrey, and called up the electronic 'chit chat' mailbox. . . . The printer began to churn out messages. 'Help!' said [a message] from her secretary, based a few miles away in Weybridge. Somewhere in the Esher area, a computer analyst was in trouble. . . . Eyles checked the team diary and her wall plan, located the analyst and the problem and set up a meeting a FI's work center in Horley, 25 miles away."

    The benefits of FI's flexible configuration to employees are obvious. But clients benefit too. Talented specialists can be called upon at a moment's notice to perform almost any task. The firm has also developed an exceptional quality record, putting to rest the idea that dispersed part-timers can't turn out top-drawer, integrated systems. FI's business is booming because its clients are heading down the same path it has. FI chief executive Hilary Cropper observes, "Before, companies tended to use FI to fill. Now they want to off-load the whole show."

11. *Globalization.* "Thinking global" is/will be the province of virtually any would-be survivor of any size. "Global players" include the small flashlight maker Maglite in Los Angeles and the penmaker A.T. Cross in Lincoln, Rhode Island, as well as GE and IBM.

Review this article and you'll realize that not only will no stones be long left unturned, but no newly turned stones are likely to gather moss in the years ahead. Perhaps the best and only defense (or offense) is to broaden your interests and become a champion for change—whether you are a London typist, small-business owner, big-firm middle manager or chief executive officer. The forces foisting all this change upon us have barely been unleashed.

Discussion Questions

1. Briefly describe the forces of globalization and information technology that are affecting the massive economic transformation.
2. What are the results of these two forces?
3. What is the overall impact of these two forces? ▼

"Why Business Managers Are Empty-handed," by David Vaskevitch

(This reading is especially suited for use in conjunction with Chapter 5 of *Information Systems*.)

Do managers really spend most of their time processing words, building spreadsheets and maintaining simple databases? That's what you'd think, looking at today's software sales and the primary efforts of the PC software industry.

The dominant software categories are word processors, spreadsheets and databases, which account for 75% of the world's PC software purchasing dollars. The next tier of applications includes presentation graphics, project management and electronic mail.

But word processors never found their way into the hearts and minds of managers. Spreadsheets can be liberating for budget-building, but most managers spend little time calculating numbers other than at budget time. And while database software is quite powerful, it can also be quite complex.

In reality, most managers use their PCs for only a fraction of the day, instead preferring copiers, fax machines, telephones, filing cabinets, secretaries and personal interaction.

In fact, while the PC is supposed to represent an electronic desk, it doesn't even come close to replacing the piece of furniture on which the machine sits. That's because today's PC software doesn't fit with what today's managers really do.

During the '90s, the software industry has to gain a clearer picture of how managers work so it can deliver useful tools.

Managers tend to work through others instead of accomplishing tasks themselves. Rather than being generators of words and numbers, managers focus primarily on the three C's: communication, control and coordination.

The computer, particularly in a networked form, can help managers concentrate on communication, control and coordination, but only if new categories of software, as described in the following pages, emerge.

A new generation of applications that will finally support a manager's everyday tasks of communication, control and coordination will make its appearance before the decade is out. With a new set of software (described on these pages), the PC could become a tool managers use all day, every day. These machines will become—finally—a central part of every manager's job.

COMMUNICATE

Managers probably spend most of their time communicating. As new PC software becomes available that more directly supports this activity, the managerial workstation will become indispensable.

Today, most managers would hardly notice if the PC on their desks were taken away—except at budget time or while writing a key memo. However, in companies with active electronic-mail systems, managers notice and complain within minutes if the mail system or their PC stops working.

E-mail, in its ability to improve the informal communications process, is the first tool to change the underlying patterns that are implicit in a manager's everyday working life.

Yet in many ways, E-mail addresses only a small part of the real need. For one thing, most E-mail systems don't remember any history. In addition, they are limited in scope, best suited for directed communications among either individuals or small groups of people.

SOURCE: David Vaskevitch, "Why Business Managers are Empty-handed," *Computerworld,* April 5, 1993, pp. 93, 96, and 97. Copyright 1993 by *Computerworld.*

Other types of communications software, namely bulletin board systems, markup packages and multiuser hypertext systems, start to address the rest of the need.

Bulletin board systems were specifically designed to remember lots of history, and they facilitate communication among medium and large groups of communicators. The system is organized around topics—that is, any subject a group of people is interested in discussing. Every message sent through a bulletin board is typically kept for subsequent display by all other interested users.

With a bulletin board system, a manager can confront an issue, come up to speed quickly, bring his longer term perspective to bear and make a decision that enables a deadlocked team to start making progress again.

A bulletin board system facilitates this process in three ways:

- The manager can stay on top of active topics by skimming the structure of the bulletin board to decide where he most needs to get involved.
- Once he has decided that an issue requires his involvement, the manager can quickly come up to speed on the context and background.
- Before making a decision, the manager can poll the team and others for additional input. The bulletin board provides both a mechanism for everyone involved in the decision to be equally up to speed and for contributors to add their input quickly, facilitating a rapid decision.

If bulletin boards are so useful, why aren't they more popular in the managerial community and among corporations in general? Part of the reason is that until recently, this technology did not really exist in a form that corporations could use internally. Lotus Development Corp.'s Notes is probably the first large-scale commercial product that is bringing bulletin board technology to commercial organizations.

But E-mail and bulletin boards are just the beginning. Waiting in the wings is an approach to communicating based on E-mail and bulletin boards that goes beyond those technologies.

To understand this communications environment, you need to understand the concept of multiuser hypertext. Whenever someone writes text, such as a memo, a story, a letter or a piece of E-mail, the author is taking a complex web of concepts and thoughts and reducing it to a linear, sentence-based form. Hypertext, on the other hand, enables users to store the original, nonlinear web of concepts directly in the computer.

Because the hypertext system maintains all the relationships between concepts, it is possible to jump from one concept to another.

Today, when a PC user communicates, he is forced to save his communication in one of three places: the traditional file system on his hard disk and network, his E-mail system or a bulletin board repository. Each of these meets a particular need, but they do not tie together very well.

Suppose you could replace all three with a single, organizationwide—or even worldwide—multiuser hypertext system?

In this new world, each time a manager communicates, what he writes would be stored in a universal shared information space. Each communication could be linked to all related communications.

Eventually, this system—in essence a synthesis of E-mail and bulletin board concepts—would be so powerful and ubiquitous that it could replace the current concept of a file system and become the underpinning of a PC-based information environment.

The file system is transformed from a passive, storage-based repository to an active communications environment that is visible to the user on a constant basis.

CONTROL

To be in control, a manager must be on top of his numbers; managers are expected to produce solid budgets and forecasts. Today's software not only falls short of supporting budget and forecasting needs, but it also fails to facilitate information access so managers can determine whether operations are on target.

You'd think budgeting and forecasting are well-served by existing tools, particularly the spreadsheet. Well, yes and no. Of course, the spreadsheet has become the primary tool used to develop budgets and forecasts, and, of course, it has simplified life tremendously compared with calculators. Yet the spreadsheet ignores two key components of budgeting: mathematical forecasting and data collection across the organization.

The standard spreadsheet leaves forecast model building, for instance, entirely up to the user. Because most people are notoriously bad at developing accurate forecasts, most business plans are based on some form of simple linear growth.

What managers need is access to some form of modeling tool that provides more sophisticated forecasting capabilities, along with built-in expert assistance in how to use them.

As for collecting data across the organization, spreadsheets again come up lacking. Most large organizations collect budget data from individuals and departments to get a corporatewide picture. Changes are then compared with overall profit targets, and managers are asked to redo their budgets. This process is repeated again and again.

The single-user spreadsheet tools available today cannot support this process. While limited facilities are provided for one spreadsheet to reference another, no spreadsheet available today has any understanding of how organizations are structured and how data is consolidated and controlled on an ongoing basis.

It is not hard to imagine a budgeting and control tool that would solve both of the problems described above. The system would start with an understanding of the organization's structure. It would also contain basic forecasting facilities, including a model for seasonal trends by product line as well as the company's master assumption about growth in the quarters ahead.

Individual managers would be able to use the system much as they use a spreadsheet today—in fact, the spreadsheet might be the basic mechanism for accessing the system. However, the underlying support structure would make all budgets and forecasts automatically part of the larger structure of organizationwide numbers without any need for copying spreadsheets or sending disks around by mail.

Such a system is not currently available. If it were, it would likely take the form of a spreadsheet front end to a database-oriented budgeting and accounting system.

Beyond sophisticated budget and forecasting, managers need to determine how their operations are doing against budget. Today—30 years after the introduction of the first computerized accounting systems—most managers have a hard time accessing that kind of performance information.

Understanding expenses often requires accessing more than accounting information; the manager must go back to the original memos, plans, proposals and status reports describing the project.

In theory, if this information is computer-based, it should be easy to find. Unfortunately, that's not the case.

Searching through multiple directories across several servers on a network is only slightly more likely to result in a retrieval than looking through file cabinets.

What managers need is a fast, friendly way of finding documents when they need them. This is an area that has received much attention during the last 20 years, yet the basic filing system most companies use continues to be based on DOS and its eight-character file names.

The kind of filing system managers need to make information access easier should have the following characteristics:

- Foldering facilities that enable documents to be filed in multiple places.
- Cross-document linking so that any document can refer to any number of other documents.
- Content-based retrieval so that documents can be located based on key words and phrases found anywhere in the text.

- Automatic archival both to migrate unused documents off the network and to bring these documents back.

Today, the only way to get the kind of filing system described here is to sweat through building it from scratch with third-party tools. Eventually, however, these types of facilities will likely become a basic part of operating systems.

COORDINATE

Coordinating the activities of a team is a time-consuming activity for most managers. This task largely involves goal-setting, schedule-setting and attending regular meetings to keep in sync with the team.

Superficially, project management software and personal information managers appear to address many of these coordination needs. Yet, even managers who depend on project management software tend to view it as a highly formal mechanism that they use only on the largest projects rather than as a vehicle for routine team coordination. Project software isn't suited for the kind of goal-setting important to the team environment.

Personal information managers, for their part, can establish and track goals and create to-do lists as well as coordinate multiple calendars to simplify meeting scheduling. But most are limited in a team setting, unable to manage the calendars of any group larger than about five to 10 people.

What business managers need is a combination of project manager and personal information manager features to yield what might be called a "team coordination system."

Such a system would include the following functions:

- **Goal manager:** *A shared forum to agree on goals, including unscheduled future objectives.*

How often have you thought of a future project that your team has no time for now and wondered how to keep track of that goal so it can be reconsidered periodically for eventual implementation? How about being able to see how all the goals for several groups, all part of a larger department, fit together?

A goal management system would deal with these kinds of problems, enabling goals set during an annual performance review to be reflected in quarterly, monthly and weekly objectives. The goal manager would enable a manager to see high-level objectives for himself, his managers and his team. He would be able to drill down to uncover the underlying details associated with accomplishing particular objectives within certain time frames.

Goal managers would be for team use. The software would provide a framework for group planning meetings, allowing the group to see high-level long-term goals or zero in on a particular area to plan a specific project.

Best of all, the system would provide a shared structure for all managers so they can share goals and coordinate activities.

- **Progress manager:** *A tracking mechanism for the timelines (strict and otherwise) associated with projects and goals.*

While the goal manager deals with the highest level planning and coordinating, a progress manager deals with the next level down. It tracks progress against objectives for a manager and his team.

Progress management software ensures that goals and schedules are in sync, it has no fixed beginning or ending date and it produces a fluid schedule that consists of multiple, unrelated activity networks. Goals, projects and tasks don't have to be part of a larger project.

Finally, progress management software has different types of output that are both simple and easy to annotate.

- **Schedule manager:** *A more detailed framework for sharing schedule information, including travel, meetings and activities related to goals.*

The final component of the team coordination system is a schedule manager. This component would include all the standard facilities of schedule, calendar and diary management, from scheduling meetings to keeping up on team travel and what project everyone is working on.

To make it all work, the system would have to exhibit some of these key characteristics:

- Fast and easy to use.
- Robust. Because calendar information, particularly for groups, is critical, it can't be lost. So a schedule manager would need the type of the integrity features found in transaction database systems.
- High throughput. Because the schedule manager has the potential for heavy use, it should be based on a highly distributed, scalable technology.

For large organizations, for instance, systems based on simple sharing of DOS files on a server would quickly run into critical performance limitations.

Some organizations have started to implement their own team coordination systems. One large government department, faced with a software project that will take eight years and involve thousands of programmers, is writing specifications for a comprehensive system. However, some companies can't afford the build-it-yourself approach.

In time, packaged software should emerge that marries personal information managers with the functionality in project management programs.

Discussion Questions

1. To what extent does currently existing software support the tasks of business managers?
2. How can managers use software to communicate, control, and coordinate more effectively?
3. What changes should be made in software to better support managers' tasks?. ▼

 **"Saving Time with New Technology," by Gene Bylinsky**

(This reading is especially suited for use in conjunction with Chapter 6 of *Information Systems.*)

If you travel a lot, how can you possible keep in touch with everybody you need to talk to? How do you avoid getting trapped in endless time-wasting games of telephone tag?

Welcome to the world of bits, bauds, modems, laptops, faxes. E-mail, on-line data service, logon names, voice mail, pagers, cellular phones, and an electronic cornucopia of new hardware. An adventurous breed of top managers and professionals—call them the wired executives—stay on top of business wherever they are, anywhere in the world, with highly portable computers and telecommunications devices that liberate them from the constraints of the office. Universally, these peripatetic executives praise their newfound freedom. More than that, their use of electronic devices has made them enormously more productive and has saved them huge amounts of time in the office, on the road, and at home.

Kenneth Olsen, CEO of Digital Equipment Corp., calls what they're doing "nomadic computing." You don't have to be a Silicon Valley techie to practice it. While many of its adepts are men and women in the computer or telecommunications industries, some you will meet in these pages operate in unmistakably low-tech venues: marketing, public relations, journalism, local government, a university. You will discover how these pioneers deploy their supergadgets, and see some of their often spectacular results.

Philippe Kahn, 39, founder and CEO of Borland International, the fast-growing software company in Scotts Valley, California, had long been frustrated by old-fashioned hotel telephones. Wired permanently into the wall, they deprive portable computer users of their umbilical connection—a phone jack—to the rest of the world. Kahn, a born problem solver, decided to do something about it. He started carrying a kit containing a soldering iron, screwdrivers, pliers, and other tools to remedy that lapse.

A French-born mathematician, musician, sailor and software genius, Kahn is not your run-of-the-mill computer user. At any given time, Kahn may be testing his company's and competitors' software on many machines (they include a Mitsubishi mobile phone, a Poqet palmtop, Sporty's E6B flight navigation computer, a Sharp Wizard Palmtop, a Sharp graphics printer, a Dell System 320N laptop, and a Canon bubble-jet printer).

Four years ago, after checking into the Hôtel de Crillon, just across the rue Boissy d'Anglas from the U.S. Embassy in Paris, Kahn ordered a bottle of Perrier and dived under the table, tools in hand. The Perrier soon arrived. Ten minutes later, so did eight husky men who barged into Kahn's room without knocking, loudly demanding to know what he was doing. They were French and American security men. Says Kahn: "It took me half an hour to explain."

He arrived in the U.S. in 1982 with $2,000. Without a green card he couldn't get a job, so the next year he founded Borland International—a huge success from the start, thanks to his Turbo Pascal software that made it possible to write programs on PCs much faster than before. This October, Borland acquired rival Ashton-Tate (best known for its dBase software) for $439 million. That turned Borland overnight into one of the world's largest software companies, with estimated sales of $500 million this fiscal year.

Kahn runs Borland by E-mail from wherever he happens to be: Paris, New York City, or Auckland, New Zealand. Sometimes he runs it from a hilltop near his office. He drives up into the woods on his dirt bike to sit under a tree and transmit messages from his laptop via cellular phone.

SOURCE: Gene Bylinsky, "Serving Time with New Technology," *Fortune,* December 30, 1991, pp. 98–104. © 1991 Time Inc. All rights reserved.

He says he's fighting the "meetingomania" of American business. Managers from his 11 subsidiaries and three sales offices around the world rarely meet in person, but the are always on-line—electronically connected. Kahn spends as much as three hours a day answering up to 150 E-mail messages. A dynamo who gets by on an average of five hours' sleep, Kahn often sends E-mail as late as 2 a.m. and sometimes prepares slides on his laptop in the middle of the night aboard the red-eye or a leased corporate jet.

In 1988, he and a crew of 11, including his wife, Martine, sailed his 70-foot sloop *Kathmandu* in the biennial Pacific Cup race from San Francisco to Oahu in typically Kahnian fashion. Using a laptop, a fax machine, and a printer on board, Kahn calculated the advantages of different routes with a program he wrote and deliberately chose the longest course. By first heading nearly as far south as Los Angeles and then cutting west, he avoided a delaying weather system called the Pacific High. He won the race in record time.

Oh yes, those hoteliers in Paris and elsewhere need not worry about their phones. Kahn usually reconnects them carefully. Sometimes, though, he'll leave a temporary connection in place so when he returns he can ask for the same room to save himself trouble. Occasionally it even works.

When he set out on business trips a few years ago, Manville Corp. CEO W. Thomas Stephens, 49, often felt like a high-tech Himalayan porter, lugging around his heavy computer and mobile phone. Now as he glides in a limo through Manhattan traffic, Stephens works on a seven-pound Compaq notebook computer. An attachment, the JT Fax made by Quadram Corp., converts the computer into a fax receiver that pops incoming messages up on the screen. Aboard his company jet, Stephens also carries a small Kodak 150 printer. On overseas trips, he has with him an 11-ounce Hewlett-Packard palmtop. At his office in Denver, Stephens uses his Compaq as a desktop.

He employs all those computers and an Epson Equity III at home for much more than instant Access to financial and other data. He has always viewed the computer as an extension of his mind. Says he: "It gives you an opportunity to be a lot more powerful and to focus on being creative rather than spending your time making charts and that sort of thing."

Stephens used the power of the computers to help pull Manville out of bankruptcy. With spreadsheets and computer graphics, he prepared clear and convincing presentations for company directors and groups of people making asbestos health damage claims. He helped restore employee morale by answering letters on his PC. Now, as he hunts for acquisitions for his rejuvenated $2.2-billion-a-year company, Stephens finds he can analyze the possibilities with unmatched versatility and speed. But he still loses more computer chess games to his daughter Anne, 8, than he wins.

"Sir, you want to send a fax to *yourself*?" That question, with its implication that the customer is slightly daft, has been asked of wired executives in many parts of the world. James E. Clark, 39, a vice president for medium-size computers at AT&T's new NCR subsidiary, faced it recently in Bombay.

Clark wanted to print out a presentation by sending it as a message to his hotel's fax machine from his hotel room—a trick clever computer addicts use to save carting a printer along. But he encountered one of those telephones permanently wired into the wall. Knowing that fax machines usually have a phone jack he could plug his laptop into, Clark sauntered over to the hotel's business office. There sat two fax machines side by side. If Clark connected his computer to one of them, he could send a fax to its sibling. It took him some time to explain what he wanted to do, but he finally prevailed.

The phone jack problem, at least on the receiving end, has been solved for Clark and other users of AT&T's snazzy new Safari notebook computer. Introduced earlier this year, the Safari is equipped with the first "wireless mailbox" to hit the market. It's a small pager that can store at one time as many as 20 messages of about 40 words each bounced off a SkyTel satellite. The messages can be read off the pager's screen.

Wireless messaging should untether the workplace even further. Clark, on the road most of the time, practices it resolutely; he calls it "anytime, anywhere computing" using "a post office in the sky."

Inside Phoenix's Sky Harbor airport, a slightly built woman sits on the floor between two elevators. Another homeless person? No, she is well dressed and busily tapping away on her Safari notebook computer. Just another wired executive at work. "It's the only place I could find a plug," explains Patricia Seybold, 42, a much traveled Boston management consultant and computer newsletter publisher. She often walks to work with her seven-pound notebook machine and her 70-pound mutt, Garlic.

What Seybold likes is the instant interaction her electronic gear provides with both clients and the equally nomadic staff of analysts at her Office Computing Group. "We publish our information electronically for a select group of customers who choose to pay more for that," says Seybold. "The customers log on in their offices. They can get our publications on-line and they can ask questions. They can interact with me about the subject matter right on the computer screen."

Soon she plans to start using a computer she can write on with a pen. She will have it programmed to read the circles, triangles, and squares she draws to portray the flow of work—insurance claim processing, say, or readying a manuscript for publishing—at the companies she consults with, many of them Fortune 500 corporations. "You could project the image on an overhead screen so that a group could see it and work together to make that particular process more efficient."

At a recent meeting of some 40 media executives and academics at a Chicago hotel, John M. Lavine, 50, director of the Newspaper Management Center at Northwestern University, surprised some of the participants by whipping out on the spot printed drafts of rather complex standards for accrediting journalism schools even as the participants continued to polish the final version. Lavine did this with a Safari notebook computer and a four-pound Seikosha LT-20 printer, shown to his right in the picture at left. Both fit in his briefcase.

Lavine took advantage of a program feature that allows him to cross out portions of text to be deleted and to indicate proposed additions by underlining them. As the changes were agreed on, he incorporated them into the text and then used the hotel's Xerox machine to make enough copies of the paper for all the participants.

Lavine is the former publisher of a chain of eight Wisconsin dailies and weeklies; among other things, he does management counsulting for newspapers. He has some hard-earned advice for managers looking to become wired. "I'm not a computer hardware freak," he says. "The goal is to have electronics serve me, not for me to become a captive of it. Executives should guard against doing on computers what their assistants can do for them, such as some of the more menial computer work. Ask yourself, 'What's the best use of my time?'"

Accordingly, Lavine centers his electronic work on the creative side. "When I'm under pressure, I can compose and edit a proposal or a presentation on a computer. When I'm done, I push a button and the proposal comes out right in a newspaper or a consulting company's office." On the go, Lavine also uses a palmtop Wizard to take notes at meetings and to store his Rolodex, his appointment calendar, and outlines of some of the major projects he's thinking about. Concludes Lavine: "Computers and telecommunications have made possible much higher quality work."

When his mother became seriously ill recently, Bernard Krisher, 60, an American journalist-entrepreneur in Tokyo, took the next plane to New York. Armed with a vintage NEC 8201 laptop, Krisher flew off without hesitation. (He later added to his electronic arsenal a palmtop Sharp Wizard he bought in New York.) Says he: "I was able to stay at my mother's bedside for six weeks, until she passed away. I kept in touch with my clients via E-mail I sent from the hospital room, and I composed messages in taxicabs on the Wizard. Many of my clients didn't even know I wasn't in Tokyo."

Fax before breakfast. E-mail at lunch. Laptop after dinner. Krisher's days and nights center around computers and telecommunications. His friends and clients aren't surprised to get E-mail, faxes, or hardcopy letters that originated in such exotic places as an express train speeding across Germany or his vacation home near Japan's Mount Fuji. He is shown at right near that home, in the process of transmitting to Tokyo and New York City via cellular phone a message he has typed into his palmtop.

He connects a modem to his Wizard and then plugs the modem into a coupler that cradles the phone. The message will cross the Pacific via MCI Mail, an electronic messaging service Krisher subscribes to. One recipient in New York also subscribes to MCI Mail, so he will read the message on his computer screen. Another, a nonsubscriber, gets the message as a letter two days later; MCI prints it out at hard copy in New York and forwards it through the Postal Service. The Tokyo recipient will get it at his hotel by fax from New York.

After he returned to Tokyo recently, Krisher used a public phone equipped with a special jack that allows a computer modem to be plugged in for message sending over telephone lines. Unhappily for wired executives, those phones are rare in Japan and only a few are available in the U.S.—so far.

Electronic devices help Krisher do a prodigious amount of work. He is chief editorial adviser to *Focus,* a popular weekly he helped start; he set up a Harry Winston jewelry salon on the Ginza and acts as a company director in Japan; he writes speeches for Japanese executives; he advises a PC users network, similar to CompuServe, in Tokyo; and he operates a service he put together that retrieves information from databases for half a dozen top Japanese corporations. To do all that, Krisher employs not a single secretary—only electronic help. In addition to the NEC laptop and the Wizard, he has four Macintoshes, a Worldport modem, and a cellular phone.

When at home, Krisher is always at his Mac before breakfast sending faxes and E-mail. Says Krisher: "Often I get half a day's paperwork done—at 2400 baud—before getting dressed." He continues his on-line activities at the *Focus* office, tapping as needed into such electronic fact repositories as Nexis and Dow Jones. Back home in the evening, he sends more faxes and E-mail to clients.

"An on-line life has freed me from the straitjacket of being confined to any given place," says Krisher. "I've become totally self-reliant so that I can easily mix business and pleasure. I'm able to receive and send messages and manuscripts to and from practically anywhere. And no one even needs to know where I am."

If, as the adage has it, the difference between adults and children lies in the price of their toys, Regis and Dianne McKenna are seriously adult. The equipment and software in the spacious computer room of their house in Sunnyvale, California, are worth about $20,000. They include two Macintosh CX's, a Macintosh PowerBook notebook computer, two text scanners, Radius large-screen terminals, an Apple laser printer, two Hayes 9600 Smartmodems, and a fax machine.

The payoff has been overwhelming. Looking much like a lepidopterist scrutinizing a rare butterfly, Regis McKenna, 52, a Caere optical digital scanner in hand, captures a paragraph of text from the *Harvard Business Review.* The scanner reads the information into his Mac's memory by translating the letters into digital language. Later, as he composes a speech, McKenna retrieves the data and incorporates it into his talk. He then electronically transmits the draft to a freelance editor in Half Moon Bay, 50 miles away.

A few days later the editor electronically deposits her revised version into a computer server, a kind of information-storing traffic cop, at McKenna's Palo Alto office, ten miles from his house. At home soon thereafter McKenna retrieves the speech electronically from the office server, makes some changes on the screen, and prints it out on his laser printer—the first time the speech has appeared on paper.

McKenna is a Silicon Valley mover and shaker whose 100-person marketing consulting and public relations firm has put many a startup on the map. (He helped fledgling entrepreneurs Steve Jobs and Stephen Wozniak find venture capital to launch Apple Computer; a McKenna designer concocted the famous Apple logo.) McKenna is electronically linked not only to his five regional offices but also to the powerful Bay Area venture capital company Kleiner Perkins Caufield & Byers, of which he is a partner, and to a number of local high-tech companies he serves as a director.

Without the pervasive use of electronics at home, in the office, and on the road, McKenna says he could not have accomplished half as much. In pre-electronics days he would often hop into his Mercedes on weekends to fetch items from his office.

Now almost everything he needs is as near as the keyboards of his computers. When he travels, McKenna takes the new Macintosh notebook with him to stay in touch. He used an earlier portable Mac to write his latest book, *Relationship Marketing*.

McKenna and his wife, Dianne, 48, often work side by side on their his-and-hers Macs. Her domain is even larger than her husband's. She is chairwoman of the Santa Clara County board of supervisors, which is responsible for apportioning an annual budget of $1.3 billion to serve 1.5 million residents. She often writes letters on her computer at night to send electronically to her staff of eight in San Jose. Next morning, she rushes off at 7:30 for a meeting in San Francisco, 50 miles to the north, safe in the knowledge that her office is humming. She makes doubly sure of that over a cellular phone in *her* Mercedes. Out of town, she usually carries along a laptop. At home, she uses a computer to do the family banking and to operate a jukeboxlike 240-disk Phoenix System CD player, changing the music at the click of a mouse. Says she, in an understatement: "Electronics makes my work and my life a lot easier and more efficient."

Discussion Questions

1. What types of electronic equipment do executives who travel extensively use?
2. How does this equipment help them perform their jobs better?
3. Give three examples of executives' use of new hardware to help them perform their jobs better? ▼

Reading 6

"In Search of the Perfect," by Steven Caniano

(This reading is especially suited for use in conjunction with Chapter 7 of *Information Systems*.)

Typically, one of the most difficult aspects of information systems engineering is selecting the software to manage the system's data. The success of a given system often hinges on the selection of DBMS software to store and control access to key business data properly.

Selecting this critical technology is very difficult. Many products are available, all claiming to be the premier DBMS. It is quite a challenge to understand each product's features, not to mention account for the differences among the many platforms and product releases.

People often find themselves in a maze of vendor hype and "expert" opinions and are left in the unenviable position of having to make a choice. This article will analyze the process of DBMS selection, presenting the key issues you should consider and questions you should ask. Obviously, as a reference guide, this article is much more generic than an application-specific analysis would be. Nevertheless, the issues presented will provide you with a solid foundation upon which to develop a more customized set of issues and, ultimately, help you make a selection.

Over time, I expect the key issues I will describe in this two-part series to evolve, as will the DBMS products' ability to address them. Readers must determine the levels at which the current portfolio of products address these key issues.

ISSUE CATEGORIES

This article defines dozens of issues that, for the purpose of clarity, I will structure into five general categories:

- System and application profile issues cover items that define the particulars of a given application. These factors are probably the most critical to consider since failure to meet application-specific needs typically outweighs the amount of features and functionality a product can provide.
- Management and vendor issues refer to items not specific to product features, but critical to understanding vendors and their services. Typical issues in this category are support, training, documentation, and financial health.
- Development and database administrator issues are those of particular concern to individuals who must use the product to design and build an application or database.
- System internals and architectural issues relate to the core components of a modern DBMS system and the implementation methods for the numerous "leading edge" features that compose it.
- Operations issues refer to the product's capabilities once it has been built in the DBMS technology and put into operation.

No one category is more important than another—that determination must be made according to the application in question. In some cases, however, issues that consider a range of product and vendor capabilities (such as vendor support) should be given more weight than a narrower product feature area. Nevertheless, the application must assign this order. Therefore, ordering these issues within a category is arbitrary and insignificant.

This list of issues is by no means a complete set for everyone who must select a DBMS product. Conceivably, you could consider hundreds of additional items, some of which

SOURCE: Steven Caniano, "In Search of the Perfect," reprinted with permission from *Data Base Programming & Design*, January 1992, Vol. 5, No. 1, pp. 44, 46–51, copyright Miller Freeman Inc., ALL RIGHTS RESERVED.

might make up new issue categories. Regardless, the issues I'll describe should help you identify potential problem areas or major weaknesses that you might have otherwise overlooked.

SIZE LIMITATIONS

The system and application profile category describes items that classify the DBMS's critical application needs. Although this category has the least number of issues, in many ways they are the most critical. You may prefer to think of them as "acid tests"—if a product cannot satisfy these needs, you should not consider using it, regardless of how well it evaluated against other issues.

The main issue here is size limitations. A critical variable in DBMS selection is how large a database (or tables) can be supported. Key questions to ask in this area are:

- What is the maximum number of tables that can be supported in a database and a partition of a database?
- What is the maximum table size in theory versus practice? (You can check actual results by examining similar computing platforms.)
- What is the maximum database size in theory versus practice?
- Can tables span physical storage devices (such as disk packs)? Can they span processors (in a distributed environment)?
- How will the product respond to potential database growth?

Perhaps the major point to evaluate is the difference between theory and practice. Often, theoretical limits are very large, if any exist at all. Ask your vendor for a reference list of other customers, preferable within your company, who have successfully built a database of a similar size to the one you are planning. If the vendor cannot produce a list, you are probably treading on new ground in terms of maximum database size for this product and should proceed with extreme caution.

BATCH PROCESSING SUPPORT

An application typically has batch processing requirements. To test how well the product meets needs in this area, you should ask the following questions:

- Does the product let you "turn off" the online system in lieu of batch processing?
- Can you execute batch jobs concurrently? (This feature may help you meet batch processing "window" requirements.)
- Are both queries and updates permitted in a batch mode?
- Can bulk data loads be performed in batch mode? Can the bulk load be segmented into pieces that are executed concurrently?
- Does batch processing support both static and dynamic SQL processing?

The major issue you should examine is whether the product will let all batch processing be performed within the window that can be allocated to batch. Of course, the product must support all types of required batch activities (such as updates, loads, queries, and so forth).

PERFORMANCE

One of the most critical aspects of any system is its ability to meet customer performance requirements. Unfortunately, this task is often the most difficult to analyze and predict. The following questions may help evaluate this category:

- What are the maximum transactions per second (TPS) ratios demonstrated on similar computing platforms?
- What types of transactions were ensured and how do they relate to the primary transactions included in the application? (Typically, vendors will cite high TPS figures that actually depict quite simple transactions. Customers must weigh these "benchmark" transactions against their actual workloads and weigh them accordingly.)
- How were the vendor benchmarks audited? (If they were not audited, the results are extremely suspect.)
- What metrics are available to describe full file scan performance; for example, time per MB and cost per MB? (This type of information will help you determine if such an activity can reasonably run within the batch window if necessary.)
- What metrics are available to measure data sorting performance?
- Is performance information available for workloads that range from online transaction processing to decision-support work, as well as combinations of the two? How closely does this resemble the applications environment?
- What is the maximum number of concurrent users supported in theory versus practice?

Obviously, performance is perhaps the most difficult area to quantify in the selection process. Nevertheless, it might be a fatal flaw to ignore it. Whenever possible, I recommend you benchmark a representative piece of the application with the product to determine the actual performance you can expect. Alternatives would be to translate other industry and company benchmarks into application terms and draw conclusions based on them.

The goal of analyzing the performance area is to feel satisfied that what needs to be done can be done. After being satisfied on this point, you can reassure yourself that work will be executed in a timely enough fashion to satisfy the application's customers.

MANAGEMENT AND VENDOR ISSUES

Management and vendor issues cover items that, while critical to DBMS selection, do not fall under any type of product feature category or classification. When you buy a product, you buy a vendor, and you must therefore consider key vendor issues, which are typically difficult, if not impossible, to quantify. In many cases, you must judge these areas by the vendor's reputation and the opinions of other customers. In some cases, however, an item is more credible if a vendor can cite examples of successes or provide supporting documentation.

QUALITY ASSURANCE

One of the major success factors for a company is its commitment to quality products and services. Many methods (called *quality assurance* [QA] *metrics*) measure product quality. These methods help better understand the vendor's level of commitment to product quality and the consistency of that quality. Some questions in this category include:

- What is the vendor's track record for quality products?
- What type of QA process is in place to assure the DBMS product's level of quality?
- Who is responsible for quality in the company? Is it a QA group that inspects the product after development or someone deeply involved in the development process?
- What metrics are in place to measure the level of customer satisfaction with the DBMS engine and the tool set? What is the ratio of closed- to open-reported problems? Will the vendor agree to time-committed fixes for severe problems?
- What test suites does the vendor currently use?
- Is the vendor willing to incorporate your test procedures into their test suites?

- What percentage of the product development staff is committed to QA of products?
- How does the vendor measure customer satisfaction?
- Does the vendor have any formal quality improvement programs in place with other customers and their suppliers?
- Does the vendor have a QA process in place with their original equipment manufacturer partners? Are they focused on a total quality solution for the customer?

The emphasis of this category is to determine how serious your vendor is about quality. Of course, they will all claim to be very serious, but unless vendors can answer a number of these questions satisfactorily, it is difficult to imagine how they will escape their "fire fighting" mode and focus on continuous quality improvements.

CUSTOMER REQUIREMENTS

Customer requirements gathering goes hand in hand with QA metrics. If you plan to deal with a vendor for a long period of time, you must understand how the vendor collects and reacts to the requirements and suggestions provided by customers. Several important questions in this category include:

- Does the vendor have a formal mechanism for collecting customer requirements?
- Who decides on the inclusion of a request? How is the response given to the customer? What measurements and time frames are included?
- What percentage of previous customer requests have been included in the product?
- How are new requirements balanced against reported problems for inclusion of product releases?
- Are past requests available for other customers to see?
- Do certain customers have priority in requests? How is the priority established?

Again, the emphasis is on determining the formality of the vendor's system for collecting and including customer requirements. This task may be a key requirement as your application evolves with the vendor.

VISION SYNERGY

Whether the application in question is critical to business operations or viewed as a strategic system, you want your vision of the future to match that of the vendor. For example, if you view distributed computing as the wave of the future and are designing architectures based on data sharing and connectivity, it would not be wise to select a vendor concentrating on traditional host-based, centralized processing and data management. Therefore, you must ask the following questions:

- Does the vendor's product architecture lend itself to processing in your current and planned architectural framework?
- Is the vendor a major player in the open systems arena or tied to a proprietary ancestry? If they are an open systems vendor, are they aligned with UNIX Software Labs (USL) or the Open Software Foundation (OSF)? How does their positioning relate to your direction?
- Can the vendor provide examples of successful partnering efforts with others in your company?
- Is the vendor willing to take extraordinary measures to guarantee success (for example, free on-site support, consulting, and so on)?
- If your company prefers a particular computer line, how well does it integrate with its current and evolving offerings?

I hope these points give you a basic idea of how well a vendor's view of the future might mesh with your own. Obviously, a long-term relationship will succeed only if both customer and supplier are moving in similar directions.

INVESTMENT PROTECTION

The vendor's historical track record in protecting the customer's software investment is often overlooked. If your company already uses this vendor, you have a leg up on getting this information. Does the vendor make their own products obsolete by regularly introducing the products that require you to purchase new licenses and convert from the "old" software? Those lacking personal experience with a vendor must rely on testimonials from other customers. Some questions to keep in mind for this category include:

- Does the vendor avoid functional discontinuity from release to release?
- When the vendor issues upgrades, do they work on the same hardware and operating system releases?
- Is the customer required to purchase new software for a new release?
- What type of database and application conversion is necessary for a typical new release?
- What is the vendor's release strategy? What is their target for quality and performance improvement from release to release? Are releases based on improving conformance to industry standards? What support commitment do they provide for older releases?

Ideally, a vendor will provide new releases on a fairly regular schedule at no charge to the customer, but keep in mind the pain involved in moving from release to release. Since it is not always possible to keep up with vendor releases, a strong support commitment for older releases is mandatory.

TEST BED FACILITY

The purpose of a test bed facility is to determine how capable the vendor is of assuring a quality product. The quality of the delivered product is very important, but the vendor's ability to recreate problems you experience in their environment is possibly even more important. To recreate these problems, they will need a similar (if not identical) test bed facility. Some important areas to consider include:

- Does the vendor have all of the processors (and their corresponding operating systems) that you use at their location?
- What priority do your computing platforms have in their porting schedules? (DBMS products tend to run in diverse environments, each of which must be ported and tested separately. If your environment is toward the bottom of the list, it can be years between the time when the vendor announces a product enhancement or release and when you actually receive it. Depending on your view, this wait can have positive or negative effects. On one hand, other customers may "shake the bugs out of a new release" so you won't have to, on the other hand, you might have to wait many months after their announcement before getting the new features.)
- What type of integration testing is performed? Does the vendor incorporate networking products and third-party software that you use in your environment into their tests? If they do not, the job of integration testing will be yours.
- Will the vendor commit to keeping their product current with your environment? As you upgrade components in your architecture, will they be working to assure efficient integration with these components? (If this testing is not performed, you may not be able to upgrade a component due to a lack of integration with the DBMS.)

In general, it is reassuring when the vendor can ensure your success because they've already demonstrated their product successfully on your equipment in their facility. Therefore, you should require a representative test bed.

SUPPORT CAPABILITY

Perhaps the single most important item in any evaluation is the vendor's ability to support the customer. Unfortunately, in today's data processing world, problems with products seem almost inevitable. The one differentiating factor among vendors is their ability to service customers in times of trouble.

Support is typically an intangible item bases on reputation and actual experience. One bad experience can often leave you with a bad impression of an entire company. Therefore, you must attempt to quantify customer support as much as possible. Ask yourself these key questions:

- What are the procedures for problem severity management? What are the hours of support? Is 24 × 7 service provided? If so, is this done through "live" coverage (for example, off-hours beepers, answering services, and so forth)?
- Are there limitations on whom can call the support line?
- Since many DBMS companies are headquartered on the West Coast, does the vendor also provide East Coast support? If so, what are the levels of expertise at each and what hours are they available?
- Is support customizable to the customer need?
- What is the procedure for obtaining on-site support during a crisis? Is there a cost to the customer? Is there a difference if it is a production versus a development problem?
- Is on-site support available on a full-time basis? If so, how is it arranged, at what cost, and what are the skill sets of the support person?
- Does the vendor provide consultation on demand? At what cost to the customer?
- Does the vendor maintain a "bug" tracking system, and is it available to customers?
- How many systems engineers are dedicated to your account? How many licenses do they cover?
- Can the vendor send granular fixes in a prompt time frame, or are fixes only available in maintenance releases?
- Will the vendor supply source code and debuggable object code for problem resolution and debugging?

Good support can be summed up in one statement: "The ability to do what is necessary to assure the customer's success." In many ways, good support is more of an impression than anything else until the customer actually needs to test it out. Hopefully, this article will help you form this impression before a crisis occurs.

DOCUMENTATION

Another nebulous but important area to consider is a product's documentation. Documentation can cover a broad spectrum of areas, and the quality in each of these areas can vary greatly as well. Although difficult to quantify, the following questions may help:

- Are product error messages documented? Are associated solutions provided?
- Are guides available that are tailored to specific user groups or functional areas (for example, DBA versus applications developer)?
- Are the guides tailored toward specific computing platforms? Is there a specialized platform-specific tuning guide?
- Is the documentation delivered prior to, in conjunction with, or later than the product?

- How accurate is the information in the documentation? (Unfortunately, this question can only be answered through experience—yours or that of other customers.)
- How is the documentation obtained, and what is its cost? Does a customer have the right to copy manuals for all interested parties or must you purchase "official" copies?
- Is there a product performance tuning guide?
- How timely and appropriate are documentation updates?
- What medium does the vendor use for documentation delivery (for example, paper, tape, online, and so forth)?

In general, successful documentation is timely, accurate, and geared toward specific functional groups and operating environments. If a vendor targets specific environments other than yours, you should be wary.

TRAINING

Training pertains to the formal education available from a vendor or a third party to build expertise in a product. Almost all vendors offer some level of training for their products, ranging from learning basic commands to full curriculums. The following points should help you evaluate training:

- What is the current curriculum offered by the vendor? Where are courses offered, how often, and at what cost?
- Can courses be tailored to meet the needs of specific customer groups? Will they "suitcase" a course to a customer location on demand?
- Is vendor training coordinated with other in-house training facilities? If not, would they be willing to move in this direction?
- Is computer-based training available? Is audio/visual (self-paced) training available?
- What are the skill levels of the instructors? How knowledgeable are they of your environment?
- Are the appropriate lab facilities available in the training sessions? (For example, if you are developing in UNIX, you don't want to do work exercises on Digital Equipment Corp.'s VAX/VMS.)
- What is the quality of the course materials? Do you have the right to copy these materials?
- Do the DBMS system and associated tools provide full "help" capabilities?
- Is there a prompted query capability in the product for the non-SQL literate?

Overall, you should look for flexible and dependable training that is customized as much as possible to the environments that concern you. Nontraditional training (computer-based and audio/visual) might be advantageous when budgets are tight.

BUSINESS HEALTH

The data processing industry is a volatile one. Technology changes at such a fast pace that a company on top today could find itself bankrupt tomorrow, unless it truly understands the marketplace and can exploit its products through continuous technological improvements. Similarly, a company with large technological advantages must not bury itself in technology, but create a business infrastructure that can support evolving customer demands and technological challenges.

Therefore, any vendor evaluation would be incomplete without a thorough analysis of the company as a business entity and its prospects for growth and continued success. Because when you purchase a product you purchase a company with it, you must believe that the company will support you as your business evolves. The following questions will give you valuable insights into the vendor's business health:

- What has the vendor's track record been over the last five to 10 years? Are they profitable? What are their revenue and profit patterns over time? What type of outstanding debts do they have? Do they have a large amount of receivables due?
- What are the vendor's plans to continue their success and improve upon it?
- What type of opinions do industry people have about this company? (Independent industry analysts and financial services companies are good sources of this type of information.)
- What is the company's investment in research and development (R&D)? What percentage of revenues does this figure represent? What percentage of R&D is put into computing platforms that affect you?
- What percentage of their revenue/income does the vendor generate from your computing platforms? How many licenses do they support per platform?
- Is the vendor having any known financial difficulties?

History has shown that you can never be certain regarding the future of a vendor in the data processing industry. Nevertheless, you must understand the business situation before deciding on a vendor in order to make an informed, intelligent decision. Remember to keep track of the vendor's situation closely throughout the life of the relationship.

THIRD-PARTY MARKETS

You might be interested in the third-party markets available for the products you are considering. Most third parties develop products for major DBMS players. Therefore, if none (or few) are available, the product may still be a minor or niche player.

Some users may prefer to not deal with third-party vendors since they are yet another variable in the equation of composing a total information solution. This point may be valid, but ignoring the third parties would overlook some of the best tools available for a product. As the third parties' main business is add-on tools, they often concentrate on the features of these tools more than the DBMS vendors (who tend to focus on the engine itself). Therefore, the best tools for a product are often marketed by a third party. In addition, you may want your DBMS to function as a server to many of your third party end-user tools. In this case, you will find more happening with the major players. If you are interested in the third-party market, the following questions should help:

- Is the engine viewed as a desirable server to many client applications? for example, does it support most of the major end-user front-end interfaces to access the DBMS as a server?
- What types of tools are available to augment and enhance the development and production environments? Who markets those tools, what is the relationship with the third party, and how successful are these companies?

A third-party market, if nothing else, usually provides a good perspective of who the major players are in the DBMS world. You should verify that the DBMS will integrate with your common front-end tools. Third-party tools may be desirable if the vendor's tools are lacking.

LICENSING ARRANGEMENTS

An area you should not overlook is the licensing arrangements in place and the flexibility of these arrangements. For example, many vendors offer volume purchase agreements to major customers. Special deals on maintenance contracts are also common. Anyone making a DBMS selection must examine these areas because the pricing available may be far different from the list prices. Some questions to ask include:

- What are the vendor's current licensing arrangements and how flexible are the terms?
- Will the vendor provide free evaluation copies to assist in the purchase decision?

- Are the licenses transportable? For example, if you purchase a license on one type of processor, can you move it to another type?
- Do you have the right to copy software? (This ability may be important if you are incorporating a vendor's product into a solution to sell to your customers.) Is a run-time license available for this purpose?

Licensing tends to be an item that is considered near the end of an evaluation. Looking at it closer to the beginning may prove valuable as the licensing restrictions may prove enlightening. This arrangement may make a very difficult decision quite simple.

STANDARDS SUPPORT

As open systems become more and more of a requirement for industry (and even more so for the federal government), standards conformance becomes a critical factor in the DBMS decision process. Those who want the flexibility of open systems require certain levels of conformance before they will do business with a vendor. If this area concerns you, you may want to consider standards support in the following areas:

- To what level of ANSI SQL (Level 1 and Level 2) does the vendor conform? Does the product also include proprietary extensions to SQL? If so, can they be "turned off" if you want to make use of ANSI SQL only?
- Is embedded SQL supported in the languages you require (for example, C, COBOL, and so on)? Is a preprocessor available for these languages? What type of limitations exist (for example, C on MVS)?
- Does the vendor participate in open standards committees working toward interoperability (ANSI SQL, X-Open, SQL Access, RDA, and so on)? Although such standards have not been agreed upon, these committees are actively pursuing them.

Although it is a new area, standards have entered the evaluation puzzle. This area may not be very important for customers who are not interested in distributed computing on multiple heterogeneous platforms with heterogeneous products. For those who care about such diverse environments, however, standards support quickly becomes one of the most important criteria.

Discussion Questions

1. What are the five categories of issues related to the selection of DBMS products?
2. What are the potential problem areas in selecting a DBMS?
3. What are three key questions to ask in each potential problem area? ▼

"The Race to Rewire America," by Andrew Kupfer

(This reading is especially suited for use in conjunction with Chapter 8 of *Information Systems*.)

Call it the first great business showdown of the 21st century: The giants of American communications are locked in a struggle to build and control a vast web of electronic networks. These so-called information highways will be of glass fiber and will deliver an abundance of services to offices and houses—video images, phone calls, helpful data in many guises. They promise to change the way people work and play. In the view of some technologists, they could affect American life as profoundly as railroads, interstate highways, telephones, and TV.

The risks are as colossal as the opportunities. Building a glass highway is moonshot expensive—by one estimate, extending the networks over the next 20 years may cost phone companies alone nearly $140 billion. Regulations are likely to change while the game is being played; technology is evolving so quickly that some highways could become obsolete before they are complete. The highways' success will depend on the revenues they generate. Yet no one knows how much consumers will pay to browse through movie libraries using their remote controls, play electronic games with far-off friends, or visit their doctors by video.

Since they control the information conduits feeding into households today, telephone and cable TV companies have the most at stake. The idea of receiving a phone call on a cable TV wire may sound as impossibly counterintuitive as, say, getting a cup of coffee out of an electrical socket. But the idea will soon be reality. New technology is breaking down the barriers between the industries. Telephone companies such as Bell Atlantic and GTE are eyeing the lucrative $20-billion-a-year cable TV business, while cable operators such as Tele-Communications Inc. and Time Warner (parent of *Fortune's* publisher) covet the vast $65-billion-a-year market for residential phone service.

The highways these rivals have started constructing are different from the electronic superhighway that Vice President Gore is promoting. His is a national network of supercomputers, linked by fiber optics, that will connect universities, hospitals, research centers, and other institutions that need to exchange vast amounts of data. Construction of this superhighway, an expansion of today's federally subsidized scientific networks, seems almost certain to proceed. But the Clinton Administration is counting on private enterprise to construct advanced networks that will serve the public generally. As a result, America's information system won't have a single owner: It will be a network of networks, controlled by many companies.

How government regulates the networks—or doesn't—will profoundly influence service and profits. Should regulators scrap rules that prevent cable TV and telephone companies from leaping into one another's businesses without constraint? Should government take the lead in ensuring that the networks all work together? If not government, who?

The most controversial question is whether business, without the help of Washington, will act quickly enough. Many people fear that the U.S. is lagging dangerously behind its trading partners in building information highways—a failing that could reduce America's competitiveness. Corning, the No. 1 maker of optical fiber, estimates that if telephone companies upgrade aging installations at their historical pace, the rewiring will take until 2037. But Japan is committed to completing a national fiber network by 2015 and believes that the resulting productivity gains will boost GNP by no less than 30%. Germany and France are not far behind in their plans. Observes Michael Morrison, manager of advanced operations testing at GTE: "These nations see how attracting and keeping companies with telecommunications helps them be competitive. We tend to trip over our own feet."

SOURCE: Andrew Kupfer, "The Race to Rewire," *Fortune* April 19, 1993, pp. 41–51. © 1993 Time Inc. All rights reserved.

Amid the debate and uncertainty, companies like Morrison's are placing billion-dollar bets. What follows is a look at the policies and technologies that will shape the new highways, the services they will make possible, and the competitive strategies of those who plan to build them.

NEW RULES OF THE ROAD

The Clinton Administration has put electronic highways on the national agenda but has yet to decide what Washington will do to get them built. One of the hottest debates is about how much the government should spend. Some people think zero. Brendan Clouston, chief operating officer of Tele-Communications Inc. (TCI), asks, "If multiple industries will create the architecture, why should taxpayers pay?"

But the highway builders face a chicken-and-egg problem that a sprinkling of government seed money could help solve. Unless fiber-optic networks can provide services that consumers want to buy, they will be just so many useless strands of glass. Useless, *expensive* strands. Meanwhile the businesses that might offer services such as movies on demand will need to invest in specialized hardware and software. Unless networks stand ready to carry their services, making these investments would be like putting up a motel before the road is built. Lee Camp, president of Pacific Bell Information Services, describes the dilemma his company faces: "Does one pursue a *Field of Dreams* strategy—'Build it and they will come'—or wait until there is proven demand?"

A modest investment of federal dollars could kick-start the industry, argues economist Eli Noam, a Columbia University professor and authority on telecommunications. Demonstration projects electronically linking, say, community libraries, schools, and universities could pique public interest and stimulate demand for high-capacity networks. Consultant Janice Obuchowski, a former Bush Administration official, advocates "applications funding," including grants to help entrepreneurs develop services to sell.

The Defense Department's Advanced Research Projects Agency or a civilian equivalent could also contribute to key technologies. In the 1980s the agency helped finance work on digital signal processing—the packing and unpacking of information for efficient transmission and reception. The technology still needs work. So does the science of translating video images into computerized form.

Regulators, meanwhile, could hurry the highway by loosening antiquated rules, especially those that hobble the telephone business. For instance, phone companies must depreciate their capital equipment over 20 years or more. That was the useful lifetime of telephone gear a decade ago, but today, when technology changes faster than governments in Bolivia, the rules deter investment.

The Federal Communications Commission and state utility commissions, which must arbitrate the networks' construction, are besieged by lobbyists from telephone and cable companies. Each side wants to gain an advantage. While the regulators deliberate, cable companies are getting into the phone companies' business and vice versa. Some cable operators have bought into companies that are laying fiber in city centers and stealing customers from the telephone network. A Bell company, in turn, just made an end run around rules barring it from the cable business in its service area by acquiring two big cable franchises out of state.

As cable and phone companies invade one another's markets, the government should dismantle the rules separating the industries carefully. So far the phone companies have won the right from the FCC to offer a "video dial tone" that enables other companies to use the phone network to transmit video programming. A few phone companies have also won relief from so-called rate-of-return regulations, which they say stifle innovation. The rules, administered by the states, limit the companies' return on assets, typically to 8% to 11%. If a company takes a chance on an ambitious new service and succeeds it must return any "excess" profits to customers in the form of rate rebates. Some states, such as New Jersey, have wisely begun to allow higher profits in exchange for guarantees that a new investment will lead to lower prices for basic phone service.

The most difficult issue government will face is how—and even whether—to make sure there is basic, low-cost service for every American who wants a phone and other essential services that the highway will provide. On the telephone network, that principle, known as universal service, has been the law of the land for 60 years. It reflects the belief that phones, like mail, electricity, and highways, unite the nation's people and make America strong.

The government achieves universal service through regulation. The phone companies are obliged to hook up everyone in their service area and charge each customer the same basic rate—even though this can mean stretching miles of wire to a customer whose payments won't cover the whole cost. High profits from some customers—such as those who pay for added services like call waiting—compensate for the money losers and enable the phone company to hit the rate of return the regulators allow.

But as competition and new technology galvanize local markets, universal service becomes harder to deliver in the traditional way. Cable companies aren't bound by universal service rules. Using leading-edge technology, a savvy cable operator could add phones to its system and target just those parts of the local market that produce the fattest profits. Indeed, Time Warner has asked the FCC to let subscribers on its advanced cable system in Orlando, Florida, use the cables to place long-distance calls. That would enable the company to claim a share of the lucrative fees that AT&T and other long-distance companies pay for connections to local customers. If the FCC approves Time Warner's plan, BellSouth would see its profits in Orlando erode—and might file for permission to raise basic rates.

What should the FCC do? Option A is to regulate local markets *more*, requiring newcomers to provide universal phone service. That would surely discourage competition and slow the development of information highways. Option B is to lift restrictions on phone companies just enough to let them counter, but not drive out, the invaders—say, by providing information services, including their own video programming, as long as such services are fairly priced. This approach involves a delicate balancing act that federal and state regulators would have to perform again and again as competing local networks pop up across the country during the coming decades. Still another option: Require new entrants to pay the phone company to help offset the cost of universal service.

Opening local markets to competition will be a difficult business because of the complex and interlocking nature of regulations affecting the industries—far trickier than opening up long distance, a process that has occupied the FCC and the courts for more than ten years. Eventually, in communities where competition flourishes, regulation may not be needed to ensure cheap and abundant telecommunications. In the meantime the government will have to be careful to modify its rules in a way that protects the public interest while giving neither industry an unfair advantage.

Letting many companies compete in building the information highway lessens the chance that the country will get married to the wrong technology. Competition will foster continuous innovation. But it also increases the risk that the U.S. will be dotted with networks that can't talk to one another.

Ah, for the simplicity of monopoly. When AT&T ran the Bell system, it kept everything working smoothly by setting detailed technical standards. When a new service appeared, it was sure to work everywhere. "But boy," says Bob Barada, chief strategist for Pacific Telesis, "was that process slow! This country can't wait for a standards body to cross every *t* before we get started."

Instead of defining standards in advance, regulators should jawbone companies into working out the details themselves. If a cable company and a telephone company operate competing networks in a community, residents should be able to reach each other no matter which network they use. But where should the physical connection between the networks occur? In a manhole? In a telephone company central office? And with what equipment? To be maintained by whom?

These are nuts-and-bolts questions that regulators aren't good at answering. Columbia University's Noam, who once served on the New York State Public Service Commission, advises regulators to bring all the parties into a room and tell them to work out their differences under threat of regulatory fiat. He says, "The arrangement works particularly well when it involves technologists—they're problem solvers." Once the rules are agreed on, regulators can codify and enforce them. If they do this job well and clear the way for competition, says Jim Chiddix, the chief technologist at Time Warner Cable, "it looks like all the forces are there for promoting tremendous innovation in technology: fear and greed."

THE GLASS HIGHWAY

"You'll be going to Cerritos, I hope," said the man from GTE. Cerritos is GTE's community of the future. Buried beneath the wide, straight roadways of the Los Angeles suburb, slender sheaths of glass guide pulses of infrared light from lasers in the switching center to two schools and 4,200 homes, bearing programs and telephone calls. A teacher summons up video lessons at the touch of a button. Some families on the network—brave Jetsons!—can call up movies on the system whenever they wish. The families can even converse with each other on the screen.

All two of them. "For years it was only one guy watching movies. It's a standing joke in the industry," says Danny Briere, president of TeleChoice, a New Jersey consulting firm, of the cautious pace at which GTE has pursued its five-year trial. But Cerritos is no joke to GTE. Billion-dollar decisions depend on what technologists and marketers learn there; other companies are conducting similar small-scale trials. They show the fitful and tentative way revolutions start.

The technology of the information highway is evolving at a furious pace. In December 1992 the FCC licensed CellularVision, a Freehold, New Jersey, startup company, to test an ultrahigh-frequency microwave radio system that may eliminate wires in some parts of urban networks. Such innovations could dramatically lower costs and reshape information networks even as they are being built.

The highways that cable and telephone companies currently envision will, in the words of GTE vice chairman John Segall, "tie the world together in a hush of photons." The network will be rich in fiber-optic cable, which has far greater carrying capacity than copper wire or coaxial cable.

Messages conveyed on the fibers will be encoded in the ones and zeros of computer language and compressed by sophisticated circuitry for easier storage and quicker transmission. Ultrafast switches will route video images as easily as ordinary phone calls. Special computers called video servers will store movies and TV programs in digital form.

These technologies will give the network its hallmark attributes. It will be "broadband." Just as a line painted with a broad brush contains more paint than a line traced with a narrow one, a broadband network can carry more information than its narrowband counterpart. Since signals on the network will all be digital, it will easily carry information of different kinds: It won't need to know whether a transmission describes a lark's song or a slasher movie. The network will also be two-way and interactive: Every user will be able to send all kinds of information—voice, video, data, and graphics—to anyone else.

Before this vision can become reality, phone and cable companies must each overcome innate weaknesses. Phone companies are experts at running networks linked by switches (powerful computers that let any customer dial any other) and at providing service with near-total reliability. But the system itself is narrowband, its thin-gauge copper wire unable to carry a high-quality video image. Cable systems, with their heavier-gauge coaxial cable, are broadband—a strength. But unlike telephone communication, which is two-way, cable signals flow in only one direction on the systems common today. They have no switches and can't relay phone calls.

GTE's experiment in Cerritos typifies the approach phone companies will probably adopt. A fiber strand runs from the phone company's central office to a curbside pedestal that can serve up to 20 houses. Inside the pedestal is an optical interface unit with a separate circuit card for each house. The card contains the subscriber's coded address and ensures that phone calls and video programs arriving on the shared fiber-optic line end up in the right place. The circuits also convert the incoming light pulses into electronic signals, which enter the household via coaxial and copper wires hooked to the TV and phone, respectively.

Cable companies, by contrast, don't need to take fiber all the way to the curb. They will run it to the edge of each neighborhood, where transmissions will feed into the coax network that is already in place. Each fiber link might serve as many as 2,000 families. By using the latest compression techniques, which can multiply tenfold the number of channels on a cable system, a company can assign channels to individual customers as needed—to deliver a movie, say, or relay a telephone call.

The fiber links are essential for two-way communication; coaxial networks alone can't handle it. In a coax system, signals pass through an amplifier every 2,000 feet or so. Each introduces a whisper of electronic interference to the line. In one-way transmission, the noise is manageable; but on the return path in two-way communication, it builds up, and the cacophony of the amplifiers drowns out the message. The introduction of fiber brings a measure of calm: Laser signals can travel for miles without a boost, so the total number of amplifiers in the system stays relatively low.

For both industries, the most expensive job will be laying down fiber. The work has barely begun. According to Corning, the U.S. now has some 12 million miles of fiber installed—compared with 1.2 *billion* of copper phone wire. Neither phone nor cable companies have put down much fiber in residential areas, which account for some 65% of the mileage of telephone networks and 75% of the mileage of cable systems.

It's hard to say how much rewiring for advanced networks will cost, partly because both industries are gradually switching to fiber anyway for their ordinary operations. Corning estimates that doubling the rate of conversion of the phone system—which would mean that the job would be finished by 2015—would increase spending over the period by $24 billion. Add the $63 billion that phone companies already plan to spend and $50 billion for new ultrafast switches to keep traffic flowing smoothly on the information highway, and the bill comes to $137 billion. That's just for the telephone network.

Until now, cable companies have held a theoretical advantage: They can make do with less fiber because they already own a broadband conduit into the home. By most estimates, a cable operator could add two-way services, including fiber to the neighborhood, for less than $1,000 per household. Installing a Cerritos-like system, including fiber to the curb, could cost its telephone rival hundreds of dollars more. That advantage will erode: As demand for two-way services increases, the cable operator will have to segment its network into smaller units and install more fiber. Eventually the two systems will look and cost just about the same. But in a developing market, the cable company's head start might be crucial.

Small wonder that Bellcore, the research arm of the seven regional Bell operating companies, has raced to find a practical way to transmit TV programs over ordinary copper telephone wire. In June 1991 it unveiled a digital compression system built to do just that. Known as ADSL (asynchronous digital subscriber line), the technology is still far from perfect. The longer the copper pathway the TV signal traverses the more the picture degrades; at best the picture quality is no better than that from an ordinary VCR. All the same, if regulations allow, phone companies can now look forward to offering video service as soon as they bring fiber to within a mile or so of a residential area.

Both industries need more breakthroughs. The greatest technical roadblock involves storage technology. In most electronic-highway plans, TV watchers will be able to scroll through menus of video libraries—Treasures of Columbia Pictures say—stocked by independent vendors. One push of a button on the remote control and the show will begin.

For such schemes to work, any company that wants to offer a video service should be able to buy a video server and hook it into the network. But servers that can store movies digitally and dish them out on command aren't ready yet. The task is crushing. Even a 95-minute film like *Wayne's World* requires billions of bits of memory. Ameritech is testing a system in Chicago that will enable Arthur Andersen, the consulting firm, to dispatch training films to clients.

Other developments, such as the evolution of wireless technology, could change the course of the highway race. In CellularVision's trial installation in Brooklyn, New York, subscribers with a decoder box receive 50 TV channels using a movable antenna only five inches square. Unlike ordinary microwave signals, which require a direct line of sight between transmitter and receiver, the ultrahigh-frequency signals bounce off concrete like a billiard ball off a felt rail, losing very little strength. So users need only move their antennas around until they get a good bounce. The system can also carry signals both ways; a test of telephone service will begin shortly.

Most telephone and cable executives dismiss the idea that any new technology, no matter how startling, will provide its owner with a sustainable edge. In the long run, the same technology will be available to all comers. TCI's Brendan Clouston gets downright testy when pressed on the pros and cons of competing schemes for an advanced network. "I don't like the way this conversation is going," he says. "Technology is not the issue. What do consumers want to buy? What do they want to pay, and when?"

THE KILLER APP

As they imagine the billions of dollars consumers might spend on electronic highways, telecommunications executives often exhibit the Pavlovian response of a gambling addict exposed to flashing neon lights. Listen to Arthur Bushkin, president of Bell Atlantic Information Services: "The marketplace is not the $20-billion-a-year cable market or the $12-billion-a-year movie rental market. It is into the hundreds of billions of dollars. It's for work force training, medical services, and shopping. It's the ability to see real estate before traveling there. It's videoconferencing and using multimedia. It's transmitting recipes. It's endless."

Maybe it will be, someday. But creating services that consumers will want to buy could make building networks seem as easy as running a string between two tin cans. Some applications are no-brainers—merely better ways of delivering services people already use. Others, the kind visionaries cite when they claim information highways will change the American way of life, pose obstacles to execution and problems in predicting how consumers will respond.

Almost without question, business demand will drive the market for advanced services at first. Manufacturers and their suppliers will use electronic highways to link their computers and collaborate on product development. Insurance companies could receive images of auto wrecks for claims processing. Video depositions and arraignments, which some law enforcement agencies already employ, would become common.

But to really cash in, communications companies will have to turn consumers on, says John Malone, president of Eastern Management Group, a Parsippany, New Jersey, consulting firm. Just as the personal computer industry languished until spreadsheet programs appeared, information highways need a "killer app"—software industry lingo for an application people are dying to use.

The No. 1 candidate for killer app status is video on demand, the armchair equivalent of a trip to the perfect video store. Viewers will be able to order movies and TV shows anytime, using remote control. TCI recently studied how such a service would compare with today's more cumbersome pay-per-view, which requires customers to phone in their orders. It found that viewers would increase movie spending three to five times.

Another likely hit: telecommuting. Despite the limitations of today's telephone networks, the number of employees working at home is rising at a startling rate. According to Malone, 14% of the FORTUNE 500 and Service 500 companies now have formal telecommuting policies; 870,000 employees work at home 35 hours or more each week, and 5.5 million do at least some home work. The numbers are growing by more than 35% a year.

The advent of information highways will accelerate the trend by increasing the number of jobs telecommuters can perform. An American Express service representative, for example, wouldn't have to leave home to field customer calls and tap into the company's immense databases. Telecommuting will get a lift in states like California, which requires companies to encourage the practice as a way of reducing auto pollution.

The educational possibilities of the advanced network are emerging in tests. Betty Hyatt, a teacher in Cerritos, uses the fiber-optic system to call up penmanship lessons for her third-grade class. That frees her from the chalkboard so she can roam the room and monitor her pupils' progress. Hyatt says, "It's changed the way I teach." Ameritech has begun a program in Warren, Michigan, that will link the homes of 115 fourth-graders to their classrooms, allowing the children to call up their homework electronically and do it on-screen. Advanced networks will eventually let students in remote areas attend college classes by wire. And they may matriculate not at Ohio State but at the Big Ten, mixing and matching video classes from any of the member universities.

For physicians, the house call may return, electronically. Using a video link on the network, a patient could see and talk to her doctor without leaving home; by placing a hand on an electronic sensor, she might relay vital readings the doctor could analyze.

The highway may be dangerous for debtaholics. Going on a buying spree will be as fun and easy as playing videogames, with no need to sit like a brass monkey before the Home Shopping Network. An armchair consumer will select a video catalogue from the on-screen menu and, by punching the remote control, ask to see a jacket in a certain size and color. A simulated three-dimensional model will rotate slowly on the screen. The subscriber can order by pushing a button; the network will have his address and credit card data on file.

Marc Porat, head of General Magic, a Silicon Valley software developer, believes the advanced network will change the way people buy information. He expects a form of publishing to emerge called electronic subscriptions. It will replace the sort of books that become obsolete as soon as you buy them—guides to New York City nightlife, for example. A broadband network could deliver an update every month by either displaying it on screen or transmitting data to the consumer's home printer.

Eventually the highway may deliver a lot more. A jovial, forward-thinking engineering colleague of Porat's predicts that people will don electronic gear and use the network to play virtual reality games. Players will have the illusion of moving through an artificial but lifelike 3-D landscape. That may put a new spin on humanity's oldest killer app. "The ultimate," says the engineer, "is when you'll be able to put on a visor and bodysuit that let you become anyone in the world having sex with anyone else in the world." Virtual reality enthusiasts call it teledildonics.

Virtual reality is the most extreme variant of so-called multimedia programming. In partnership with GTE, the Discovery Channel is already transmitting coded instructions in its TV signal that add graphics to the station's science and nature programs when they appear on the Cerritos system. Viewers may see a map superimposed on the screen, or a fact about an animal habitat. The information comes from a miniencyclopedia on a CD-ROM that plays in a device connected to the TV; the codes in the TV signal summon up relevant bits during the show. Only 50 or so families receive the disks now; nationwide rollout may begin next year. When advanced networks are ready, the disks will be unnecessary; the extra information can travel over fiber.

But like other services upon which the information highway will depend, multimedia is having trouble getting off the ground. Production is awkward and enormously expensive; most CD-ROM programs are as primitive as the *Groucho Marx Show* in TV's early days.

That's one reason network builders are having a tough time predicting customer interest. TCI's Clouston says: "Traditional marketing is done with products that exist. What we're doing now is like asking a horse-and-buggy driver whether he'd pay $100 more for a car with an air bag. He'll ask, 'What's a car?' Nobody knows what people will spend."

That leaves cable and phone companies with high hopes and gnawing doubts, like city leaders who erect a lavish sports dome in hopes of landing an expansion team. Are the network builders in for a nasty case of that queasy feeling you get when you wake up in a bad, bad place?

GIGADOLLAR GAMBLES

Gaining an advantage in 21st-century telecommunications won't be cheap. Stewart Personick, a networking information services executive at Bellcore, explains the cost of simply entering the race: "If you want to make a commitment, you have to have a million customers. The investment in optical fiber, network hardware and software, automated billing, and advertising is a minimum of $1,000 per customer. You've got to go for a billion dollars."

If technology, regulations, or business relationships change unexpectedly, that billion could vanish. Yet companies that hesitate could lose out completely. Even with imperfect technology, a big enough player making a big enough bet could stake out a dominant position. As a result, says Personick, the competition is like an Olympic bicycle sprint: "All of these guys are on their expensive racing bikes going five miles per hour, waiting for someone to make a break. And then they all go like mad."

The break has clearly begun. Last October, TCI announced it would soon begin offering some subscribers 500 channels. In January, Time Warner upped the ante with its Orlando plan to build a two-way network for 4,000 families. Then Cablevision promised a similar system in the New York metropolitan area—for over a million subscribers. Meanwhile, US West unveiled plans for fiber-to-the-curb systems in its 14-state region; Bell Atlantic won permission to replace with fiber all the copper wire in New Jersey by 2010. Virtually every other big communications company has an information highway plan in the works.

Among the contenders, Bell Atlantic stands out for aggressiveness and astute politicking. Its plan to rewire an entire state is a first. It convinced regulators that New Jersey needs the expensive new systems to maintain competitiveness. Bell Atlantic wants to time the installation of fiber to suit local markets in each of the seven states it serves. In a few neighborhoods, where marketers believe there is ready demand for interactive service, the company is extending fiber to the curb right away.

That has thrown a scare into at least one cable company. The owner of a housing development in northern Virginia says, "When the cable people found out Bell Atlantic was putting fiber optic in, they had a fit." Where the company thinks TV watchers will embrace an alternative to cable, it plans to take fiber to the neighborhood and send ADSL transmissions the rest of the way over existing copper wires.

US West is betting that the fastest way to roll out advanced networks is by cutting costs. The company has challenged suppliers to tighten their belts and help it build fiber-to-the-curb systems in new neighborhoods for no more money than a standard copper-wire system. (Right now putting in fiber costs about 30% more.)

TCI, the largest cable company, will switch to digital signal transmission in dozens of communities starting next year and has ordered one million state-of-the-art converter boxes to let customers tune in. The investment could serve as the foundation for two-way networks that can deliver video on demand. Archrival Time Warner has focused its attack more narrowly, concentrating on showcase projects designed to push network technology as far as it will go. The system planned for Orlando will have 600 digital channels for video on demand and phone calls, as well as 75 regular channels for ordinary TV. Construction is set for next year, even though crucial components such as video servers aren't yet available.

GTE, which owns local systems in 40 states, is maneuvering to cash in on a key advantage over other regional phone companies. Since it was never part of the Bell system, GTE is not bound by the federal consent decree that bars Bell companies from owning information businesses. GTE is testing interactive video services it can market through systems like the one in Cerritos. One lets customers pay bills by filling in on-screen checks; another helps students prep for SAT exams.

AT&T, finally, is poised at the edge of the field. It no longer owns a wire into the home, but with its proposed $3.8 billion investment in McCaw Cellular Communications, it could again be a powerful force in local markets, especially if wireless technology emerges as a way of delivering advanced information services.

As they circle one another warily, phone and cable companies are like predators at a jungle water hole, wondering, Will it try to eat me, or will it kill some other animal and let me share the meal? Conflicting motives leave them torn between competition and cooperation.

Phone companies could easily afford to put broadband wire into people's homes—regulators permitting. But the job would take a long time, and the companies lack experience in programming. Cable operators are in a position to skim off lucrative telephone business. But they have little experience with network management, and none with switching or billing phone calls. The industry's fragmentation also suggests a need to cooperate: Most metropolitan areas have several cable systems, which would probably have to work with the phone companies to provide local service.

Temporary alliances are taking shape. In Denver, for example, AT&T, US West, and TCI have teamed up to test-market video on demand. Viewers at home browse through a catalogue of 2,000 movies and punch in a code number on their remote controls. Exactly five minutes later the film starts playing, as if fetched from a computer's memory bank—though what actually happens is that a worker at the test center steps up, finds the proper videotape, and views it in a bank of VCRs. Customers pay $4.99 per showing, about $2 more than for a rental cassette.

Which companies clash will depend partly on the speed of deregulation. If state regulators move slowly, phone companies may move outside their service areas to get into other businesses, invading one another's areas. Southwestern Bell, for example, recently bought two cable systems near Washington, D.C., putting itself on a collision course with Bell Atlantic.

Where regulators are most flexible, phone companies will simply upgrade their own networks. They may even ally with local cable operators to economize. In such an arrangement the phone partner would handle switching and billing for calls and interactive services delivered through the cable system. Eli Noam of Columbia University thinks regulators should be leery of such plans, lest they give rise to powerful monopolies in local service: "Phone and cable companies should be beating each other over the head in their home service areas." But Clouston of TCI argues that alliances would speed network building.

In fact, technology is evolving so quickly that monopolies seem unlikely. Cellular-Vision, with its capable little antennas, has sent strategists scrambling at phone and cable companies alike. The household antenna and decoder box cost only $300 to install, much less than any glass highway hookup. Such innovations could alter the balance of power. Alarmed, several Bell companies tried to squelch Cellular-Vision's license application by filing objections with the FCC, saying the technology wouldn't work. But it does. During a recent demonstration in

Brooklyn, the picture quality was good, except when a moving crane passed before the window.

Among the would-be builders of information highways, it's too early to pick winners. At a recent press conference about Time Warner's ambition to build glass highways and fill them with photons bearing movies and recipes and homework, CEO Gerald Levin showed a flash of grim realism. Reflecting on the company's multimillion-dollar losses on Time Teletext, an early electronic information service, he said: "A lot of people are going to lose a lot of money." No doubt. But the bounty will be great for those who marry the right technology to the right services at the right time.

Discussion Questions
1. What is a telecommunications highway?
2. What technologies likely will make up a U.S. telecommunications highway?
3. What factors are hindering the developing of an effective U.S. telecommunications highway? ▼

"A Multimedia Solution to Productivity Gridlock: A Re-Engineered Jewelry Appraisal System at Zale Corporation,"[1] by Julie Newman and Kenneth A. Kozar

(This reading is especially suited for use in conjunction with Chapter 9 of *Information Systems*.)

ABSTRACT

Zale Corporation once melted down most of its damaged, returned, or repossessed jewelry, resulting in substantial lost revenues. It was determined that additional revenue could be produced from salvageable jewelry if the value of the items could be accurately determined. This meant the jewelry had to be appraised by experienced gemologists to determine the most profitable disposition. The gemologists' productivity suffered because the appraisal was extremely labor intensive. To address this problem, an automated multimedia system utilizing electronically linked measuring instruments, voice recognition, and interconnected LAN databases was developed. Although the unique voice recognition feature of the system was later abandoned, the use of the system enhanced productivity. This paper describes the systems development, its subsequent evolution, and the lessons learned from the process.

INTRODUCTION

The world of gems, jewelry, and diamonds is a fascinating one. Even though most of us at one time or another purchase these items, the jewelry industry has been given little attention in the business or information systems literature. Some problems of the jewelry industry are common to many businesses, but others are unique. Unlike many other products, the component parts of a piece of jewelry as well as the composite item have intrinsic market value. Not many items sold in retail outlets could be melted down and sold for their salvage value. This uniqueness creates both problems and opportunities for Zale Corporation.

THE PROBLEM/OPPORTUNITY

Zale Corporation, the world's largest jewelry retailer, has a jewelry processing center in its world headquarters building in Irving, Texas. Each year the center receives about 300,000 unsalable pieces of discontinued, damaged, or repossessed fine jewelry from its 1500 stores. In the past, a lack of sufficient processing ability forced Zale to ship these goods periodically to a local smelter to be melted down in acid baths. The smelter returned to Zale a check for the value of the recovered gold along with glass bottles containing the diamonds and other precious gemstones recovered from the melting process.

Almost all of the Corporation's so-called "surplus" jewelry was melted. Because the value of melted jewelry is far below its original cost, disposing of unsalable jewelry in this manner resulted in significant losses for Zale. Much of the original damage to this jewelry, if any, was slight—a loose prong or a scratch. However, determining a more profitable means of disposing of damaged jewelry is a very complex process. Experienced gemologists must perform a detailed appraisal of the jewelry. Scientific measuring devices, complex calculations, and subjective analysis are used to derive the current salvage value of each item and assess its potential for additional recovery. The gemologists also must look up current commodity prices for gold and gemstones to determine their salvage value. Since a good gemologist can

SOURCE: *MIS Quarterly* March 1994.

FIGURE 1 The Gemologists' World

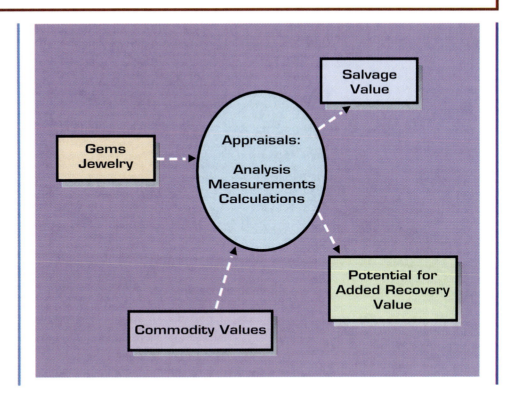

manually evaluate only about 25 pieces of jewelry per day, traditional methods are not a cost-effective process for appraising a high volume of jewelry.

In addition to the possibility of recovering additional revenue from intact damaged jewelry, there is an opportunity to recover more from the components of the jewelry that must be melted. Zale was paying "finders' fees" to various vendors for locating specific gems to satisfy insurance claims and customer repairs. Tens of thousands of dollars each month could be saved if Zale maintained an accurate inventory of the loose gemstones that were recovered when large quantities of jewelry were melted. The diamonds and gems recovered from the smelting process were being sold through brokers in large batches with little understanding of their individual size and quality. A perpetual inventory that identified the size, shape, and quality of precious gemstones would allow them to be reused, thus greatly enhancing their value to Zale.

The consequence of not knowing the actual value of salvaged jewelry was clearly illustrated when one of the authors was handed a bottle of loose diamonds and told that their total value was "probably about one million dollars." After appraisal, it was determined that the value of the diamonds in the bottle was closer to two million dollars.

A still greater potential for increasing the revenue produced by the disposition of distressed inventory came from refurbishing the jewelry and then retailing it at reduced margins through liquidation outlets. But first the rather daunting problem posed by the high volume of items that must be subjected to a gemologist's scrutiny had to be overcome.

To address the appraisal problem, Zale considered the possibility of automating the process in order to improve the productivity of the gemologists. At first glance, appraising jewelry appeared to be incompatible with automation. However, closer examination and revision of the gemologists' processes, combined with a concern for the end user, resulted in a creative and unique application of modern technology that led to dramatically increased productivity.

AN AUTOMATED SOLUTION TO JEWELRY APPRAISAL

An automated system to receive and appraise the unsalable inventory that accumulates in Zale Corporation jewelry stores was proposed. The end result was an intelligent, multimedia system named "MEDUSA."[2] MEDUSA was designed to run on a local area network and utilize voice recognition as the primary vehicle for capturing data. All of the activities performed by the gemologists were supported by voice commands, including the use of ancillary tools-of-the-trade such as calipers and diamond scales. Barcodes were used to track items as they made their way from receipt through a multitude of possible detours and destinations. This system allowed expert gemologists to increase their productivity by 600 percent, and Zale's recovery from distressed merchandise has increased by millions of dollars.

To build the system, three criteria were identified that in combination were expected to have the necessary impact on productivity: (1) allow the gemologists' hands and eyes to be used solely for evaluating jewelry, not for completing forms or performing keyboard data entry, (2) eliminate as much as possible the need to evaluate every item, and (3) provide decision support for the gemologists throughout the entire appraisal process. The first objective was realized to be of pivotal importance after conducting simulated evaluations and observing that the gemologists' hands and eyes were continually occupied with instruments and of course, the jewelry itself. Each objective was met by integrating new technology with leading-edge systems already in place at Zale Corporation.

The system has evolved since its original design—the gemologists no longer use the voice recognition feature. But the development and evolution process are nonetheless instructive. The following describes Zale Corporation's experiences with this new process for dealing with unsalable jewelry.

THE PROCESS OF EVALUATING UNSALABLE JEWELRY

The purpose of the gemologists' evaluation is to ascertain accurately the actual salvage value of each piece of jewelry. This value is used as the basis for determining the greatest revenue-producing disposition for each item by estimating the resulting profit or loss and accurately assigning the results to the appropriate cost center.

The merchandise that is processed through the MEDUSA system is comprised of four types of unsalable jewelry: (1) damaged or defective items, (2) discontinued items, (3) repossessed items, and (4) trade-ins. The 1500 retail stores periodically return these items to Zale Corporation headquarters in Irving, Texas. Store personnel produce a shipping document by entering a transaction into their point-of-sale system. This transaction also updates a host-based file with the details of the shipment.

When the jewelry is received in the processing center at Zale headquarters, a unique barcode is affixed to each item. A receiving auditor enters the number of the accompanying document into MEDUSA, and the shipment information is retrieved from the host-based file and displayed on the auditor's LAN-based workstation.

The auditor receives each line of the shipment by scanning barcodes until the quantity scanned equals the quantity shipped. For instance, if the quantity of an item on a shipping document is "3," the system expects the auditor to scan three different barcodes before proceeding to the next line. After all items in a shipment are received, they are sorted into common categories (watches, gold jewelry with stones, gold jewelry without stones, etc.) and staged for evaluation by the gemologists.

thetical (speculative) models. Removed from both the factory and the sales floor, executives are drawn to systems that summarize the graphically present every larger collections of indicator variables that purport to reveal "what's going on." Finally, baffled by what all of the numbers mean in terms of choosing a concrete course of action, executives are grasping at the canned wisdom offered in expert systems.

TWO ILLUSTRATIONS

Just two reviews in the trade press of current offerings from the EIDS product genre will serve here to illustrate. In the May 15, 1989, issue of *Infoworld*, "The Politics of Executive Information Systems" by David Raths reports that top-level management in some large firms have authorized expenditures of $500,000 and more to acquire systems that reproduce the capabilities of previously installed software with more automated interfaces. The trade-off for reducing the skill required for the executives to operate the system is a corresponding reduction in the range of outputs and ability to construct novel analyses.

As Raths asserts, "What most of these products do is provide canned screens for an executive to look at. If he wants to go beyond that, somebody has to do a lot of work so that you can turn that next layer into a canned report." He apparently must depend on them to "make it look pretty before they pass it up the line." The thrust of the article is that data processing personnel "must educate top management about computer technology and its expanding capabilities to provide competitive advantage…," apparently without imposing upon top management the necessity of mastering the technology themselves.

At the small end of the business scale, Mike Falkner reviewed a $1,000 microcomputer package in a June 27, 1989, *PC Magazine* article called "CFO Advisor: Financial Analysis Beyond Spreadsheets." To use this package, substantial "manual" labor is required to get data into a form the program can handle. Thereafter, the program applied the "Du Pont return-on-net-assets-model" and provides goal-seeking and sensitivity analyses to compare alternative plans of action. "On three screens you get 15 analyses that show what a change to a key performance factor will do to six key-result areas."

The "…novice business user…may want to read the financial reference section…before getting started. It provides a good overview of the Du Pont theory…" An obvious fallacy here is that an analyst can proceed by just fiddling with numbers. An infinite number of monkeys seated at an infinite number of word processors would indeed eventually turn out all of the works of Shakespeare along with gigabytes of drivel and random nonsense. But the monkeys would have no way of knowing when to quit. CFO Advisor's advantage, then, is that it offers bells and whistles to signal success and to guide the novice in the right direction.

But the question remains: success at what? How is a novice to determine which of the many operating ratios should move in whatever direction to achieve what goals, and by when? Further, all of these manipulations imply (advise) real-world actions: the hiring and firing of real people, the buying and selling of real goods and services. How is the novice to know when the real world is being cantankerous, refusing to behave as theory predicts? Even more important, one wonders if goal-setting is covered as well as goal-seeking? Is the issue of to what to be sensitive covered in CFO Advisor's tutorial on sensitivity analysis? And what about effects that were never anticipated or intended by the designers of the expert system?

THE CASES OF FORD AND EASTERN

Consider whether, by using CFO Advisory, Eastern Airlines would have discovered that the public may be more concerned about flying in planes maintained by happy mechanics and flown by satisfied pilots than about the airline's bottom line to labor costs? Would Ford Motor Company have been warned when planning production of the Pinto about the potential of outraged public sensibilities, or would an EIDS system confine the analysis to the sensitivity of per-unit profit to closely shaved material and labor costs? In both cases, it is clear that the computer bean counter would reproduce the advice of the human bean counters.

The human cost-benefit analysis at Ford projected the per-unit cost of death benefits for customers "burned" to be less than a few dollars worth of protective hardware for the Pinto gas tank. This led to Ford's decision to forgo installation of minimal safety-enhancing features. The assumption by Ford's expert of no trend in the per-settlement cost over time was more than a technical error.

The experts at Ford and Eastern both failed to appreciate that the "inexpert" car-buying and flying public does not think stockastically. Each individual buyer makes an idiosyncratic purchasing decision. What in the aggregate means millions for the seller, amounts to only a few dollars either way to fly with happy crews and drive non-explosive cars for the consumer. It was the model of the customers' utility itself that was at fault. Had the risk benefit analysts from Ford left the office and gone down to a local dealership for just one evening, things would have gone very differently. They could have tried floating their cost-saving concept with a few customers. One can imagine the pitch:

> "I'm going to build two different cars. The Pinto will be priced at $1900 (late 1960s prices, remember) and the Nino will be $1910. Now these two will be exactly the same car except for one tiny detail. In order to bring the Pinto in at $10 less than the Nino, we will leave off a bracket and a few bolts that keep the bumper from folding in, causing the gas tank to explode if the car is hit from behind at relative speeds of 15 miles per hour or more. We will put this extra safety stuff on the Nino so it won't explode, although, we all know that if you are in a car that is hit from behind at relative speeds of much above 40 or 50 you likely won't survive even if you aren't fried. So, what do you think Mr. and Mrs. Average Customer, is an extra 25 or 30 miles an hour of survivability worth $10? Which car do you want, the Nino or the Pinto?"

Obviously, one evening of frank discussion at the local dealership might have averted disaster for Ford Motor Company, and saved some lives. It is hands-on knowledge of the material with which one is working—in this case, customer—that distinguishes craft from factory work.

Hands-on knowledge provides a means of judging the limits of models. What is addressed in this case is the issue raised earlier: that management must not confuse a model with reality. There is a price/volume relationship, no doubt. But neither customers' utility for money, nor what each added dollar buys, is uniform when the typical purchase is a single unit instead of so many pounds of potatoes at so much per pound. A model of the aggregated likelihood of sales of single units to many individual customers behaves on the computer screen much as a model of the likelihood of selling many units to a single customer does, but these two cases are fundamentally different. Leave out a critical component to reduce cost in the expectation of increasing volume, like the steering wheel or a few bolts and a bracket, and your marketing plan just might blow up in your face.

In computing, this means that an executive information system that isolates management from the underlying reality will inevitably lead management astray. When data are gathered for analyses and models built, the users of the models must possess the experience to identify critical aspects of the process under analyses that are not incorporated in the model.

Experience is also a guide to roughly what range of outcomes to expect before an analysis is run. Abstractions in models don't always act in the same way as are the real-world components they purport to represent. An unexpected analytical result leads an experienced manager to suspect the model first and their internal sense of the process last. The opposite tends to happen to an inexperienced manager. Prior knowledge of the processes producing the data being analyzed, and how well the indicators being tracked actually capture the fundamentals of those processes, helps an experienced manager to resituate the findings of an analysis in the real world. The significance of results must be evaluated on more than statistical grounds, and only hands-on experience can provide that "something extra."

Experience includes learning the jargon and nuances of categories: In order for analysis to proceed, the events of the real world must be scored and tallied into appropriate categories. This is perhaps the most critical step in any analysis, yet is one that top management typically leaves for others.

SUMMARY

It is hoped that the information presented here provides a sobering appraisal of executive and decision support systems. It is a poor craftworker who blames his tools for poor results. Above the minimal level of tool quality, it is clarity of purpose and conception, understanding of the material with which one works, and coordination of mind and hand that explain the bulk of the variance in the quality of results. If managers seek effective, efficient computer applications, they must themselves master the tools. If there are to be gains in productivity, there must be intimate knowledge of the tasks to be carried out. If systems are to stand and deliver, those who design and implement them must constantly observe, reflect upon and correct the methods of operation.

Discussion Questions

1. What is the quality of information that DSS and EIS can provide?
2. In what ways do business communities demonstrate the "empirical bias of science?"
3. How can managers judge the validity of models inherent in the information systems?
4. How can a manager improve the use of executive and decision support systems? ▼

"Networking with the Enemy," by Rochelle Garner

(This reading is especially suited for use in conjunction with Chapter 12 of *Information Systems*.)

Harry Brown was not amused. Word had gotten back to him that one of the companies invited into his carefully wrought network of suppliers and, yes, competitors wasn't playing fair. It was going after projects on its own instead of with the team.

"I said, 'If you can't abide by the rules, then you should leave.' They agreed and walked out."

Big mistake on its part.

The renegade manufacturer lost business because it didn't have the clout of Brown's network—an informal team of companies from around Erie, Pa., in the same small-parts business.

In contrast, Brown's EBC Industries, Inc. (Brown is its president) and all of its 11 allied suppliers and competitors have been growing at 12 percent to 15 percent every year since he cobbled together the network in 1988. EBC has grown from 68 employees to its current 93 and from less than $4 million in sales to $8.4 million expected by year's end.

That incident highlights the glories and potential pitfalls in the growing trend of "co-opetition."

Not familiar with the term? Get used to it—the word could become as prevalent as the phrase "virtual corporation."

Both embrace the concept of companies reaching across corporate boundaries to engage in mutually beneficial projects. But co-opetition, management pundits say, goes even further to include the notion of competitors working together toward a shared goal while continuing to compete.

For example, EBC gladly shares its electronic data interchange (EDI) expertise and inventory database with team members working on the same job. But should any member step on another one's territory, the members politely but firmly tell the violator to stop.

SOME UNSUCCESSFUL

Not everyone has had Brown's success. Others have ventured into collaborative waters only to find themselves mired in a swamp of distrust, churning through investment dollars without earning a single cent of return.

Take Electronic Joint Venture (EJV) Partners. Like the Erie network, New York-based EJV Partners embodied the shared vision of competitors. But rather than laid-back, small-parts manufacturers from the green valleys of Pennsylvania and Ohio, these companies were six of Wall Street's leading bond-trading firms.

Their goal was enormous profit. The result so far has been an industry joke.

Three years ago, the bond-trading market hungered for data and analytical tools to more confidently buy and sell bonds. Sure, Bloomberg Financial Services, a financial news service, provided some information. But only some.

London's Reuters Holdings PLC, one of the largest market data companies in the world, approached New York-based Goldman, Sachs & Co.'s senior bond traders with a deal. Help us start a service to compete against Bloomberg. The business side called in James K. Burns, then Goldman, Sachs's chief information officer, to evaluate the prospect.

SOURCE: Rochelle Garner, "Networking with the Enemy," *Computerworld*, November 29, 1993: pp. 83–85. Copyright 1993 by *Computerworld*.

The idea looked great. So great, in fact, that Burns, along with Salomon Brothers, Inc.'s Mark Sternberg, with whom he discussed the project, decided to eliminate the middleman.

"We both agreed: Why share this with Reuters?" said Burns, now president and CIO of SHL Systemhouse, Inc., a systems integration and outsourcing organization based in Canada and New York. "But we also said whatever we would do would start off behind Bloomberg, so we needed more partners."

Eventually, Goldman and Salomon recruited CitiBank NA in New York, The First Boston Corp. in New York, Morgan Stanley & Co. in New York, and Lehman Brothers, Inc. in New Haven, Conn. Each partner would donate data and software that the resulting service company—EJV Partners—would turn into a data and analytics system powerhouse certain to lure business away from Bloomberg.

Only it hasn't turned out that way. Every partner had a different idea of how to deliver the information: with a cutting-edge system that would take time to build or with a "reasonable" package that it could sell almost immediately. Cutting-edge won, and Bloomberg continued to gain ground with more customers.

But the problems ran deeper. While EJV Partners won't confirm or deny it, word throughout the halls of Wall Street hold that the six partners continually bickered over what facts, analytics, and software they would give to the venture, holding out the best information for themselves.

Whatever the reason, the initial bond-trading system sucked eggs.

"When we evaluated EJV's system, it became clear that the marginal benefit for Bloomberg just wasn't worth the rest," says Tony Coffey, portfolio manager at Franklin Resources, Inc. in San Mateo, Calif.

In more than a year and a half, not one customer bought the system. Zip. EJV Partners employment fell from 180 to its current 110. The firm's chief executive officer also felt the ax and was replaced last summer by Thomas Wendel. However, EJV Partners released a new, more capable system last summer that is finally winning customers.

"We've gone from [having] no paying customers to between 15 and 20 in the past four months," says Dick MacWilliams, EJV Partners' head of sales and marketing. Six of those paying customers are EJV Partners' original partners. What went wrong?

AGREEING TO AGREE

"It's always difficult getting competitors to agree on common goals, common standards, and common methodologies," MacWilliams says. "And when you have partners contribute more than just money, decision-making becomes even more complex."

EJV Partners management operated like the multiheaded Hydra, each with its own idea of how things should work.

That, maintains Jessica Lipnack, co-author of *The Team-Net Factor,* can be a common source of failure. Lipnack, who actively promotes the idea of co-opetition, says participants must define with hard-edged clarity the purpose of their project. "That purpose is the glue holding the teamnet together," Lipnack says. "Without it, the project will fail."

Her point transcends mere platitude. After all, a traditional hierarchy contains rules, regulations and policies that people can follow. "But in a [teamnet] network, all you have is the shared agreement of what needs to be done," she says.

Perhaps one way to ensure clarity of purpose is with a disinterested arbitrator. That's one role Electronic Data Systems Corp. is playing as it helps four California managed-care plans develop the California Health Information Network (CHIN).

Initially, Dallas-based EDS and its partner, Health Information Technologies in Princeton, N.J., were setting up an EDI system to transmit uniformly formatted claims/encounters, eligibility information and referral authorizations among health care plans, independent physicians associations (IPA), and medical groups. For the competitors—PruCare, HealthNet, TakeCare, and Blue Cross/Blue Shield of California—the challenge is to discover what they have in common without revealing proprietary data.

"I constantly have to weigh in the back of my mind what is competitive information," says Joseph Sinsangkeo, manager of information systems technology at HealthNet in Woodland Hills, Calif. "That's where EDS and [Health Information Technologies] play a role—as keepers of company-specific information. And a lot of times they'll come back and say, 'You all have a lot more in common than you realized. Are you willing to share?'"

And while EDS's role as information broker is important, so is the relationship among the four partners. Every week, IS representatives from the four, along with representatives from EDS and Health Information Technologies, hold conference calls to work out implementation concerns.

Every month, CIOs and top business executives meet to hash out larger issues, such as choosing where the January pilot will roll out. Each member has an equal voice, which it exercises loudly and clearly. It's as if the project leaders had read Lipnack's book, with its admonition to meet regularly, push information both up and down the hierarchy, and create more leaders (and fewer bosses) throughout the team.

FEWER THE BETTER

It is also wise to limit the number of partners in the group at the outset and let the membership increase as it learns to work together.

For example, when CHIN finally goes on-line, partners will pay per transaction. And since volume will lead to volume discounts, participants hope to recruit as many competitors, IPAs, and medical groups as possible.

That, however, will be much later. For now, the aim is to keep the process running, which means limiting the players to four.

"I think the difficulty of reaching agreement increases exponentially as you add people," says Linda Hutchinson, senior systems consultant at PruCare. "But the nature of the project is that by having four of us cooperating, we will accomplish more than any one company could do alone."

This kind of openness and lack of formality among members is what's so intriguing about a network of erstwhile enemies, says Brown at EMC. "We all just call, ask to come over, and discuss the topic."

TAKING THE TEAM APPROACH

Interested in a particular job? Just tell the other players; they might want to vie for it, too. Want a new computer-numeric control program for your milling machine? No problem. EBC's programming staff will send one over.

The team approach has helped each member reach independent goals in ways otherwise not possible. In Brown's case, his goal was big, lucrative contracts that were beyond his reach. Brown, quite simply, needed help.

When he first took over what was then called Erie Bolt Corp., the manufacturer of parts for the transportation and defense industries was losing $100,000 a year.

Worse, much of the shop floor equipment had been cannibalized to keep other machines operating. Then an order came in that EBC couldn't fill.

"So I went to my competitors, explained my dilemma, and proposed that we go after contracts together," he says.

As it happened, one of those competitors, Joseph Dyson & Son in Painesville, Ohio, saw this as the opportunity to expand. It was the beginning of a beautiful relationship—one that eventually grew to include up to 12 suppliers and competitors that team up against much larger forces bidding on the same contract.

"We still compete. But we cooperate on areas where individually we couldn't do it alone, either because of equipment or capacity reasons," Brown explains.

THAT'S THE TICKET

That attitude is just the ticket needed to succeed and one that is obviously not being lost on the CHIN group. Chances are, the four players in the CHIN group will succeed. Somehow, whether through common sense or just plain luck, they've established a way of interacting that promotes trust, open communication and a constant eye on the project's objective.

Those ingredients—crucial for any co-opetitive venture—are damnably difficult to instill among allied competitors. Just ask EJV Partners' members.

So before you enter the oh-so-brave world of collaboration, ask your gut if you and your potential partners can work together. If the answer's yes, prepare to work long and hard. If it's no, back out.

Discussion Questions
1. Define and illustrate *co-opetition*.
2. What are the benefits and pitfalls of co-opetition?
3. What problems did EJF Partners experience?
4. What factors contribute to effective cooperation among competitors? ▼

**"The End-user Developer: Friend or Foe?"
by Jeff Papows and Joe King**

(This reading is especially suited for use in conjunction with Chapter 13 of *Information Systems*.)

USER DEVELOPERS BUILD BETTER BUSINESS SYSTEMS

It's too late to debate whether end users should be invited into the application development process. They have already arrived.

Groupware, with the power it gives to end users, is the phenomenon that is forcing the development rules to change. Groupware products are both technologically and dynamically in tune with the user developer: The level of complexity varies with users' needs and knowledge. Entry-level users can whip built-in templates and examples into simple applications, while power users can take advantage of macros to help develop more sophisticated tracking and work-flow applications.

In this way, end users can become the most effective weapon against an applications backlog that can mount up to several years at the typical Fortune 1,000 company. And people who work in glass houses shouldn't be throwing stones at this idea: Information systems needs to stop hoarding development and realize the best thing that could happen to an organization is for users to develop what they need.

The benefits of harnessing user power in to the development process are clear. For starters, no one has a keener insight into what makes an efficient and effective business application. It stands to reason that end-user developers will create—or quickly add—a necessary function once they know they need it.

There is no opportunity for the messy and costly miscommunication that sometimes occurs in the typical development life cycle when users hand in their requirements and pass system specs to programmers, who hand applications back to users and so on.

Even more importantly, as users develop these systems, they can discover flaws in work flows the applications address.

At one New York-based advertising company, for instance, a cross-functional team of businesspeople, with little help from IS, planned to develop an automated traffic control system for projects. The groupware-based system was to replace the company's manual, nine-step time- and paper-intensive work-flow process. As the team mapped the work flow, it realized the process was a mess. It would be a mistake merely to automate it. For instance, there was no formal way to specify who would be a member of which project, to assign team duties or to set up teamwide briefings.

Because the developers were professionals integrally involved in the business, they picked up on the poor processes. IS would never have been able to.

This is heady—and empowering—stuff for users. "Suddenly, they see their own information needs being met and quickly envision myriad specific applications to be implemented," says the IS director at an accounting and consulting firm. He says the appeal of this kind of development is "almost visceral."

As users, excited and enabled by groupware, flock to the application development party, business organizations are starting to see quantifiable results in terms of reduced time to action and improved quality in business processes, including product development, account management and customer service.

SOURCE: Jeff Papows and Joe King, "The End User Developer: Friend or Foe?" *Computerworld*, November 15, 1993, pp. 180–182. Copyright 1993 by *Computerworld*.

One leading scientific equipment manufacturer I know of got a 20% increase in response after putting in a prospects and sales tracking system that an applications engineer and the company's director of training created.

On the basis of this improved response, the company estimates that if each rep makes one additional sales call per week it can bring in $4.3 million more in revenue annually.

As users are brought into the development mix, the loudest applause should come from savvy IS professionals. Only those with their eyes on the past will bemoan the rise of groupware as the fall of the IS profession. There's a chance for users and IS to work together.

That's because, as Mark LaRow, a consultant at the Ernst & Young Center for Technology Strategy, points out, there is a shift occurring. Command, control and communications are no longer the driving forces in companies.

Users in the development process can't be ignored anymore.

IF YOU WANT TROUBLE, THEN LET USERS DEVELOP

Don't be swayed by the popular myth that users are your programming resources of the future.

With the PC applications backlog what it is—at least three years, by my reckoning—it would be great to think that end users are the answer to the information technology group's prayers. What information systems manager would turn down a bunch of extra helping hands if it meant faster development?

But getting end users involved will do more harm than good.

I'm not talking about end-user development with personal productivity tools, such as spreadsheets, word processors and personal databases. That's baby stuff, stand-alone and isolated development that rarely has any ripple effect on applications and communications companywide.

Rather, the danger is letting end users go wild with new enterprisewide multiuser application systems of which Notes, Objectvision and Visual Basic are all a part. Combine user-controlled development and the workgroup computing nature of such tools and you have the makings of a technological Molotov cocktail.

Such products are a siren song to end users. They promise simplicity and ease. (Perhaps a new Dale Carnegie course is in order—"Yes, You, Too, Can Be an Application Developer.") Users don't have to wait around with their hair turning gray to get an application built. But are you prepared to have your users "simply" and "easily" handle complex communications software, administer a client/server environment, ensure security over multiplatform systems, distribute databases over a wide-area network and master multiple programming languages?

Yet these are all part and parcel of what it means to develop applications with Notes or Visual Basic or whatever. It's been my observation that the learning curve for Notes—and I'm talking about the learning curve for technical professionals—is long: about six months. Users take twice that time to come up to speed—if they ever do. Can your organization afford to have your users spend up to a year learning to be competent developers?

I'm not kidding when I say development can get complicated. Notes, for instance, doesn't sit there by itself; building a complete application often requires, say, Visual Basic or Objectvision. I know of one project that needed as many as seven separate products to build a single system.

You can't really expect users to master all of these tools. Even if they did, issues of design, data integrity, and quality come into play.

I know one company whose business users built a slick shared database application on a LAN. But it took so much effort to maintain that the support staff doubled. And then it doubled again. The system duplicated the existing corporate systems' data entry functions, and the company was left with data that did not balance. Data integrity has become a major issue.

While the rigors of design, analysis, testing and methods are second nature to professional developers, users haven't been versed in these areas. And you can kiss documentation goodbye.

Also, when companies let their users take on development, users quickly discover that for their applications to have value (surprise!) they either have to get data from or talk to older systems. So it ends up spending a good chunk of its time figuring out how to integrate new and legacy systems. What starts out as a way to shorten an applications backlog ends up adding to it instead.

I don't want to give the impressions that I'm not a big fan of these new development tools. Quite the contrary. The tools can have a profound impact on the development life cycle. But *only if* development is in the right hands.

It's not like users won't be involved in development at all; in fact, one of the things these tools have going for them is iterative and rapid development, which brings users and developers together in a real-time "conversation." Users participate actively, but control stays with IS.

I can't see why companies want to create more development headaches than they already have.

Discussion Questions

1. What advantages do user developers offer?
2. What role does groupware play in users' developing software?
3. What disadvantages do user developers create?
4. How can an organization achieve balance in the involvement of users in systems development? ▼

Reading 13: "No Set Rules for Systems Design," by Kathleen A. Gow

(This reading is especially suited for use in conjunction with Chapter 14 of *Information Systems*.)

Many factors, including geographic origins and locations of foreign sites, influence the manner in which multinational corporations handle systems planning and acquisition.

Japanese companies, for example, tend to encourage local autonomy wherever they operate as a means of staying close to local markets, according to Christopher Bartlett, professor of business administration at Harvard Business School and author of *Managing Across Borders, the Transnational Solution*. "If you shook a Japanese manager out of sleep today, he would be mumbling 'localization,' not globalization," Bartlett says.

In other instances, multinationals allow greater latitude for local decision-making in certain areas of the world. Many, for example, give Latin American business units and subsidiaries much more local control over systems planning and acquisitions than their North American or European counterparts. There are a number of reasons why Central and South American sites are accorded this special treatment. One is that systems and communications software used in other parts of the world are either unavailable in these areas or incompatible with the local standards. Another is that stringent government regulations frequently restrict the flow of information across borders.

Bartlett describes the challenge for multinational firms as being able to balance the need for local differentiation with the seemingly contrary objective of achieving integration and coordination on a worldwide basis.

Achieving this balance calls for a certain amount of flexibility in weighing the cost and efficiency advantages of centralization and standardization against the requirements of individual areas.

At Gillette Co., for example, David Lawless, assistant director of international systems, says Gillette Europe is handled very differently from Gillette Latin America. Europe has centralized planning and direction coming out of the Isleworth, UK, facillity for every function, including IS. Latin America, on the other hand, looks like Europe did seven years ago: Although the region adheres to the framework of centrally developed hardware, organizational and procedural standards, there is much more local autonomy.

"Local control is useful to the degree that business requires resident systems, but it can mean higher costs and the risk of mismanagement," Lawless says.

At Stockholm-based Alfa Laval AB, local control is encouraged but within certain limits. In the early 1980s, Alfa Laval sought to counter a structure that was too cumbersome by decentralizing control of its business units, which are arranged by product area. The only requirement imposed on these units, says John Tower, a rate manager of MIS at Alfa Laval, Inc. in Park Ridge, NJ, is that they maintain systems compatibility with headquarters.

Alfa Laval uses an IBM communications network and range systems that vary locally. The seven business areas use different processes and manufacturing equipment, but some systems have come out of headquarters, such as electronic mail and the in-house-developed Global Inventory File.

Corning, Inc., takes a very broad view of IS diversity. "We're opportunistic," Harvey Shrednick, vice-president of information services, says of the Corning, N.Y.-based conglomerate's approach to IS. "We share where we can and manage by prevention."

SOURCE: Kathleen A. Gow, "No Set Rules for Systems Design." *Computerworld*, October 1, 1990, pp. 98–99. Copyright 1990 by *Computerworld*.

Shrednick holds overall responsibility for corporate IS worldwide. He says Corning has not come up with a global strategy that it can use across the board. Rather, the strategy varies depending on the needs of the industry and the people involved in each unit.

In North America, IS operations are centralized and report directly to Shrednick. In Latin America and Europe, however, systems control for the consumer products groups is much more local. The central IS function provides advice and guidance, but decision-making authority for hardware and applications software rests locally. "We have chosen not to legislate what people use," Shrednick says. It is each group's responsibility to purchase equipment and software that will communicate with headquarters.

Although achieving worldwide coordination in this type of an environment is not easy, Shrednick says he stresses that individual freedom does not always lead to a choice to be different. He gives the example of a U.S. plant floor reporting system that was taken to Japan and adapted for Japanese plants, complete with a hot key between English and Japanese versions.

MANAGING BY CONSENSUS

Many multinationals have set up international IS management groups to help achieve coordination through consensus. At Xerox Corp., for example, the Corporate Information Management (CIM) group brings together senior information managers from business units worldwide to make decisions on issues such as architectures, operating system software and primary database modules.

According to Judi Campbell, manager of strategic technology deployment at Xerox in Rochester, N.Y., the CIM group can also serve as a catalyst for resource sharing. In one instance, she says, a member—the liaison for Latin America—was able to identify an opportunity for adapting a set of systems developed for a European region to the requirements of a Mexican unit.

Bartlett says it is impossible to overemphasize the value of forums that permit face-to-face meetings. Globalization is not just to gain access to markets, he says, but also to gain information such as competitors' activities and government regulations.

"In the old role, the subsidiary served as a delivery pipeline, essentially acting as a dumb terminal," he says. "Now, they capture and transfer knowledge—not just raw data processing, but information" and, for that reason, "it is better to manage through socialization," he maintains.

Bartlett stresses that this transfer shouldn't just be between headquarters and subsidiaries but from one subsidiary to another: "That's what drives transnational innovation."

Discussion Questions

1. What factors influence the way multinational corporations handle systems planning and acquisition?
2. Do multinational companies have uniform systems architectures and sites in different continents?
3. What advantages and disadvantages does localized versus corporate control create?
4. Offer three illustrations of decisions about systems architecture by multinational companies. ▼